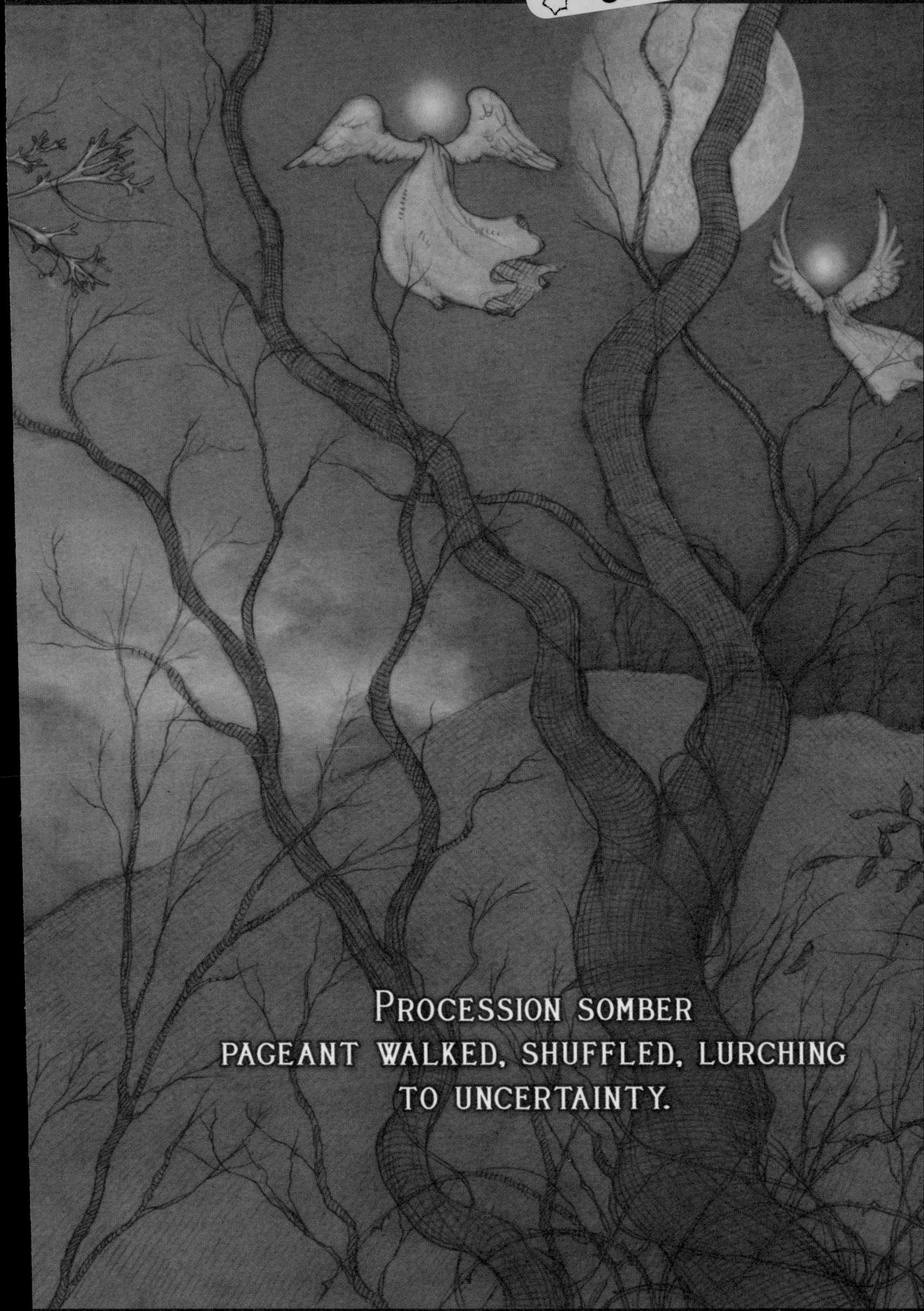
Procession somber
pageant walked, shuffled, lurching
to uncertainty.

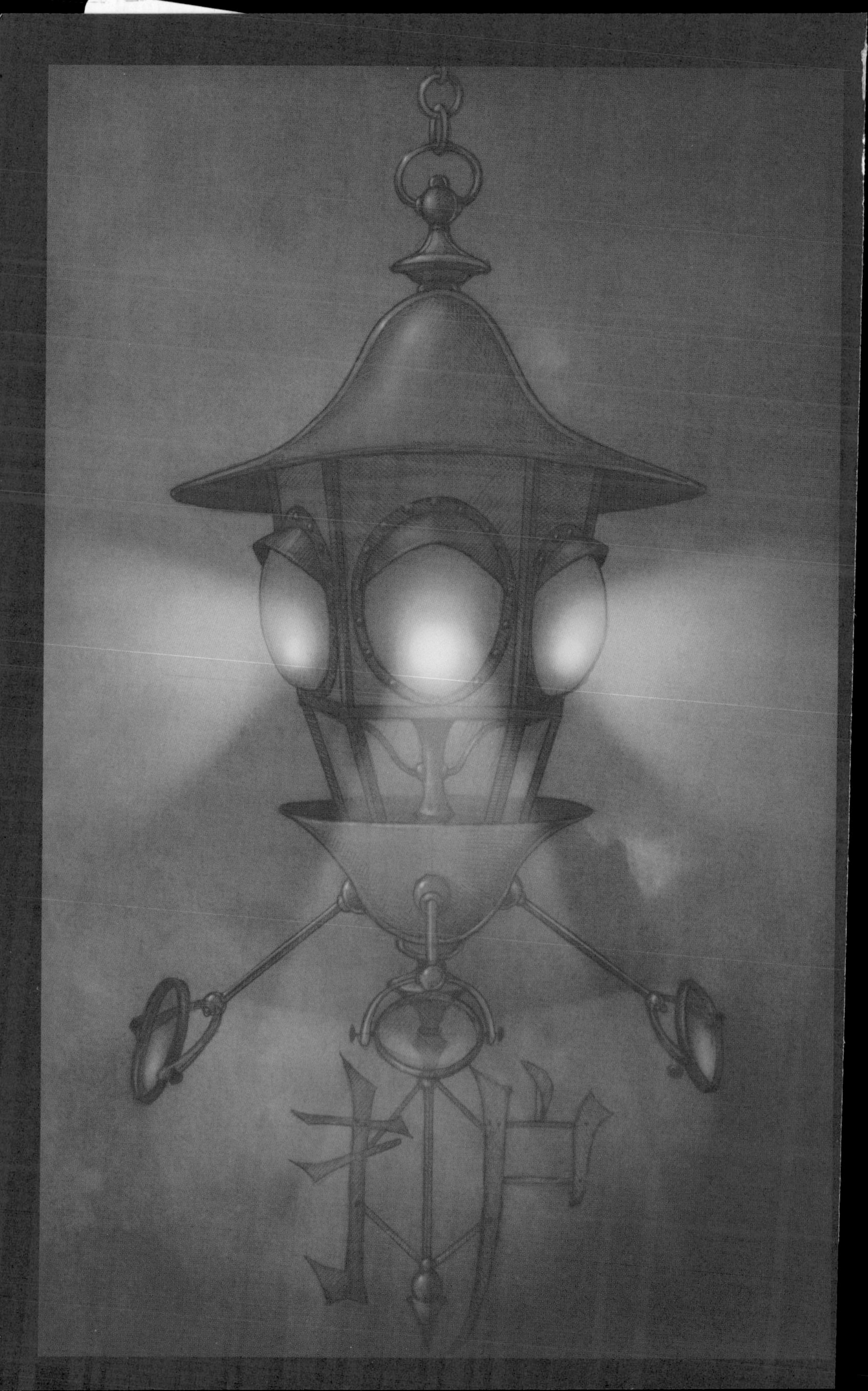

HOPELESS, MAINE
+INHERITANCE+
™

TOM & NIMUE BROWN

ARCHAIA ENTERTAINMENT LLC
WWW.**ARCHAIA**.COM

HOPELESS, MAINE™
•INHERITANCE•

CREATED BY
TOM & NIMUE BROWN

WRITTEN BY
TOM & NIMUE BROWN

ILLUSTRATED BY
TOM BROWN

LETTERED BY
DERON BENNETT

Rebecca Taylor, *Editor*

Archaia Entertainment LLC
Jack Cummins, *President & COO*
Mark Smylie, *CCO*
Mike Kennedy, *Publisher*
Stephen Christy, *Editor-in-Chief*
Mel Caylo, *Marketing Manager*
Scott Newman, *Production Manager*

Published by **Archaia**

Archaia Entertainment LLC
5670 Wilshire Boulevard, Suite 450
Los Angeles, California, 90036, USA
www.archaia.com

ARCHAIA™
NEW STORIES. NEW WORLDS.

HOPELESS, MAINE Volume Two INHERITANCE Original Graphic Novel Hardcover. October 2013. FIRST PRINTING.

10 9 8 7 6 5 4 3 2 1

ISBN: 1-939867-03-7
ISBN 13: 978-1-939867-03-2

Printed in **China**.

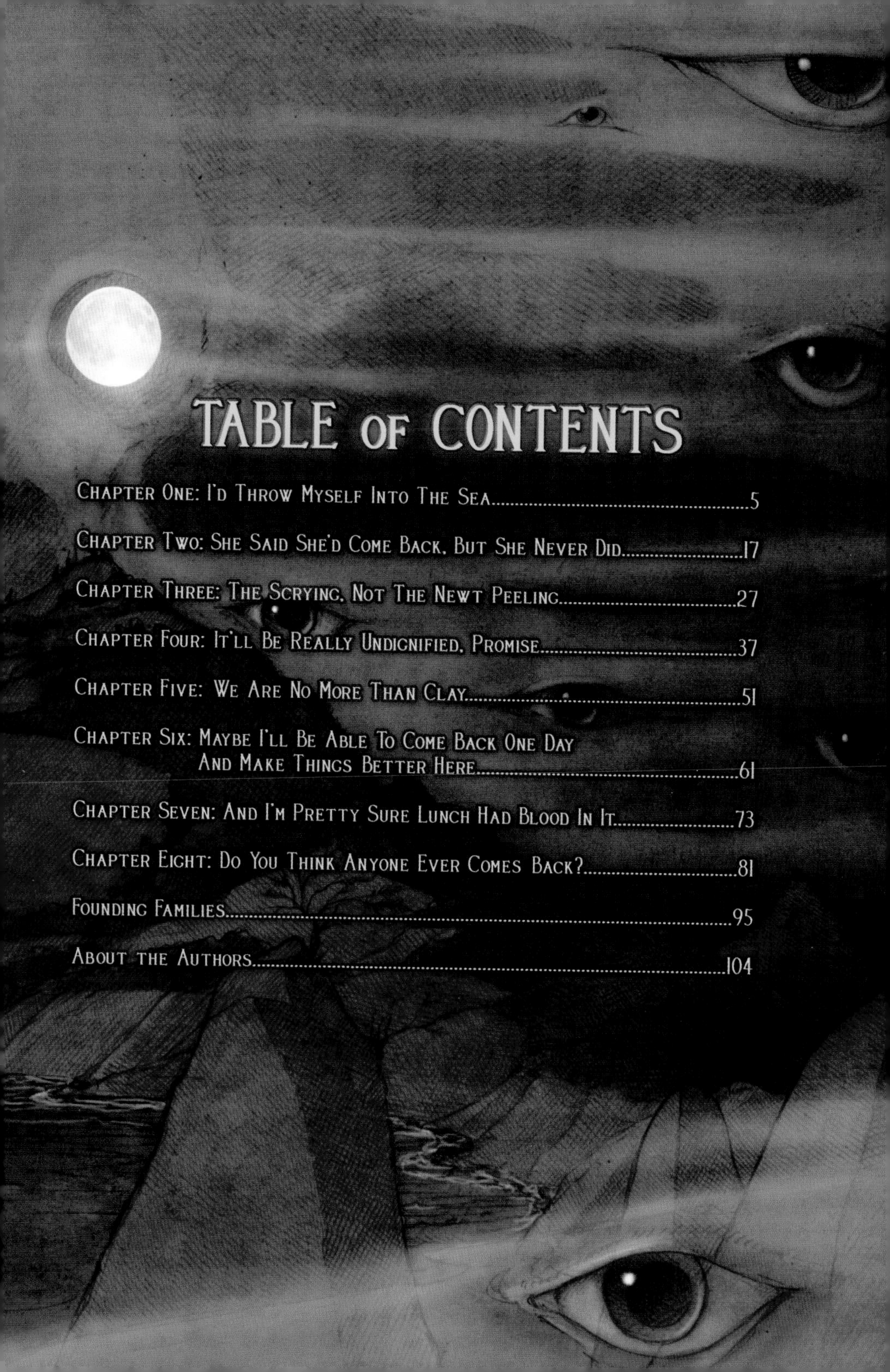

TABLE of CONTENTS

There are dead ones who walk, restless, and others who sleep.
There are the oblivious living and those who pause to think.
There are the missing.
The might-be-dead.
Walking.
And not walking.

Growing up magical,
growing up hoping that your parents are a nightmare
from which you have finally surfaced.
Growing up to find your parents were a dream
from which you must now awaken.

We are from them, not of them.
Our lives a tangle of what was, knotted through
with naive hope, forlorn nostalgia.
We are tied to each other with shackles made out of air,
and pinned against the land by a relentless sea
that does not let us leave.

We were children in Hopeless.

Now we seek after the trappings of adulthood.
The rites of passage.
Casting off old skins and taking the form our future will wear.

Once upon a time, we fought demons together.
Now we are older, wiser.
We give our demons different names.
And no names at all.

This is not a story about growing up.

It is a story about thinking you had grown up already.

And finding it wasn't that simple after all.

CHAPTER ONE

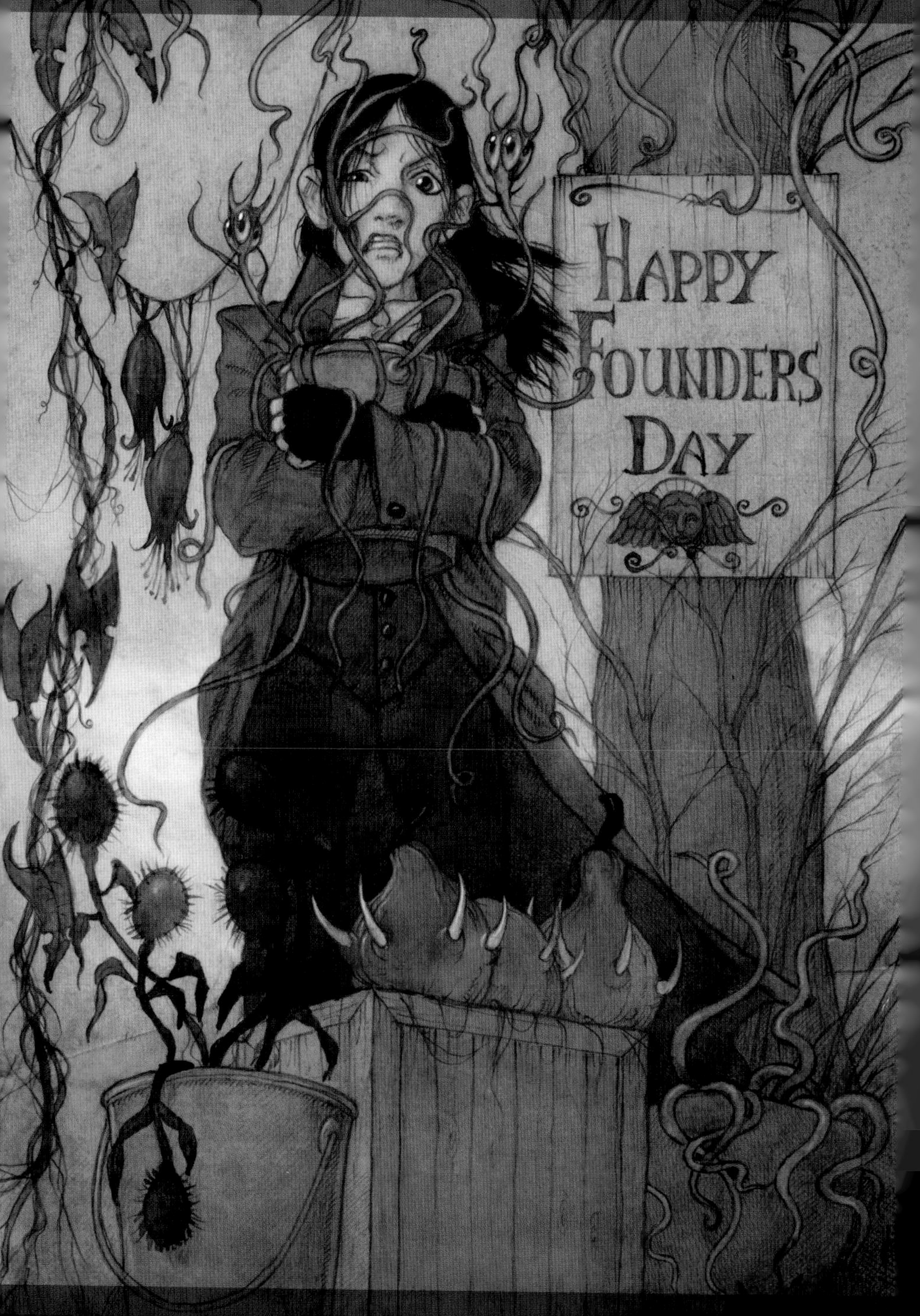
HAPPY FOUNDERS DAY

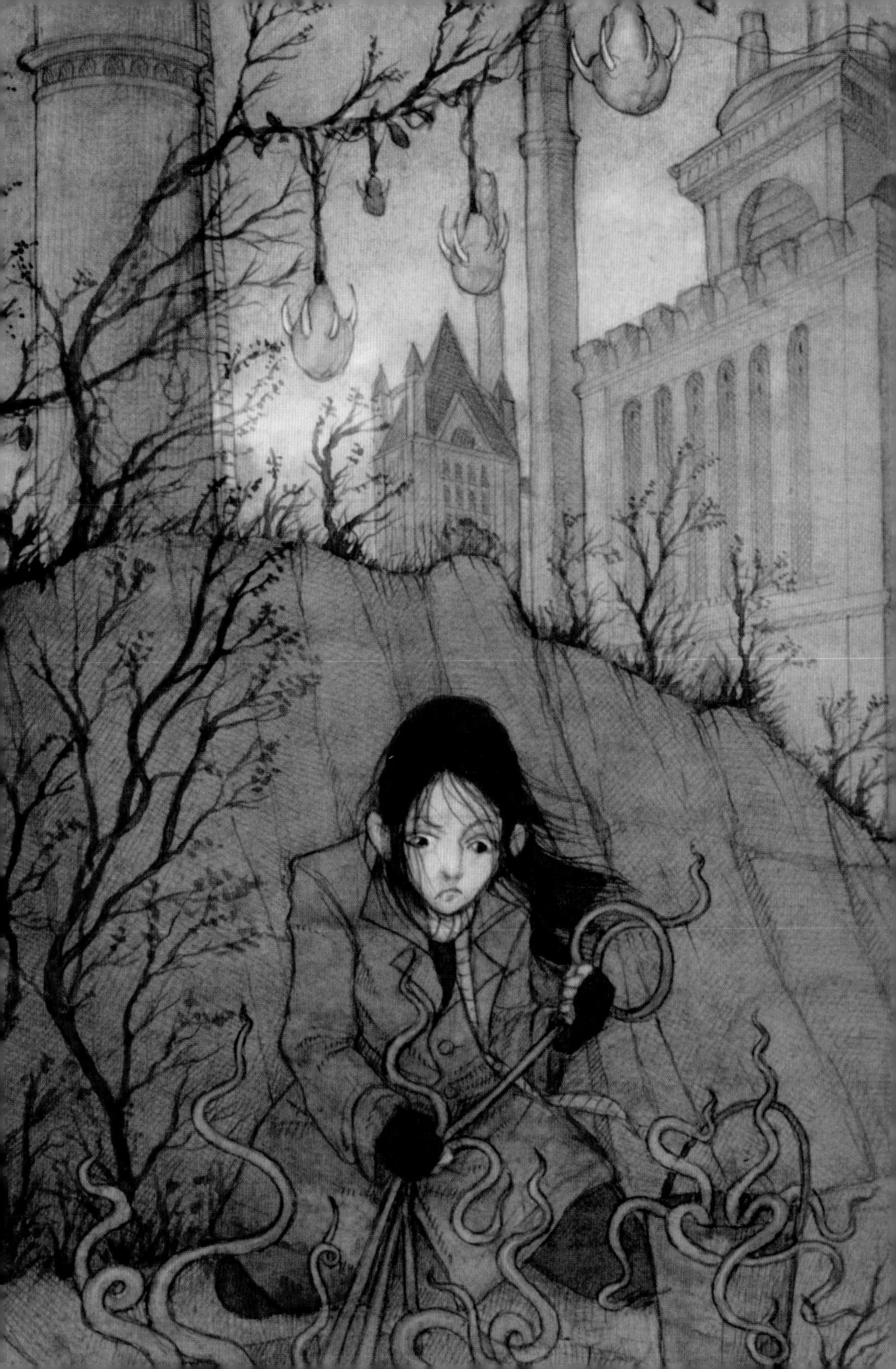

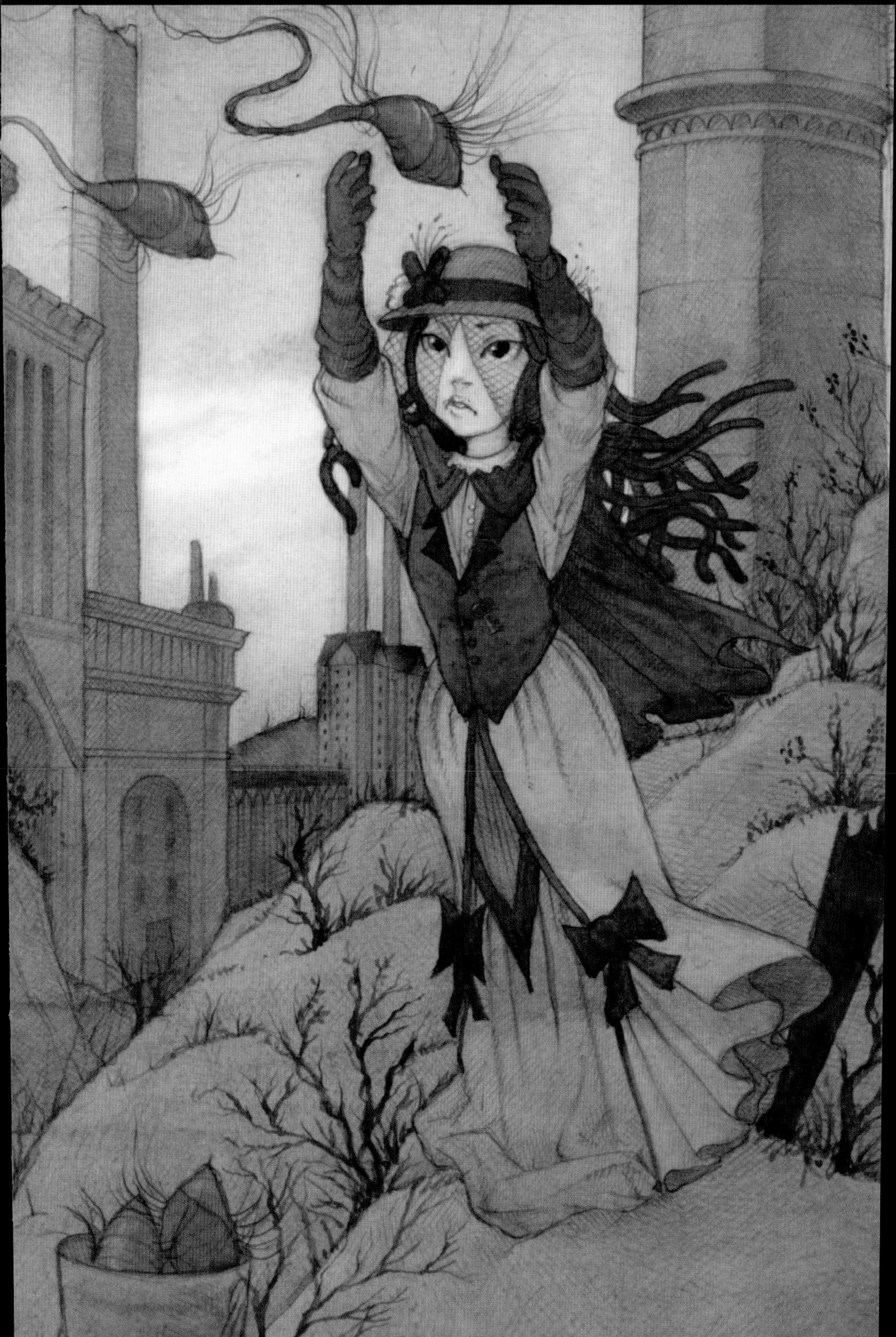

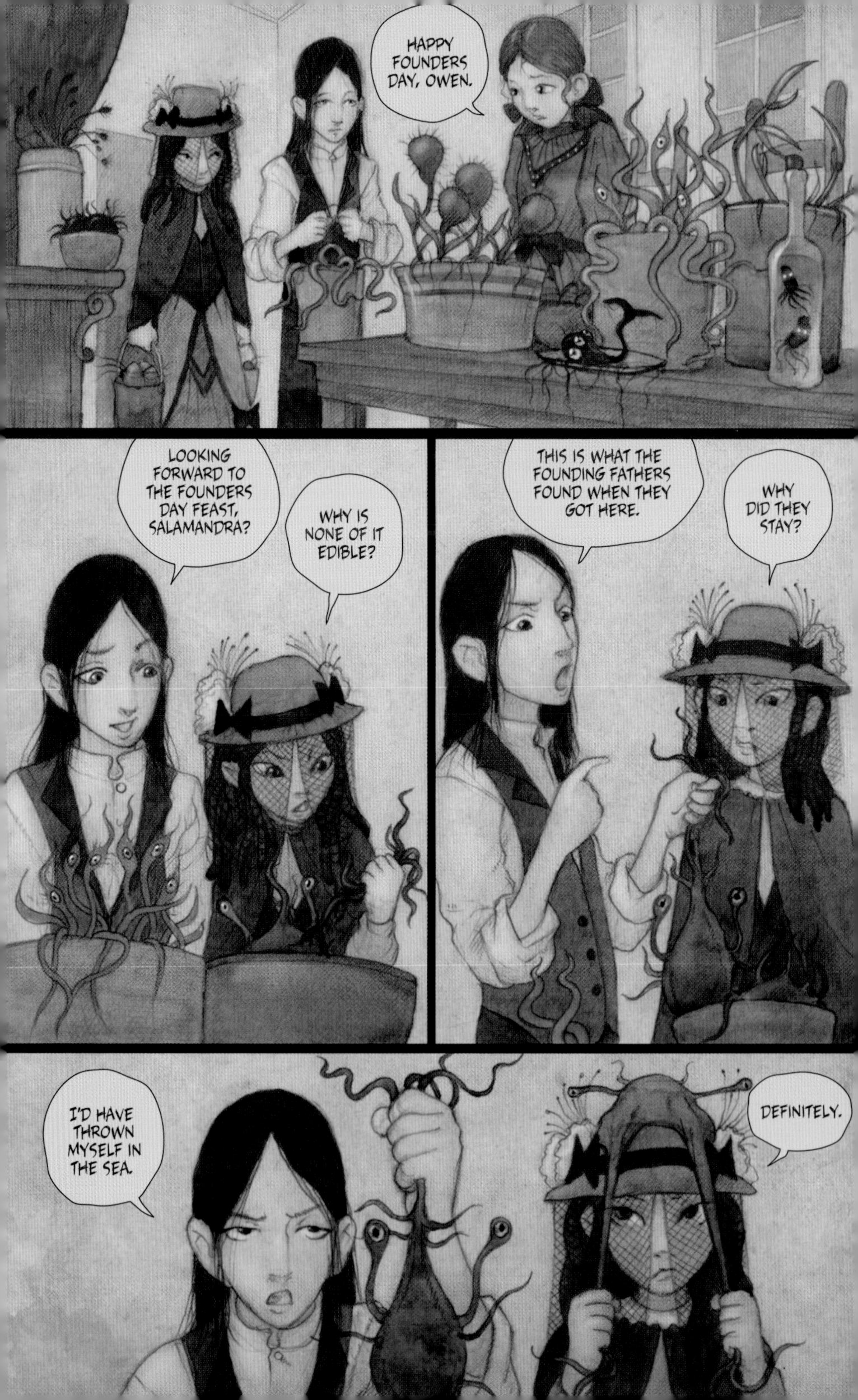
HAPPY FOUNDERS DAY, OWEN.
LOOKING FORWARD TO THE FOUNDERS DAY FEAST, SALAMANDRA?
WHY IS NONE OF IT EDIBLE?
THIS IS WHAT THE FOUNDING FATHERS FOUND WHEN THEY GOT HERE.
WHY DID THEY STAY?
I'D HAVE THROWN MYSELF IN THE SEA.
DEFINITELY.

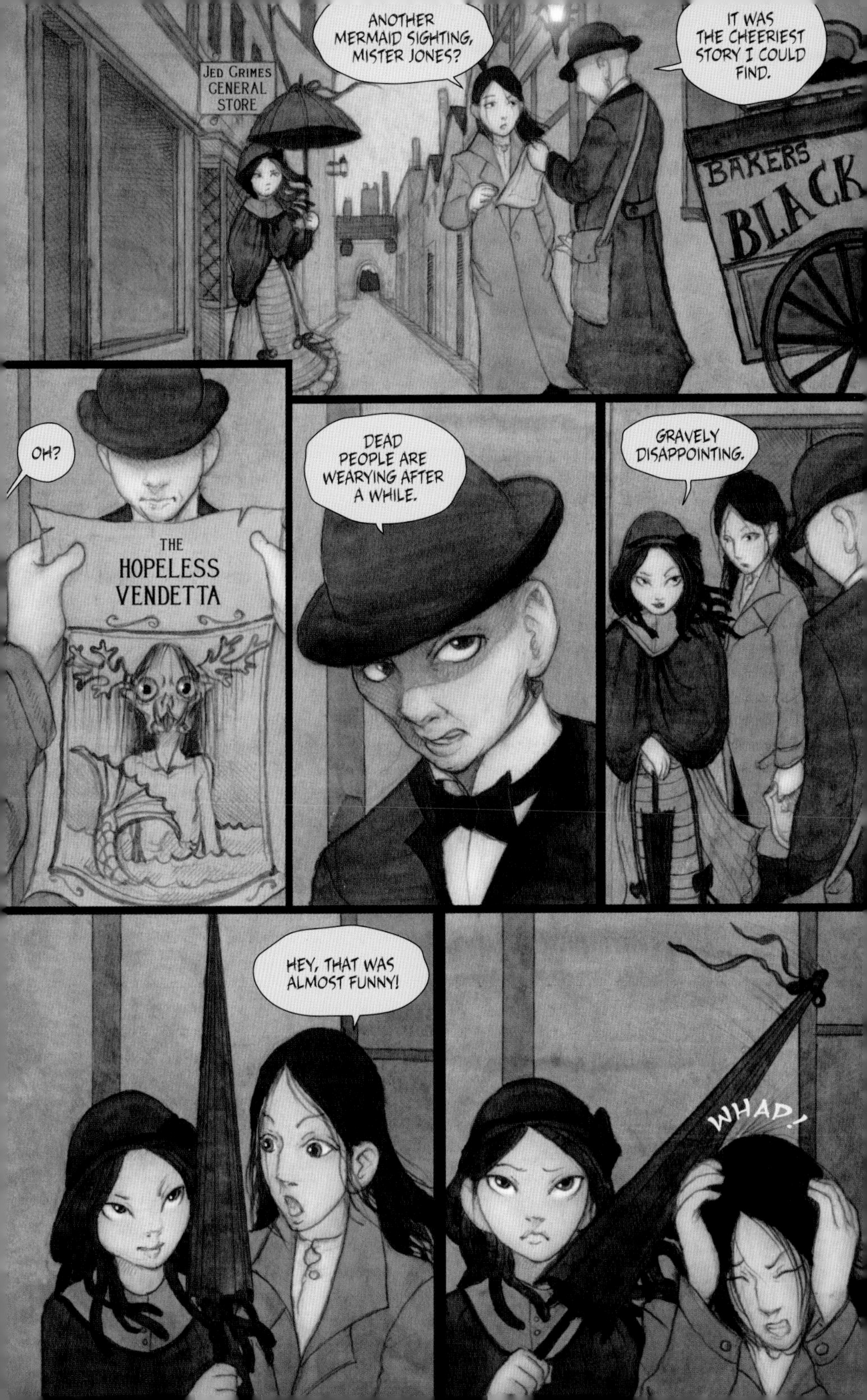
JED GRIMES
GENERAL
STORE
ANOTHER MERMAID SIGHTING, MISTER JONES?
IT WAS THE CHEERIEST STORY I COULD FIND.
BAKERS
BLACK
OH?
THE
HOPELESS
VENDETTA
DEAD PEOPLE ARE WEARYING AFTER A WHILE.
GRAVELY DISAPPOINTING.
HEY, THAT WAS ALMOST FUNNY!
WHAP!

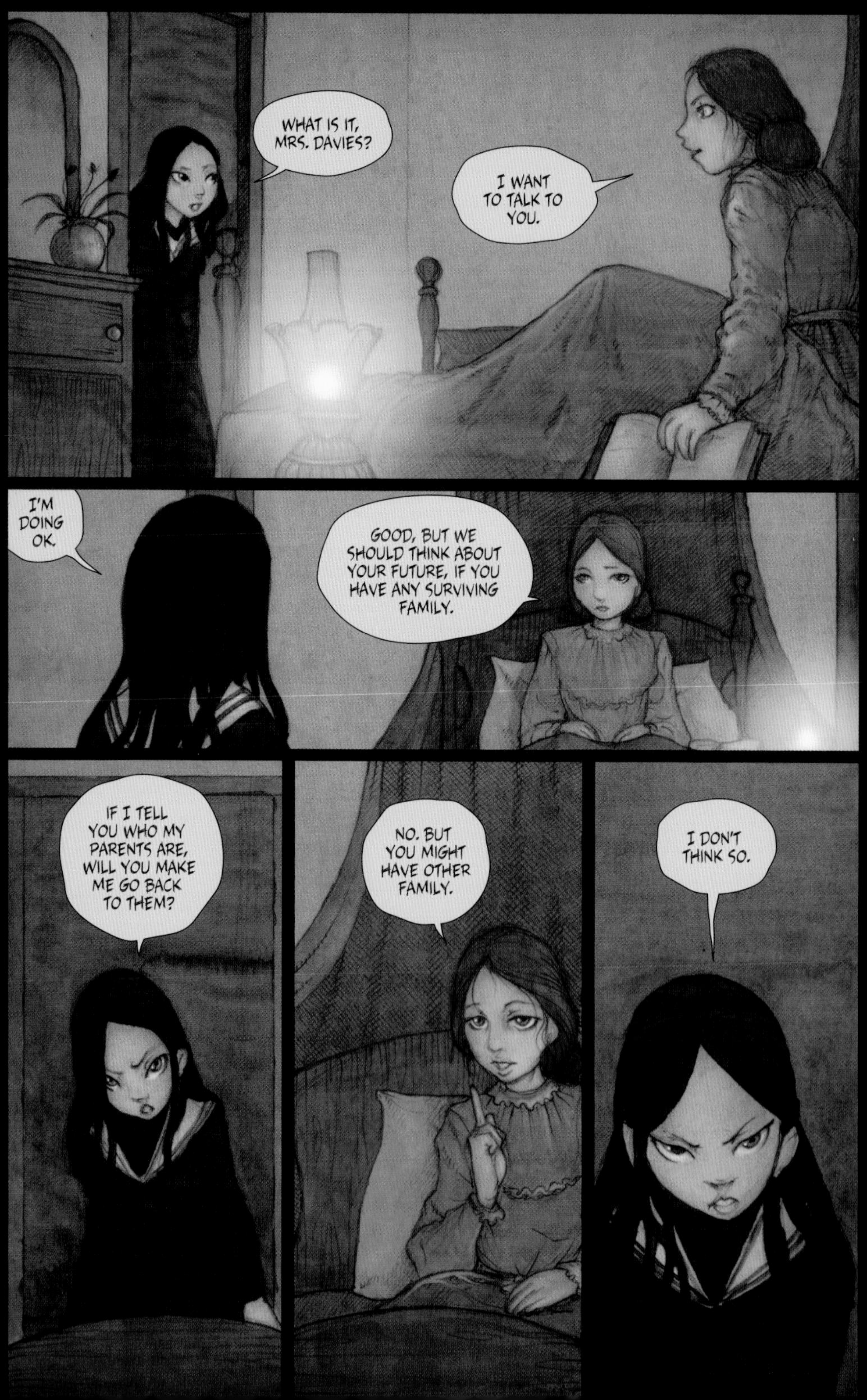
WHAT IS IT, MRS. DAVIES?
I WANT TO TALK TO YOU.
I'M DOING OK.
GOOD, BUT WE SHOULD THINK ABOUT YOUR FUTURE, IF YOU HAVE ANY SURVIVING FAMILY.
IF I TELL YOU WHO MY PARENTS ARE, WILL YOU MAKE ME GO BACK TO THEM?
NO. BUT YOU MIGHT HAVE OTHER FAMILY.
I DON'T THINK SO.

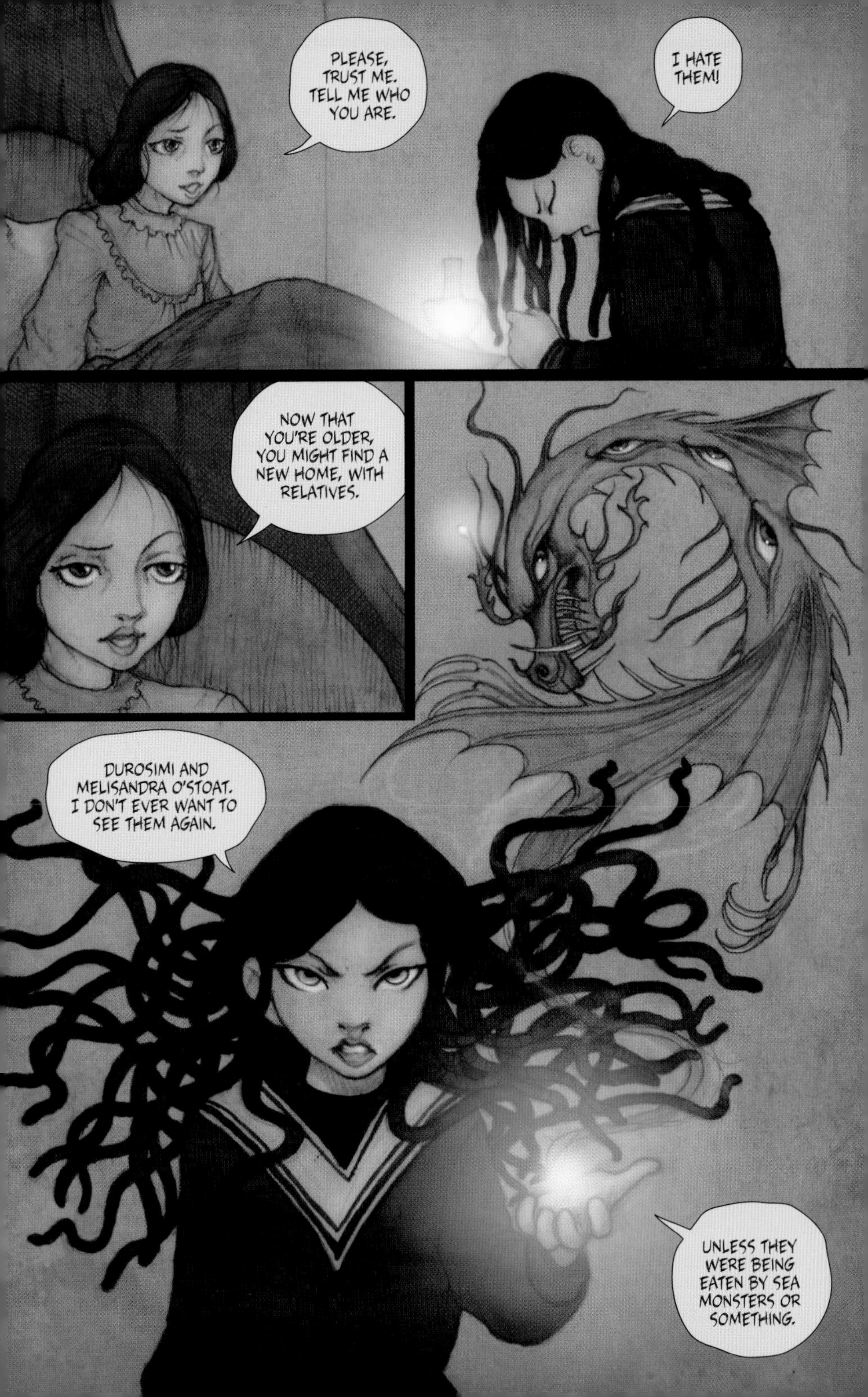
PLEASE, TRUST ME. TELL ME WHO YOU ARE.
I HATE THEM!
NOW THAT YOU'RE OLDER, YOU MIGHT FIND A NEW HOME, WITH RELATIVES.
DUROSIMI AND MELISANDRA O'STOAT. I DON'T EVER WANT TO SEE THEM AGAIN.
UNLESS THEY WERE BEING EATEN BY SEA MONSTERS OR SOMETHING.

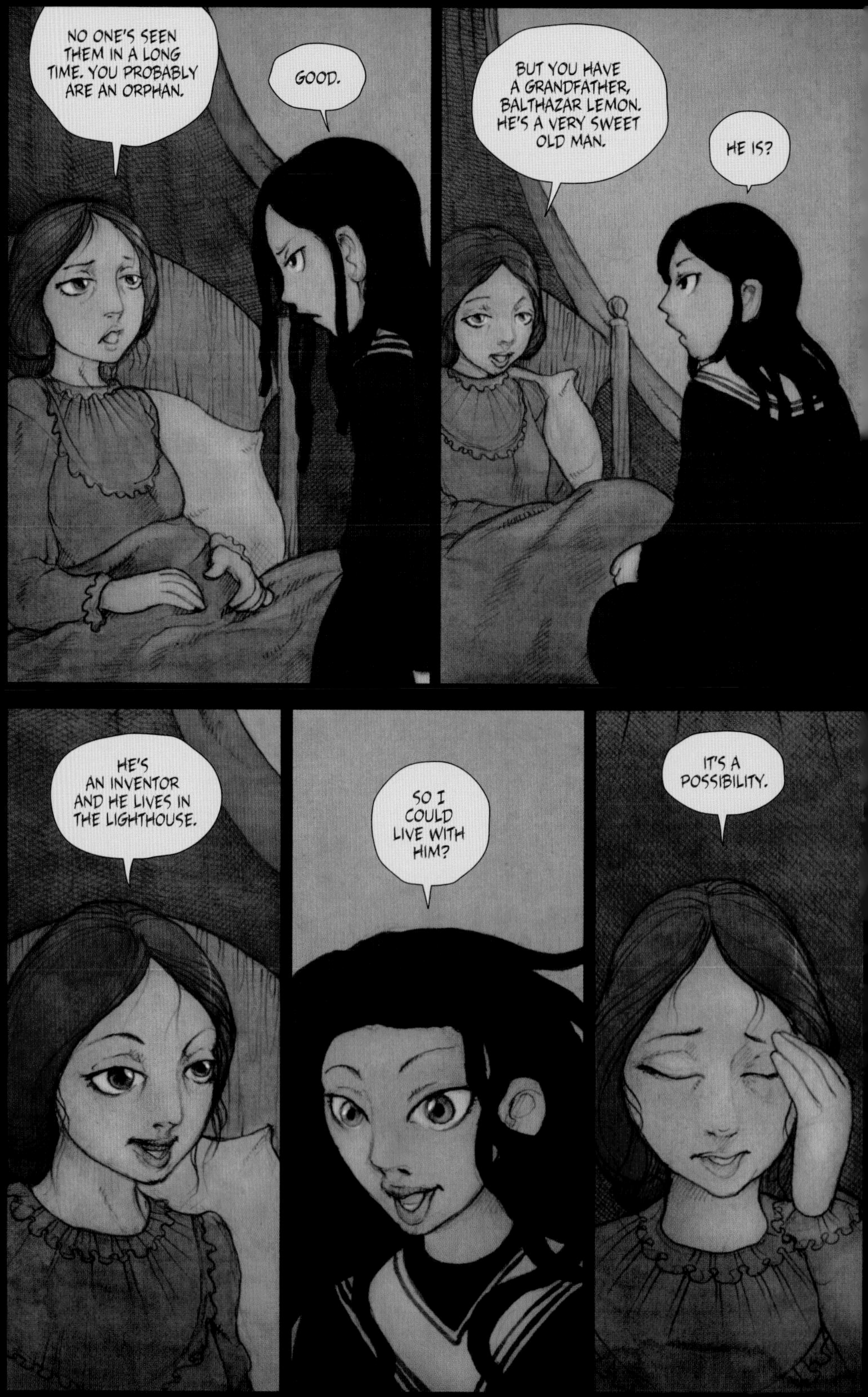
NO ONE'S SEEN THEM IN A LONG TIME. YOU PROBABLY ARE AN ORPHAN.
GOOD.
BUT YOU HAVE A GRANDFATHER, BALTHAZAR LEMON. HE'S A VERY SWEET OLD MAN.
HE IS?
HE'S AN INVENTOR AND HE LIVES IN THE LIGHTHOUSE.
SO I COULD LIVE WITH HIM?
IT'S A POSSIBILITY.

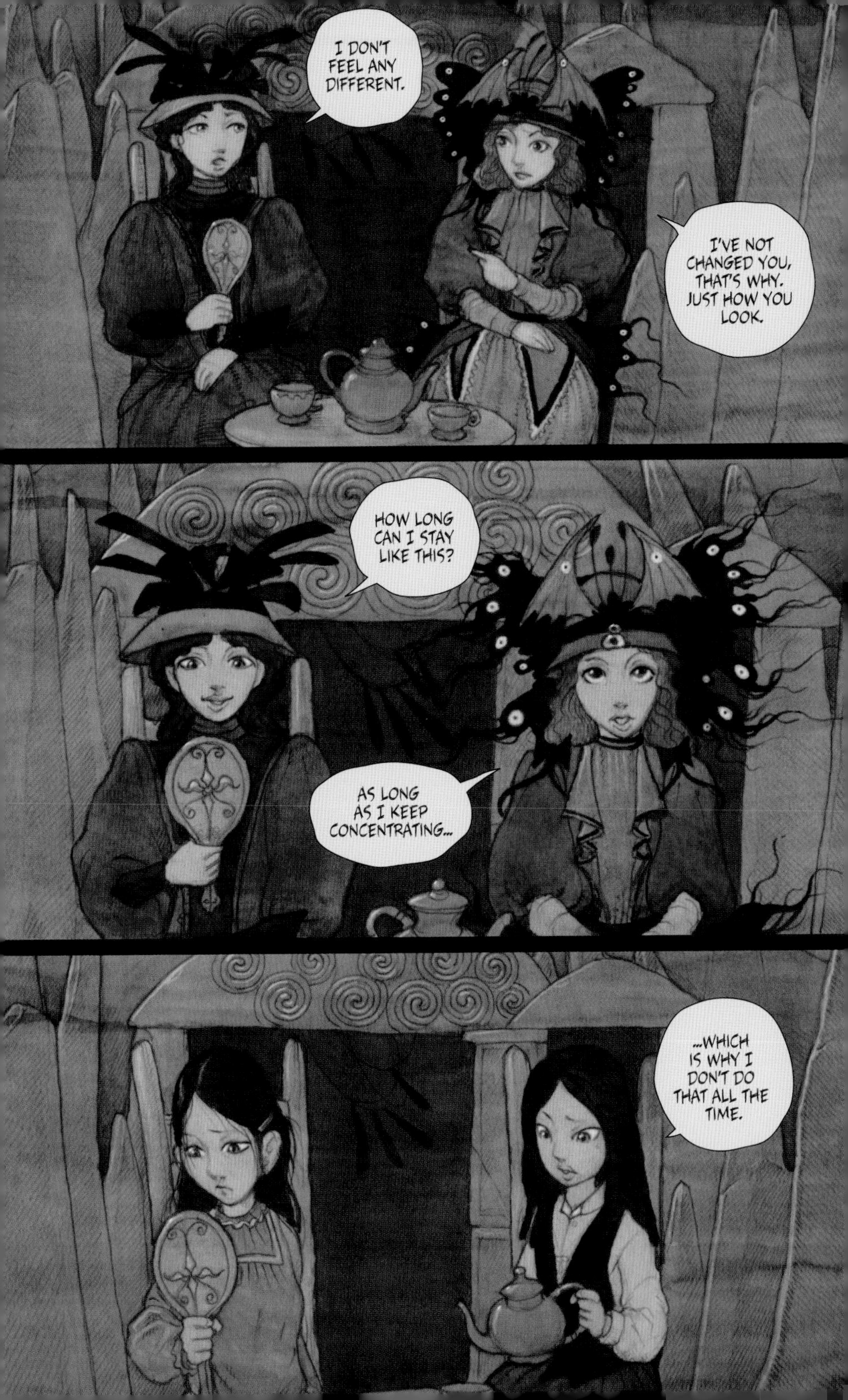
I DON'T FEEL ANY DIFFERENT.
I'VE NOT CHANGED YOU, THAT'S WHY. JUST HOW YOU LOOK.
HOW LONG CAN I STAY LIKE THIS?
AS LONG AS I KEEP CONCENTRATING...
...WHICH IS WHY I DON'T DO THAT ALL THE TIME.

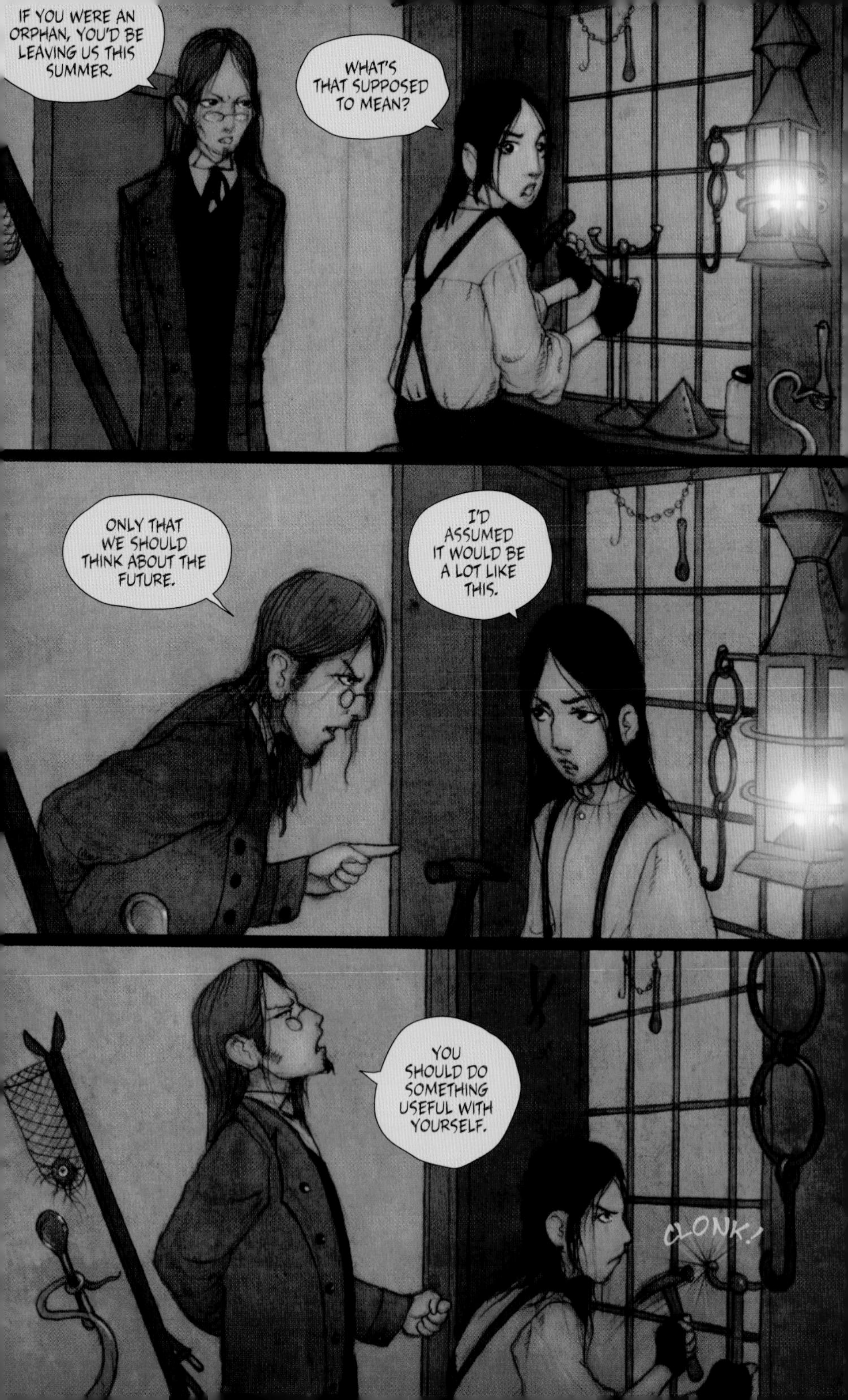
IF YOU WERE AN ORPHAN, YOU'D BE LEAVING US THIS SUMMER.
WHAT'S THAT SUPPOSED TO MEAN?
ONLY THAT WE SHOULD THINK ABOUT THE FUTURE.
I'D ASSUMED IT WOULD BE A LOT LIKE THIS.
YOU SHOULD DO SOMETHING USEFUL WITH YOURSELF.
CLONK!

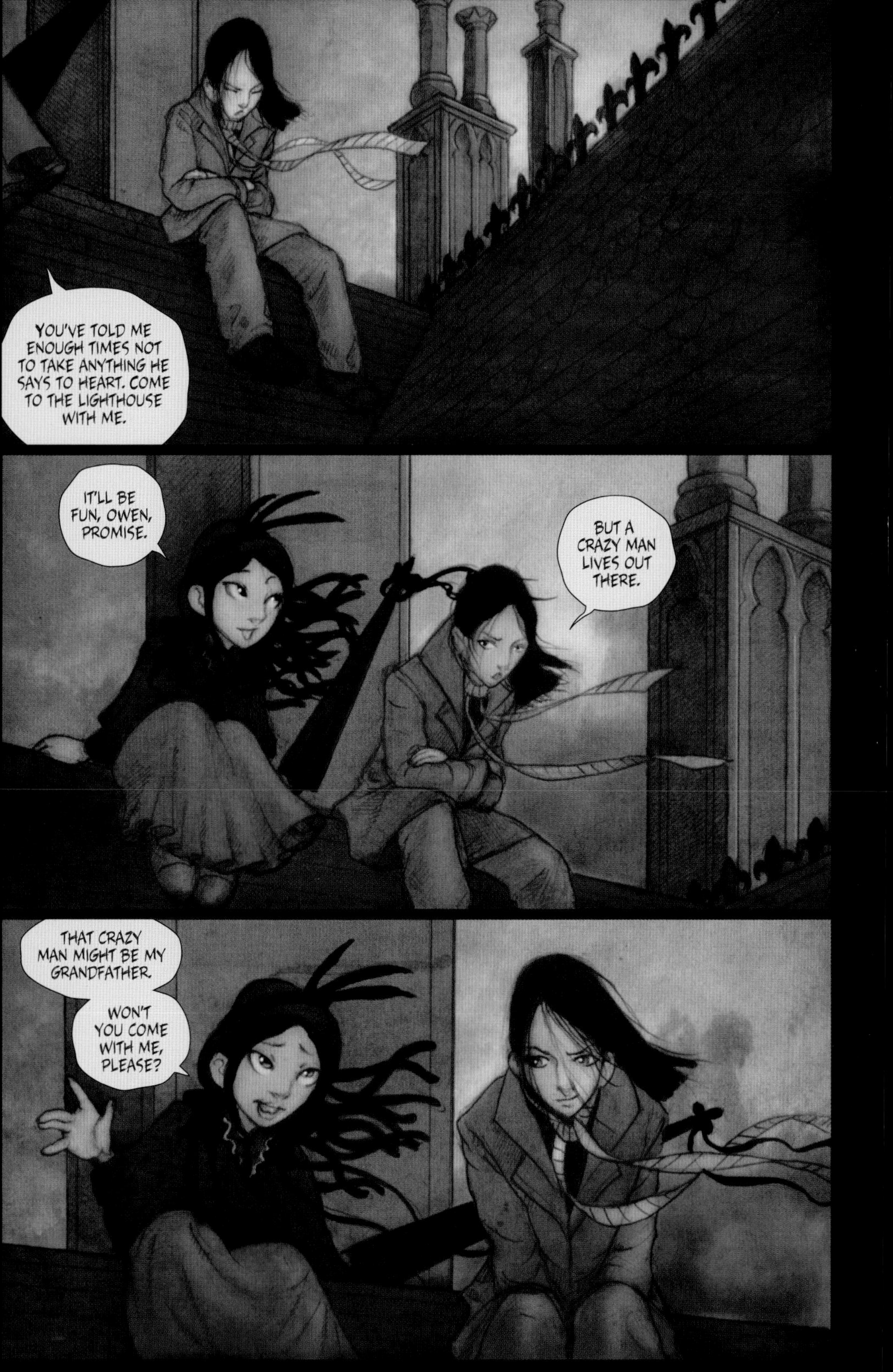
YOU'VE TOLD ME ENOUGH TIMES NOT TO TAKE ANYTHING HE SAYS TO HEART. COME TO THE LIGHTHOUSE WITH ME.
IT'LL BE FUN, OWEN, PROMISE.
BUT A CRAZY MAN LIVES OUT THERE.
THAT CRAZY MAN MIGHT BE MY GRANDFATHER.
WON'T YOU COME WITH ME, PLEASE?

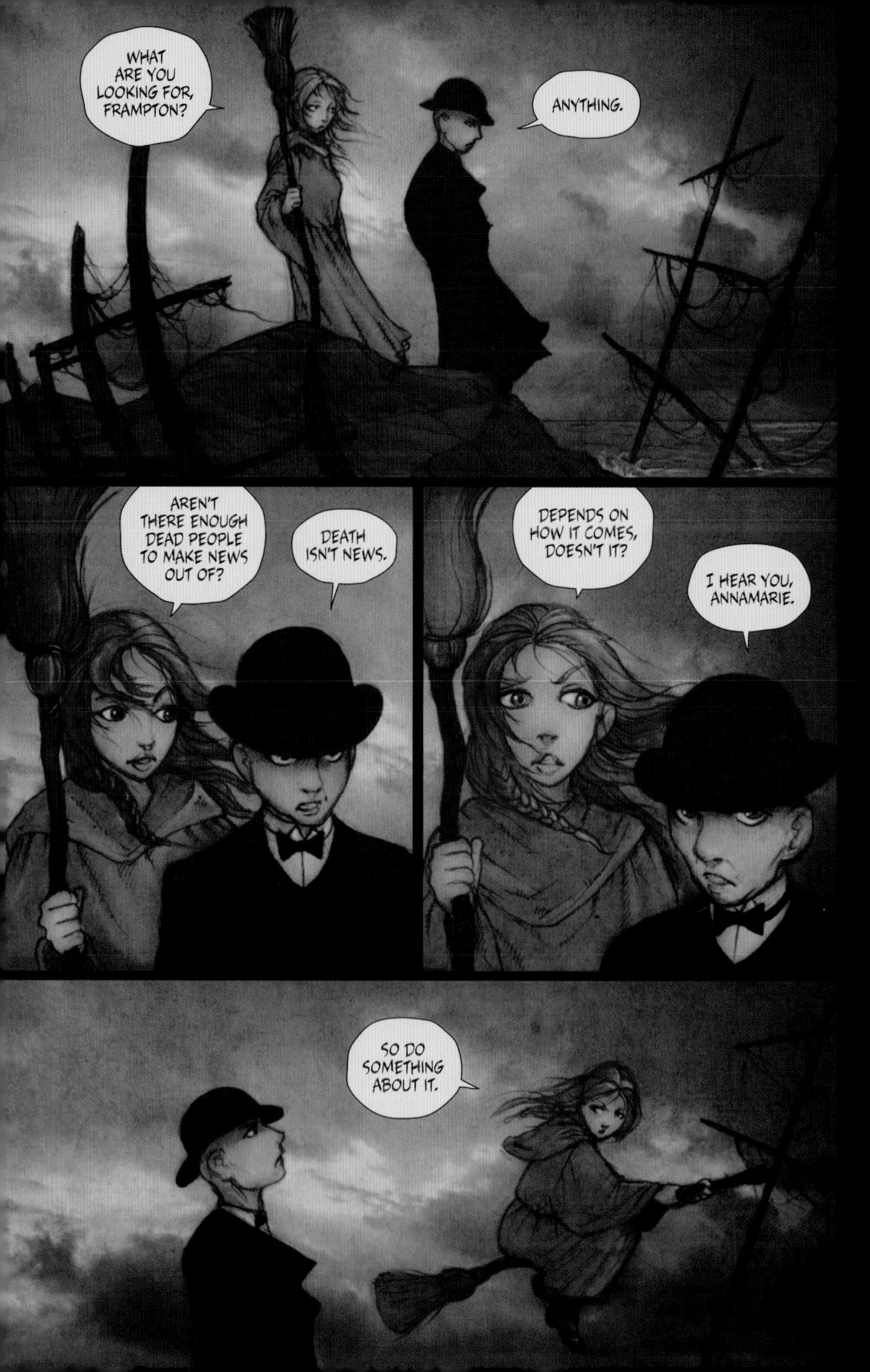
WHAT ARE YOU LOOKING FOR, FRAMPTON?
ANYTHING.
AREN'T THERE ENOUGH DEAD PEOPLE TO MAKE NEWS OUT OF?
DEATH ISN'T NEWS.
DEPENDS ON HOW IT COMES, DOESN'T IT?
I HEAR YOU, ANNAMARIE.
SO DO SOMETHING ABOUT IT.

CHAPTER TWO

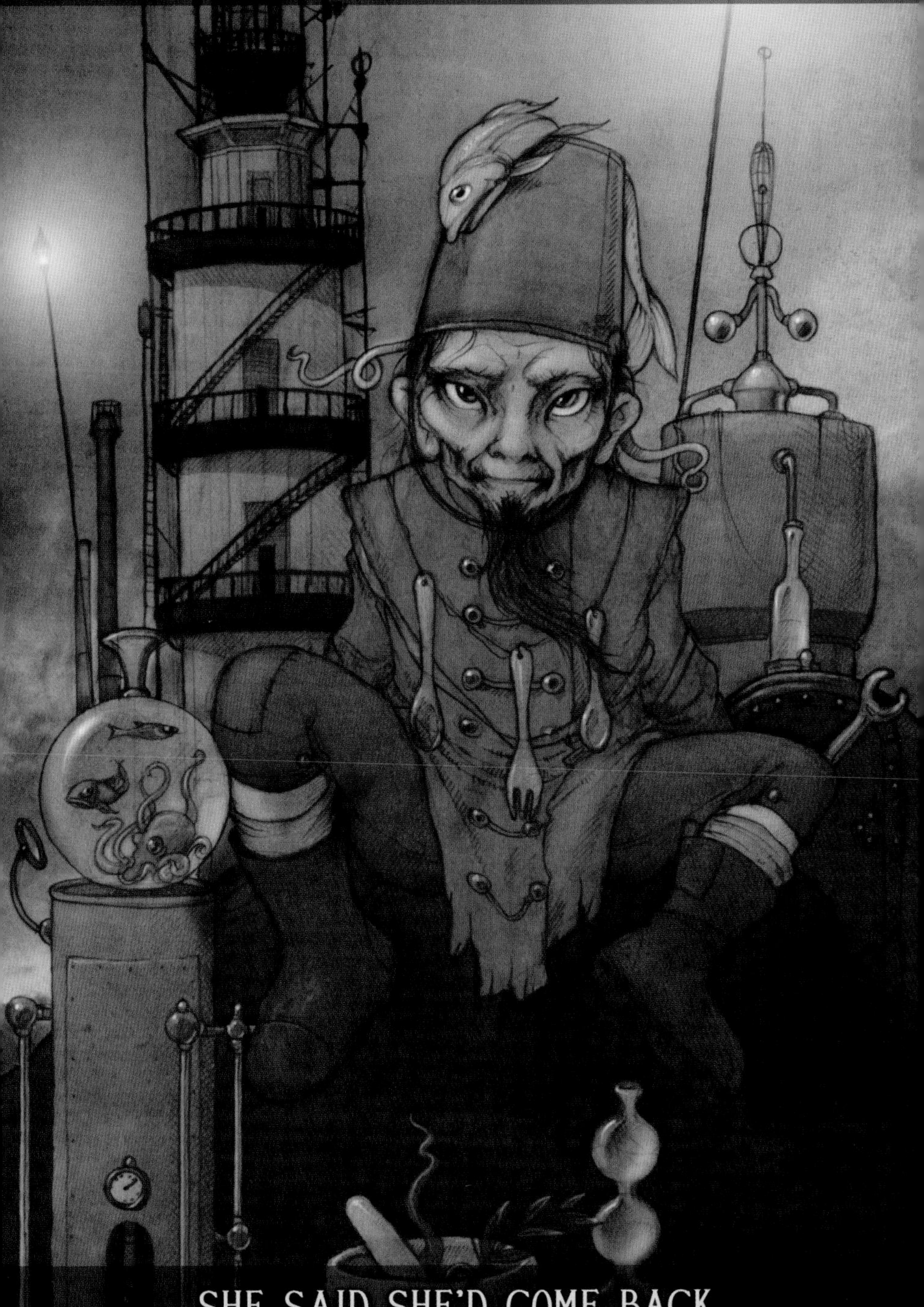

SHE SAID SHE'D COME BACK, BUT SHE NEVER DID

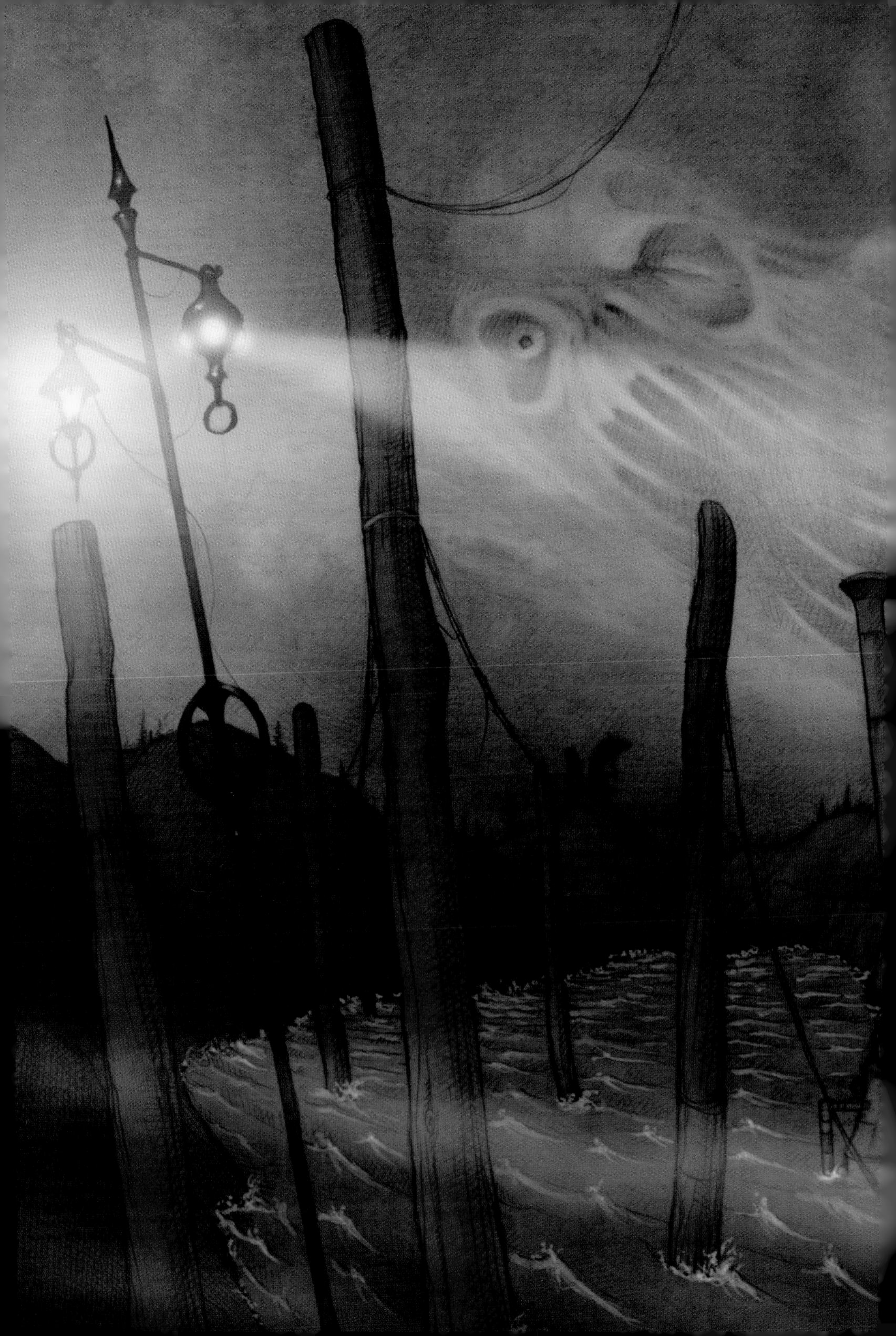

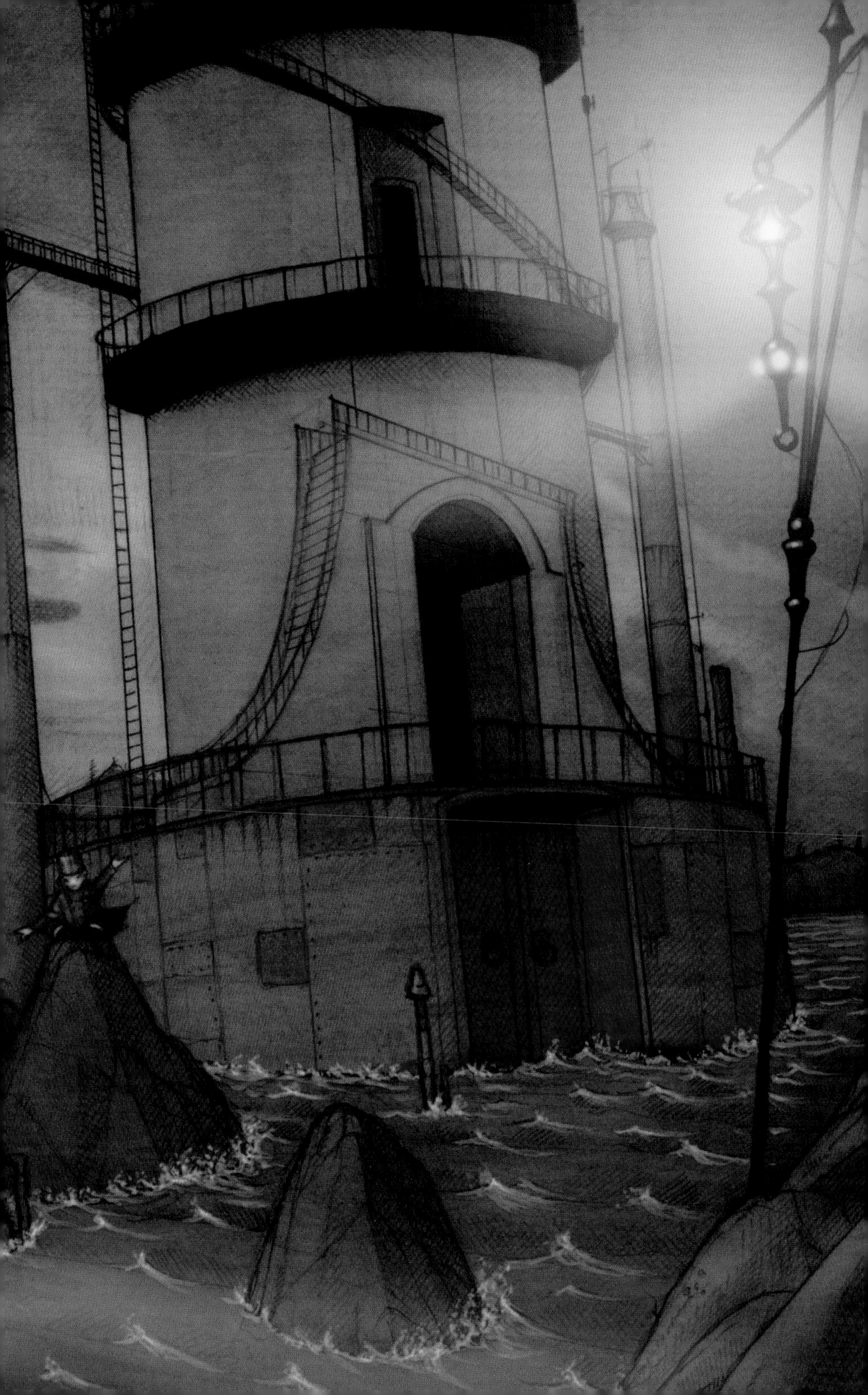

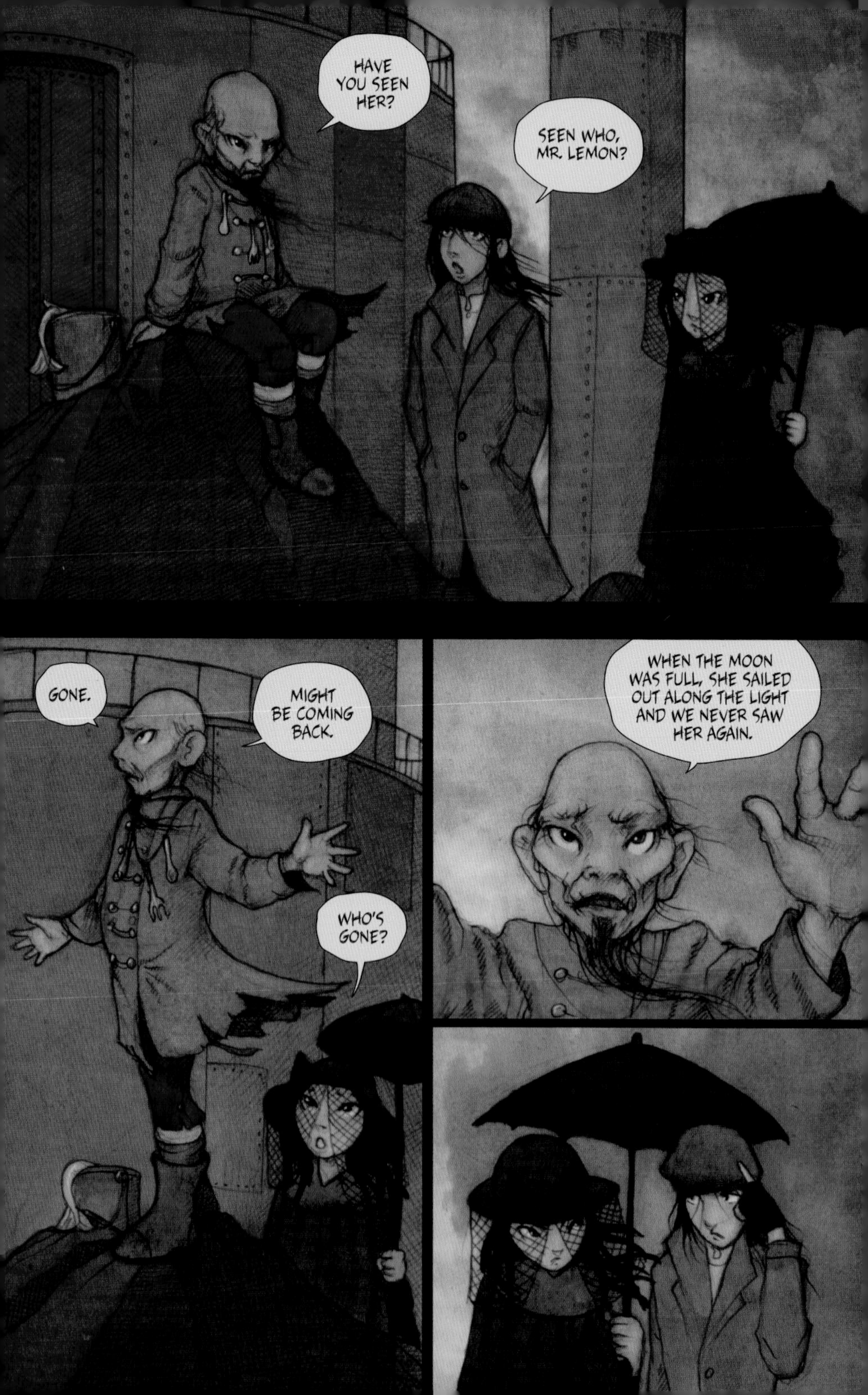
HAVE YOU SEEN HER?
SEEN WHO, MR. LEMON?
GONE.
MIGHT BE COMING BACK.
WHO'S GONE?
WHEN THE MOON WAS FULL, SHE SAILED OUT ALONG THE LIGHT AND WE NEVER SAW HER AGAIN.

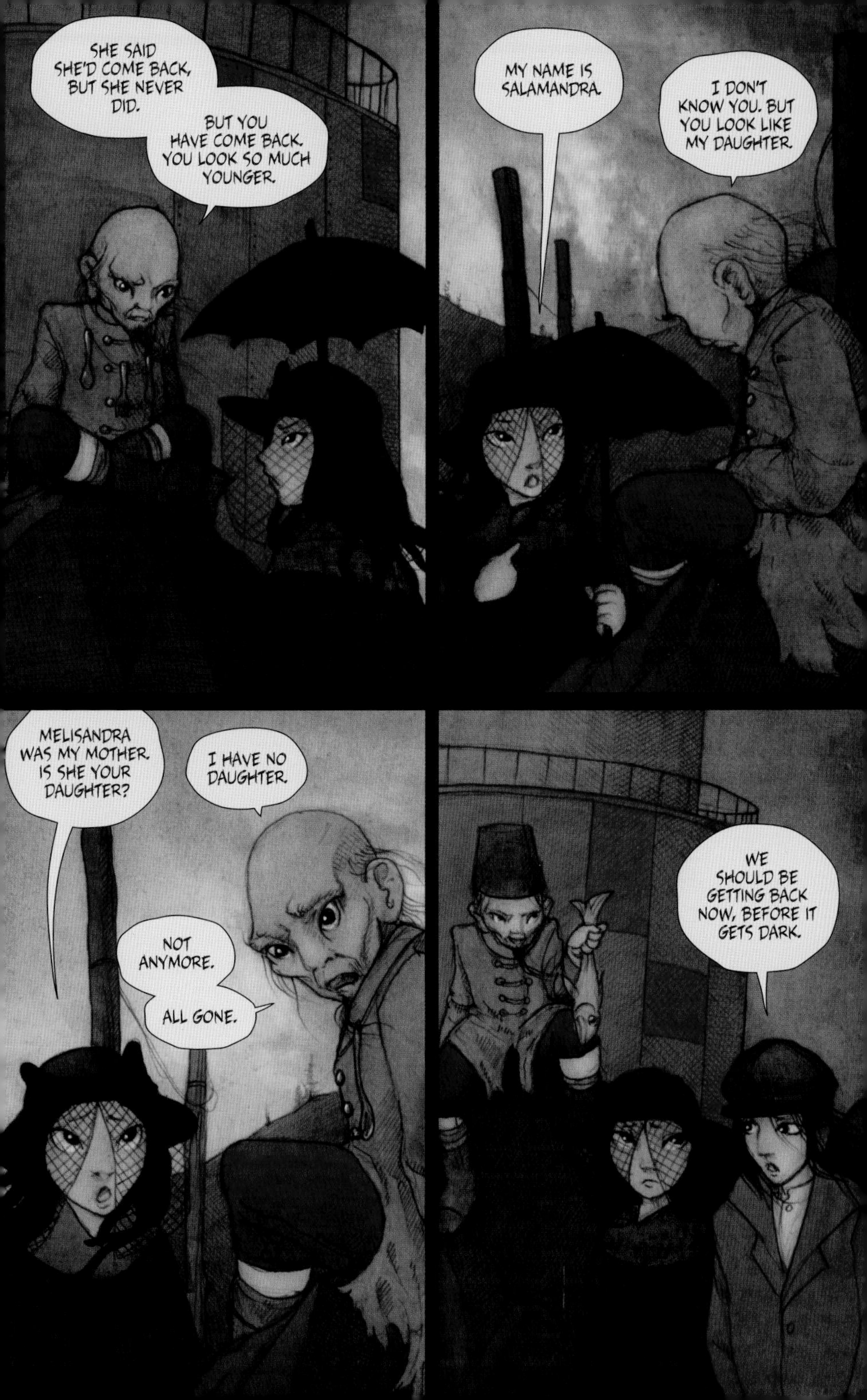
SHE SAID SHE'D COME BACK, BUT SHE NEVER DID.
BUT YOU HAVE COME BACK. YOU LOOK SO MUCH YOUNGER.
MY NAME IS SALAMANDRA.
I DON'T KNOW YOU. BUT YOU LOOK LIKE MY DAUGHTER.
MELISANDRA WAS MY MOTHER. IS SHE YOUR DAUGHTER?
I HAVE NO DAUGHTER.
NOT ANYMORE.
ALL GONE.
WE SHOULD BE GETTING BACK NOW, BEFORE IT GETS DARK.

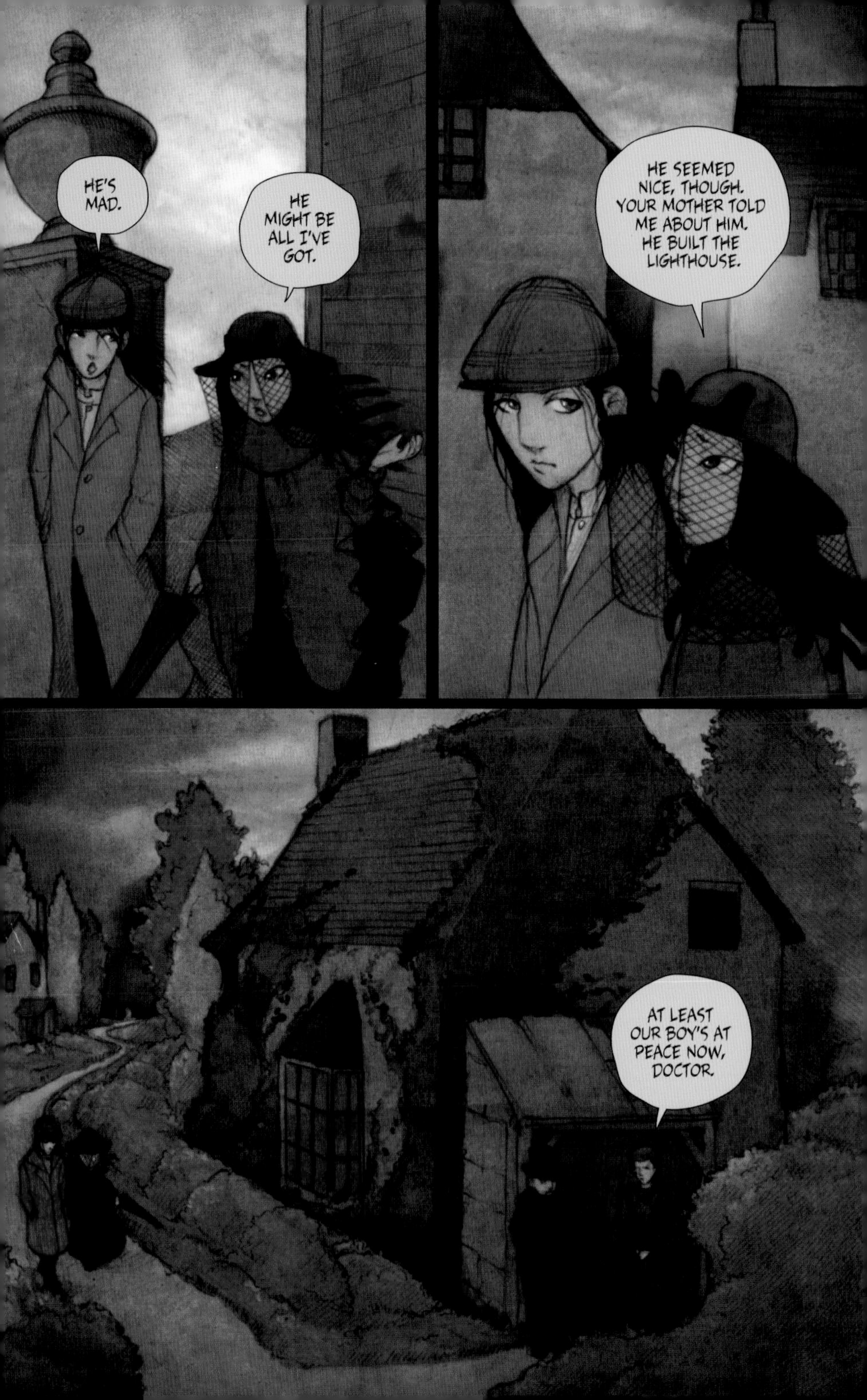
HE'S MAD.
HE MIGHT BE ALL I'VE GOT.
HE SEEMED NICE, THOUGH. YOUR MOTHER TOLD ME ABOUT HIM. HE BUILT THE LIGHTHOUSE.
AT LEAST OUR BOY'S AT PEACE NOW, DOCTOR.

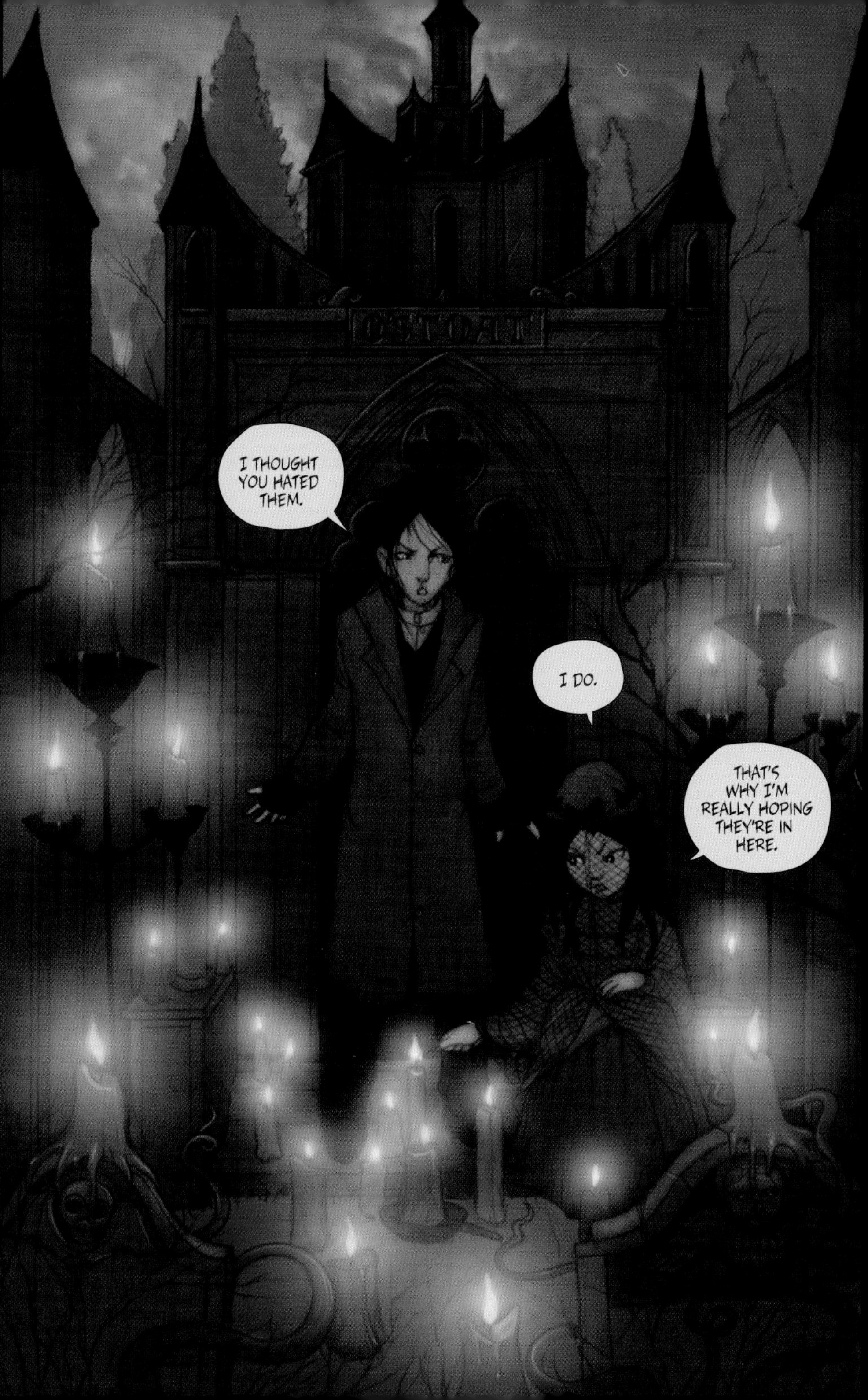
I THOUGHT YOU HATED THEM.
I DO.
THAT'S WHY I'M REALLY HOPING THEY'RE IN HERE.

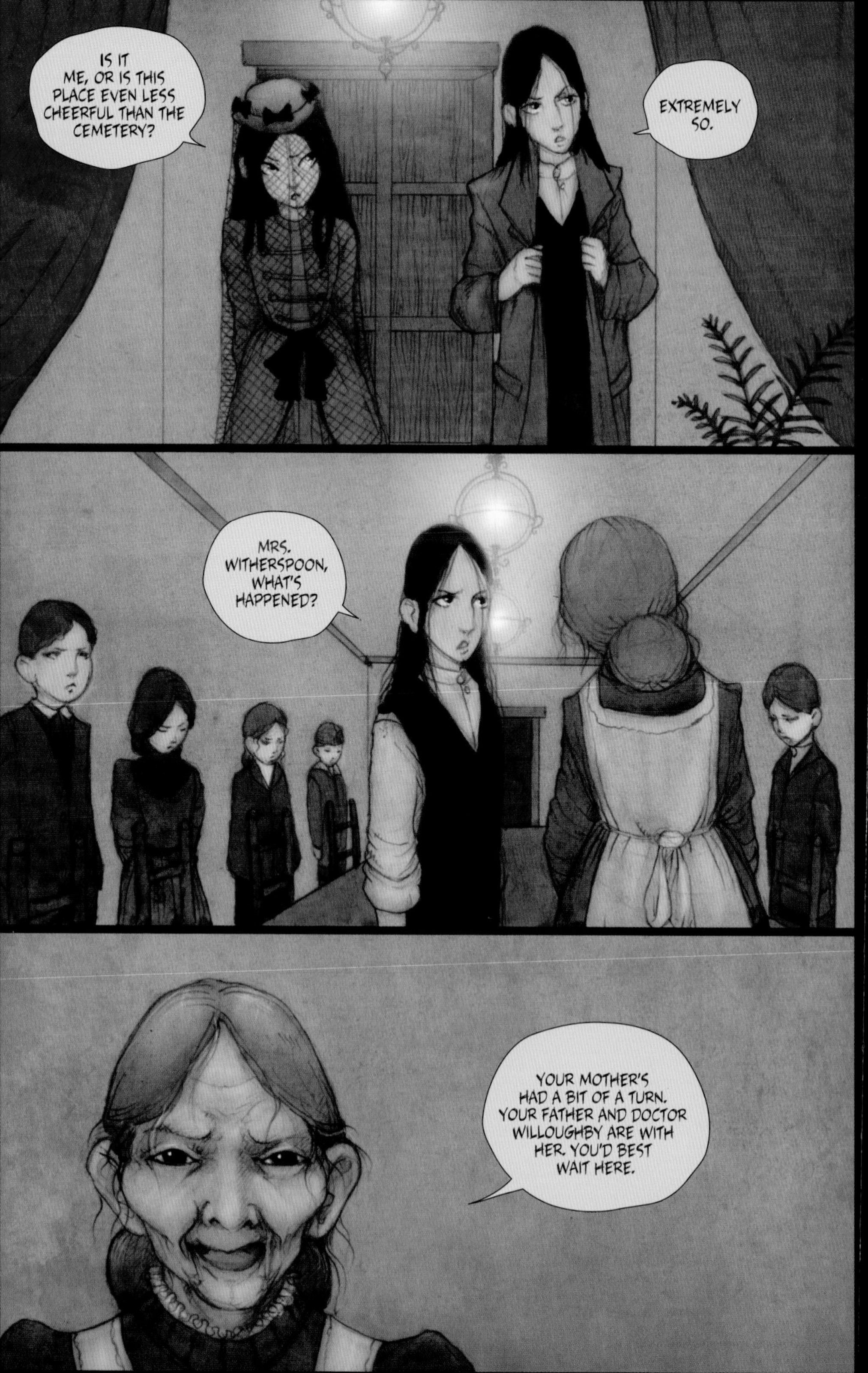
IS IT ME, OR IS THIS PLACE EVEN LESS CHEERFUL THAN THE CEMETERY?
EXTREMELY SO.
MRS. WITHERSPOON, WHAT'S HAPPENED?
YOUR MOTHER'S HAD A BIT OF A TURN. YOUR FATHER AND DOCTOR WILLOUGHBY ARE WITH HER. YOU'D BEST WAIT HERE.

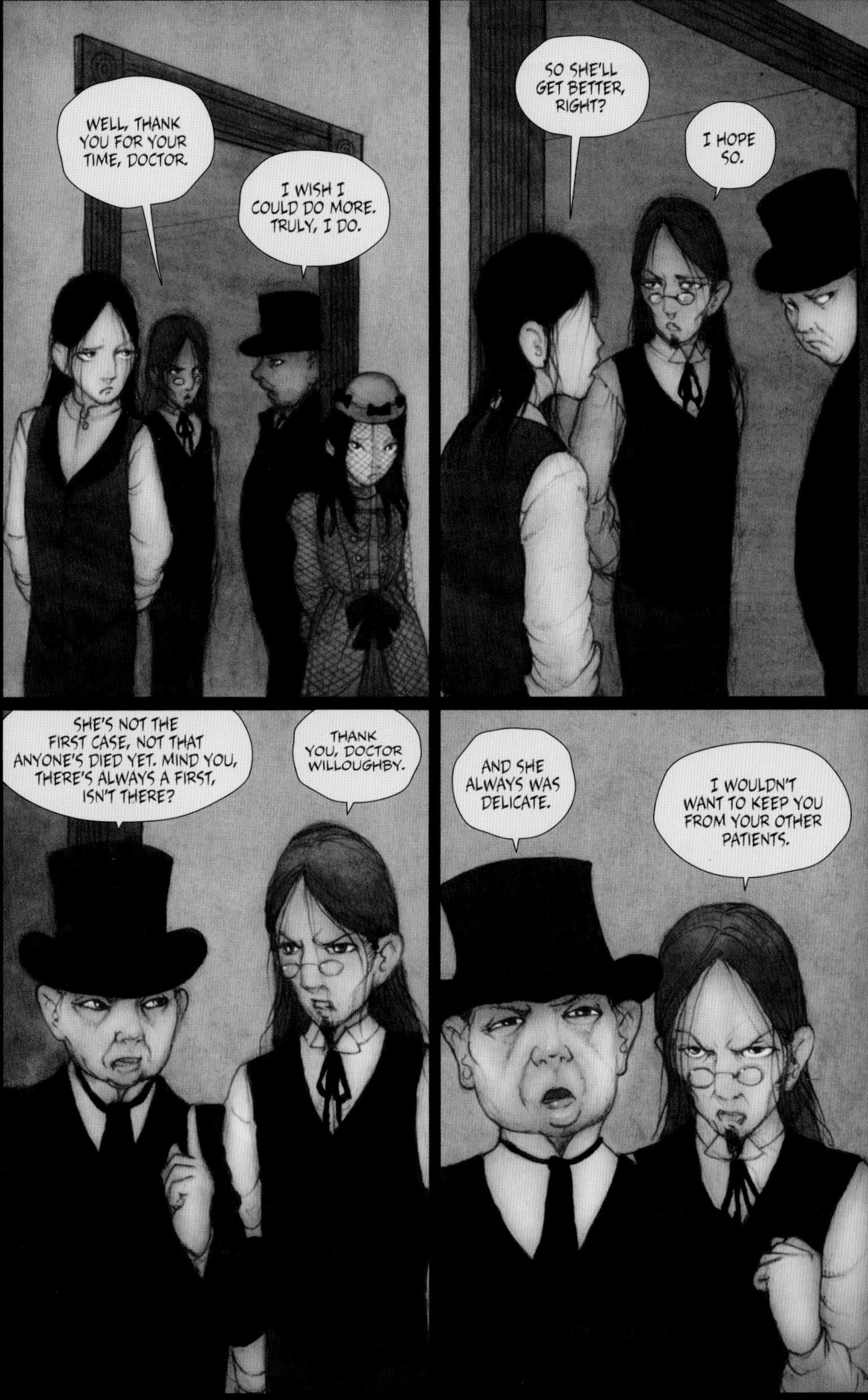
WELL, THANK YOU FOR YOUR TIME, DOCTOR.
I WISH I COULD DO MORE. TRULY, I DO.
SO SHE'LL GET BETTER, RIGHT?
I HOPE SO.
SHE'S NOT THE FIRST CASE, NOT THAT ANYONE'S DIED YET. MIND YOU, THERE'S ALWAYS A FIRST, ISN'T THERE?
THANK YOU, DOCTOR WILLOUGHBY.
AND SHE ALWAYS WAS DELICATE.
I WOULDN'T WANT TO KEEP YOU FROM YOUR OTHER PATIENTS.

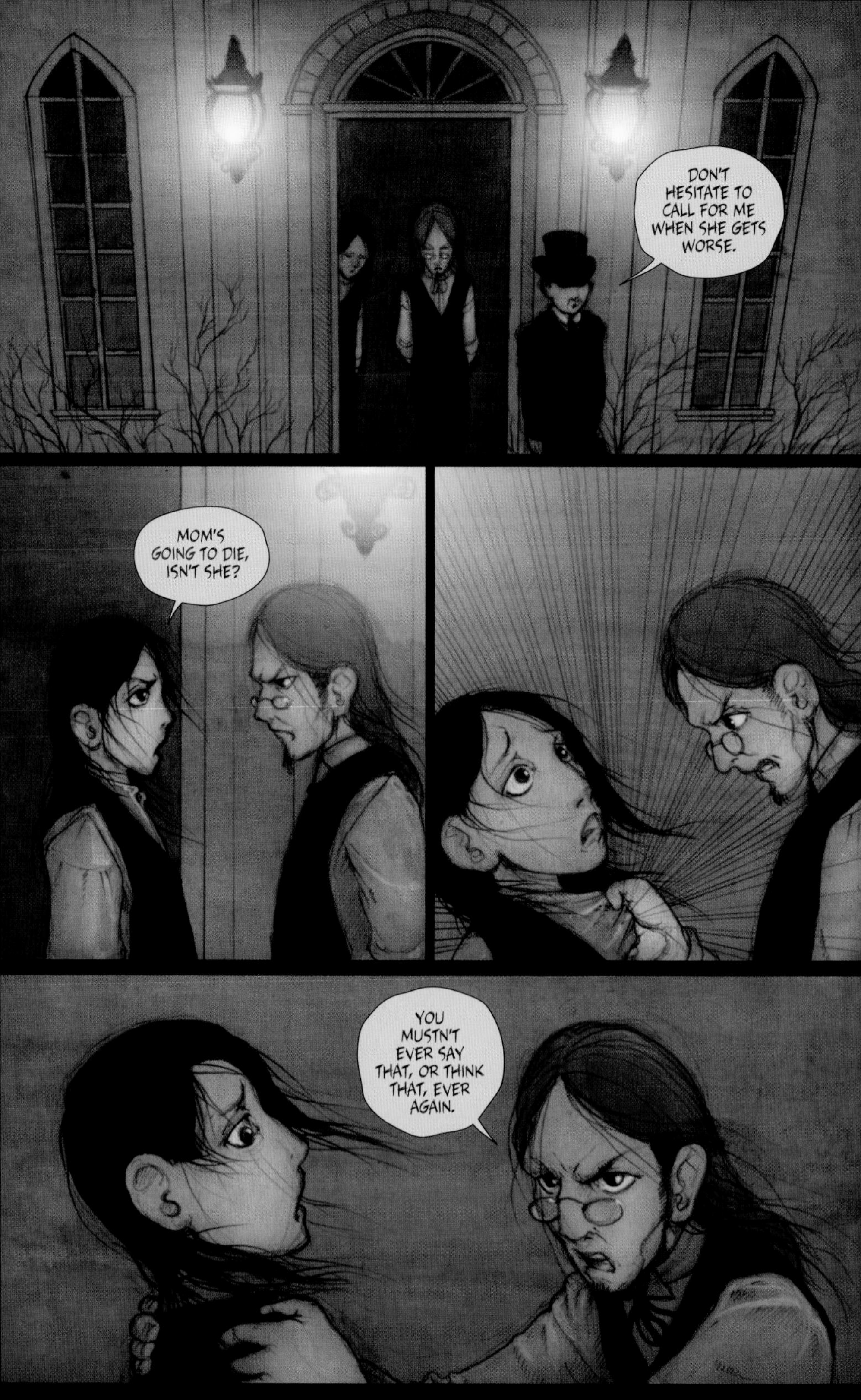
DON'T HESITATE TO CALL FOR ME WHEN SHE GETS WORSE.
MOM'S GOING TO DIE, ISN'T SHE?
YOU MUSTN'T EVER SAY THAT, OR THINK THAT, EVER AGAIN.

CHAPTER THREE

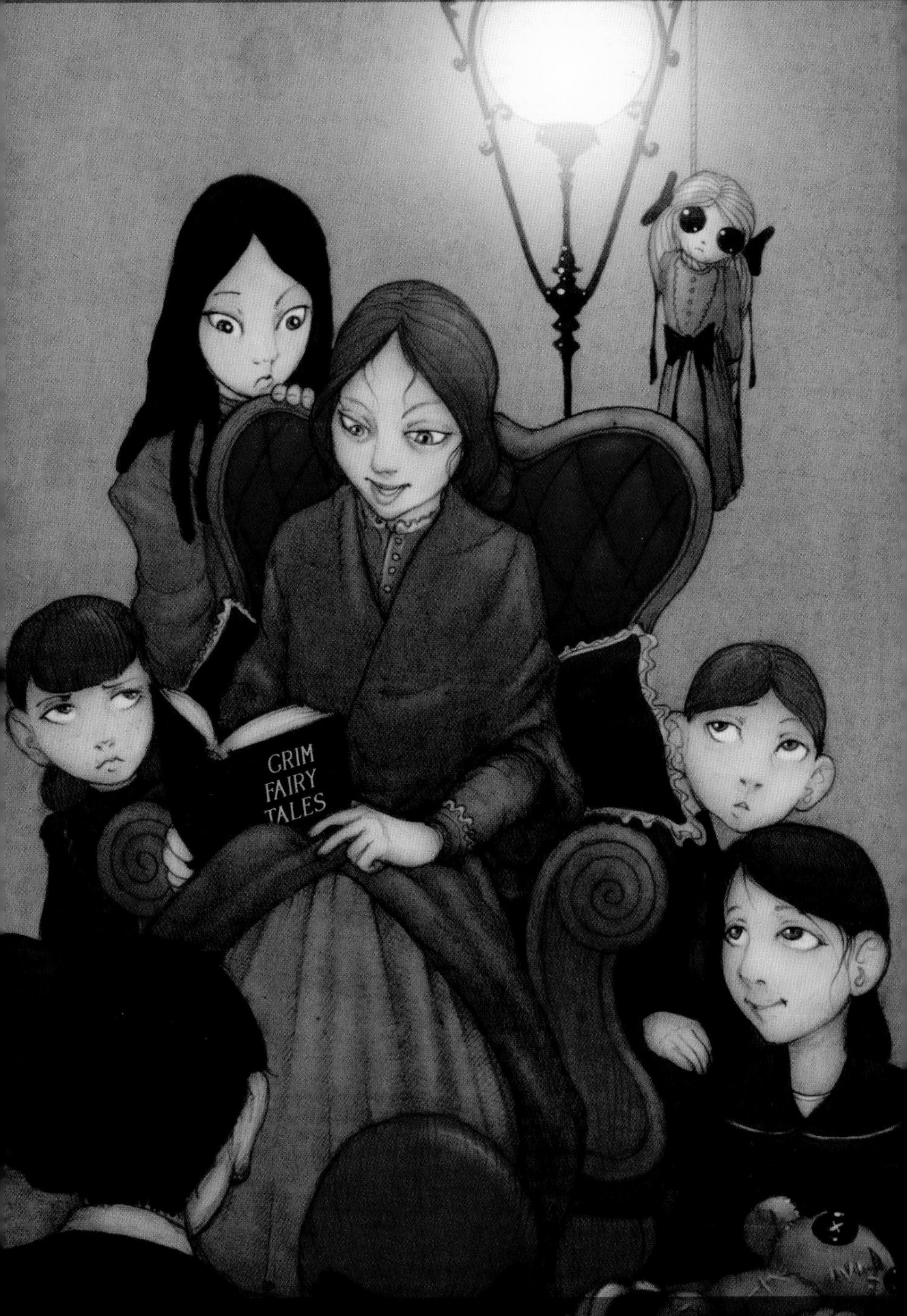
GRIM
FAIRY
TALES

THE SCRYING, NOT THE NEWT PEELING

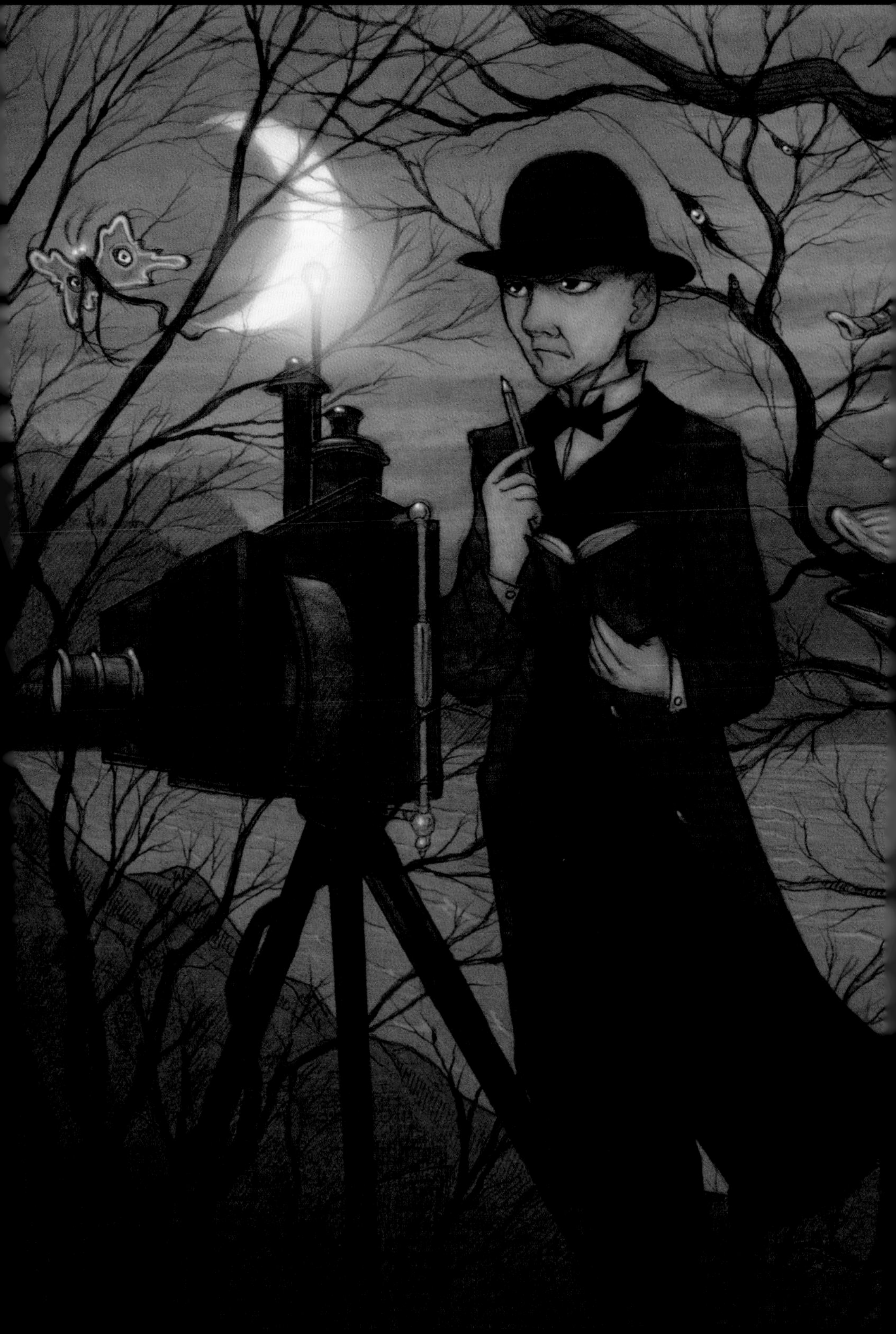

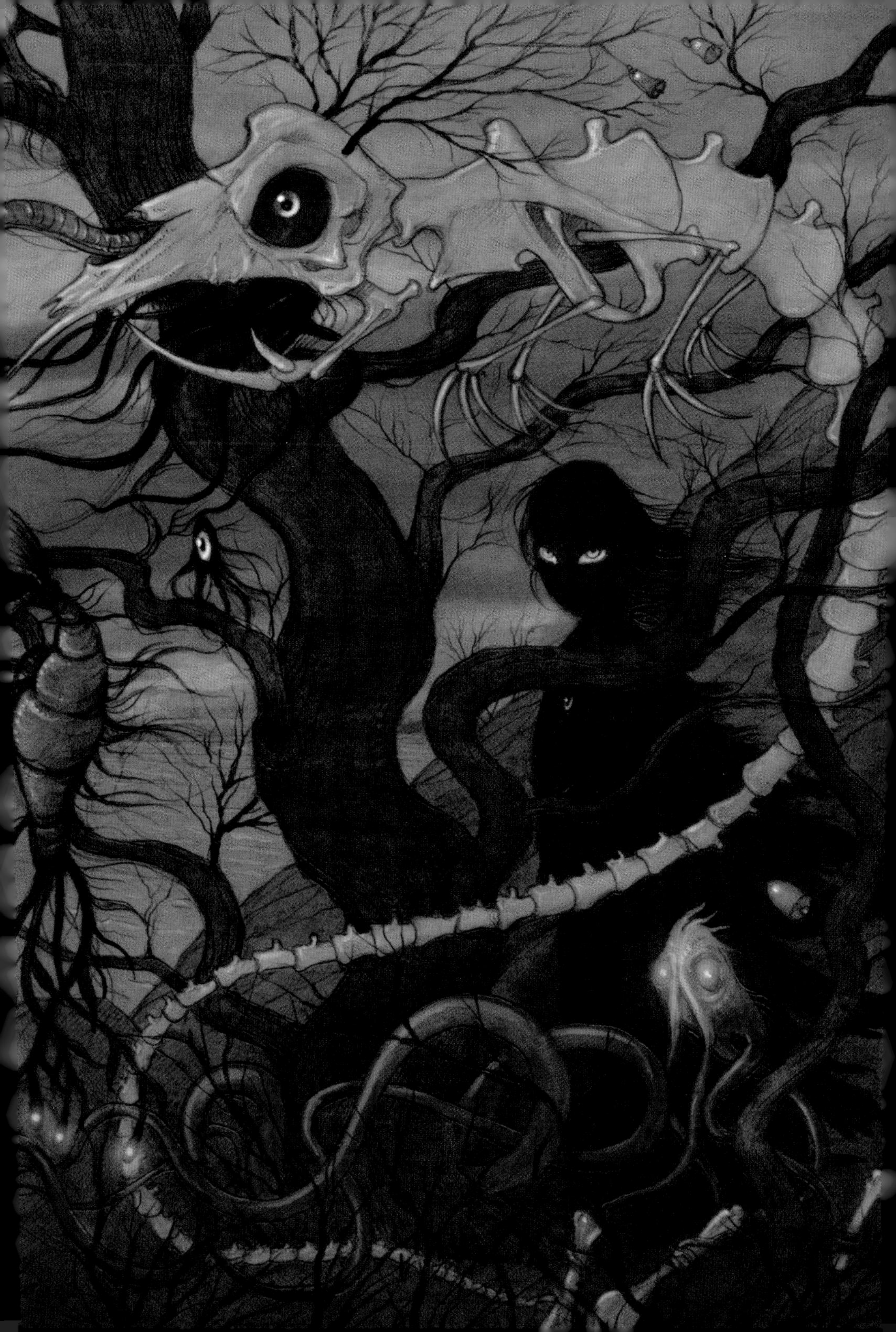

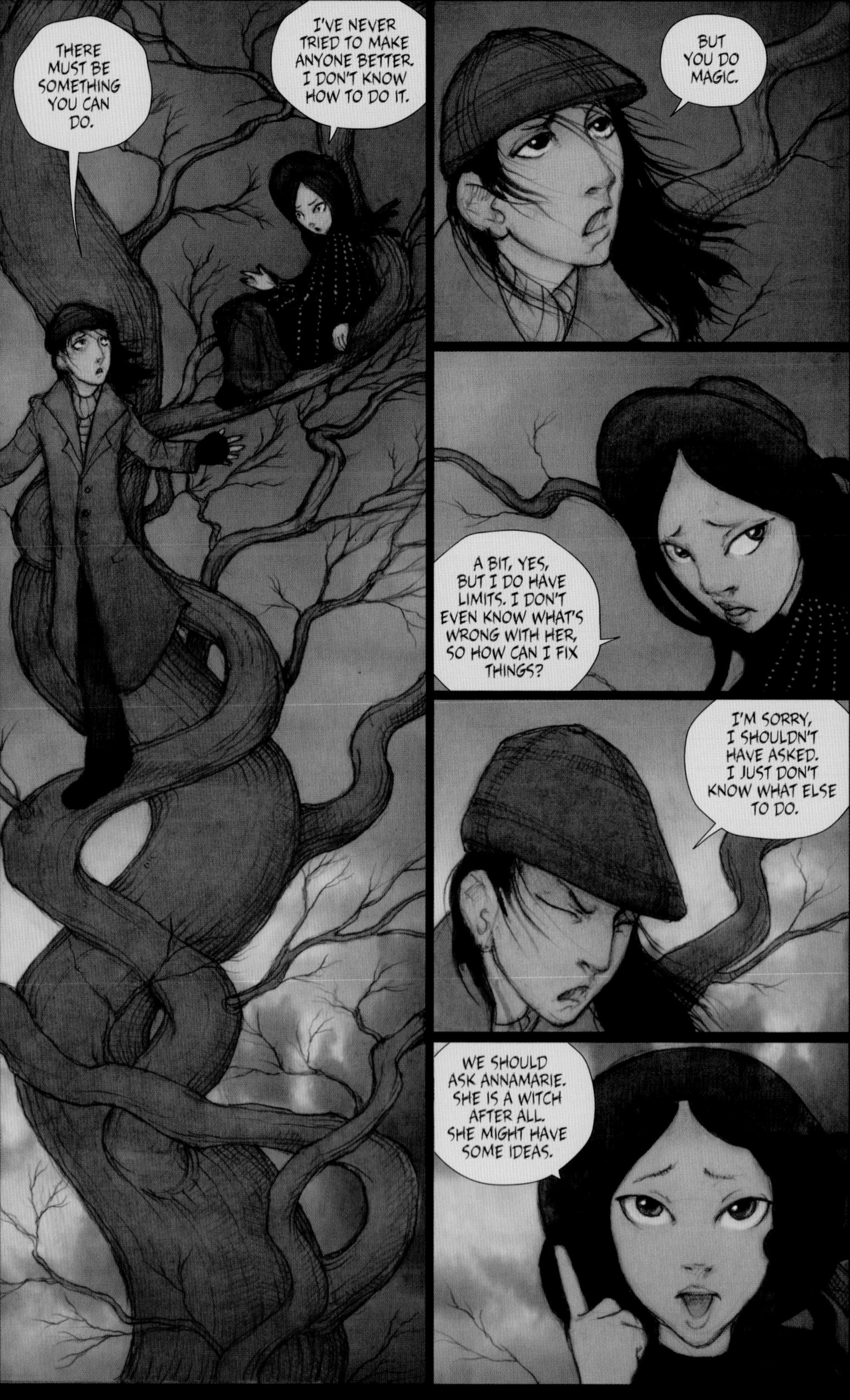
THERE MUST BE SOMETHING YOU CAN DO.
I'VE NEVER TRIED TO MAKE ANYONE BETTER. I DON'T KNOW HOW TO DO IT.
BUT YOU DO MAGIC.
A BIT, YES, BUT I DO HAVE LIMITS. I DON'T EVEN KNOW WHAT'S WRONG WITH HER, SO HOW CAN I FIX THINGS?
I'M SORRY, I SHOULDN'T HAVE ASKED. I JUST DON'T KNOW WHAT ELSE TO DO.
WE SHOULD ASK ANNAMARIE. SHE IS A WITCH AFTER ALL. SHE MIGHT HAVE SOME IDEAS.

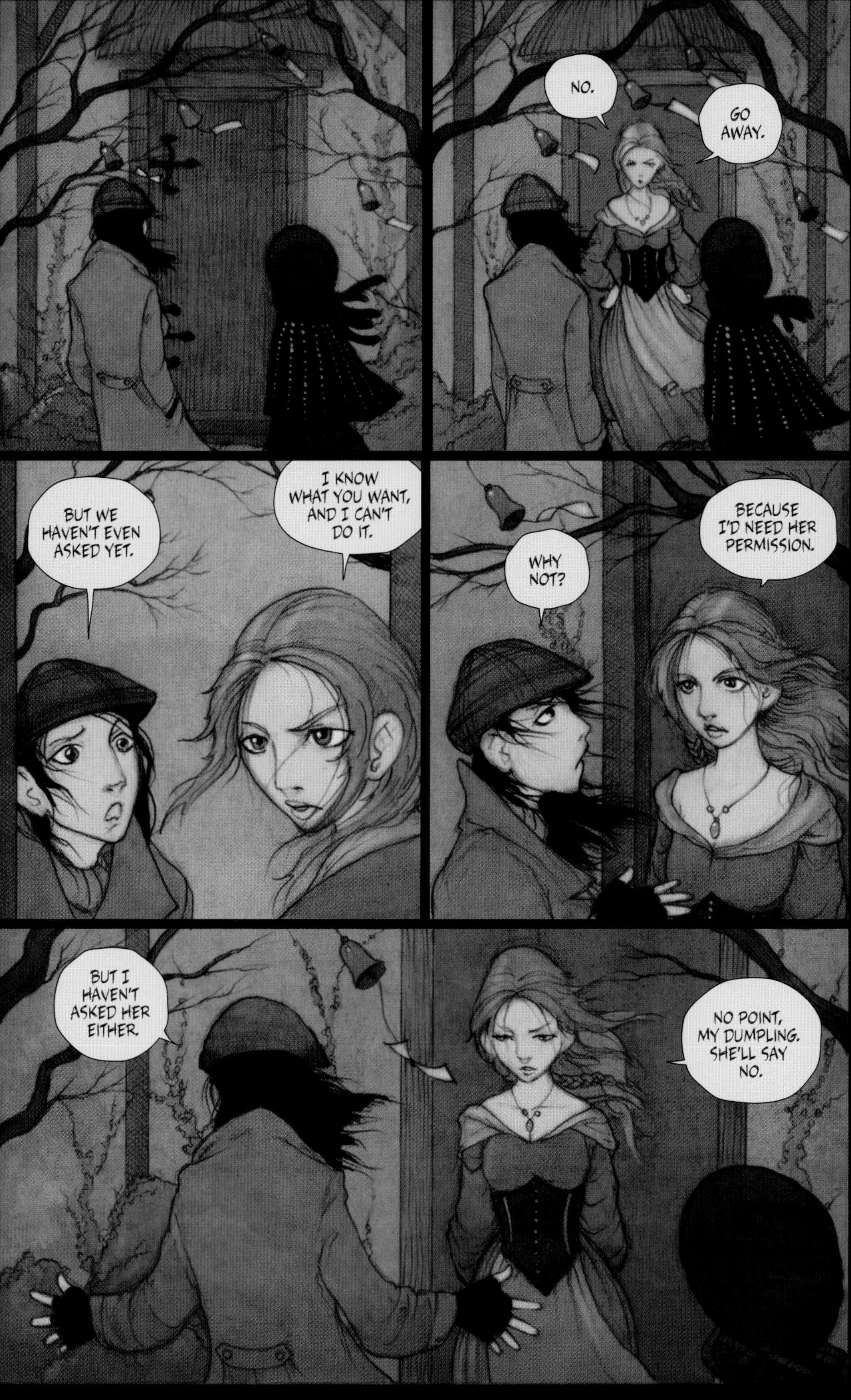
NO.
GO AWAY.
BUT WE HAVEN'T EVEN ASKED YET.
I KNOW WHAT YOU WANT, AND I CAN'T DO IT.
WHY NOT?
BECAUSE I'D NEED HER PERMISSION.
BUT I HAVEN'T ASKED HER EITHER.
NO POINT, MY DUMPLING. SHE'LL SAY NO.

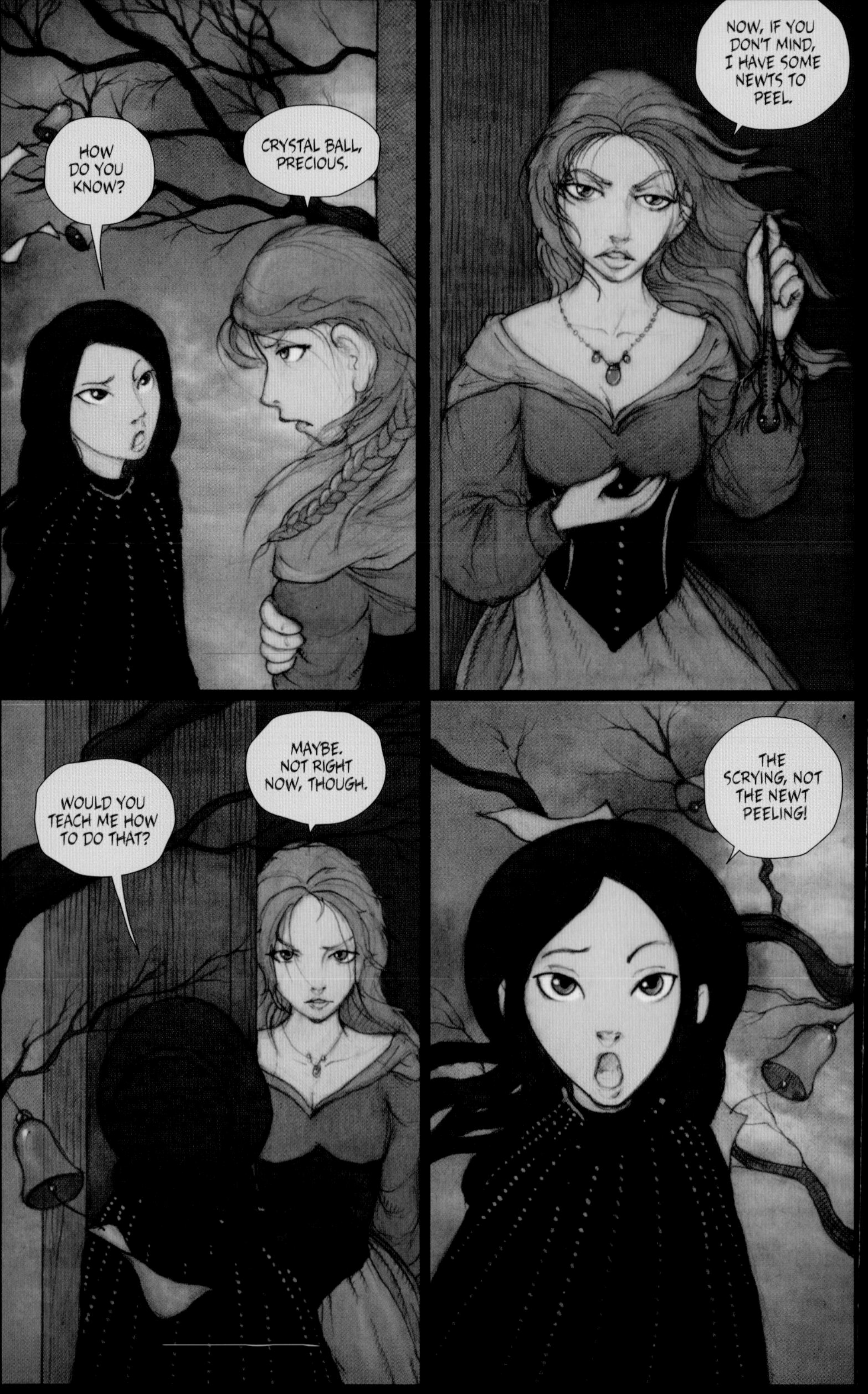
HOW DO YOU KNOW?
CRYSTAL BALL, PRECIOUS.
NOW, IF YOU DON'T MIND, I HAVE SOME NEWTS TO PEEL.
WOULD YOU TEACH ME HOW TO DO THAT?
MAYBE. NOT RIGHT NOW, THOUGH.
THE SCRYING, NOT THE NEWT PEELING!

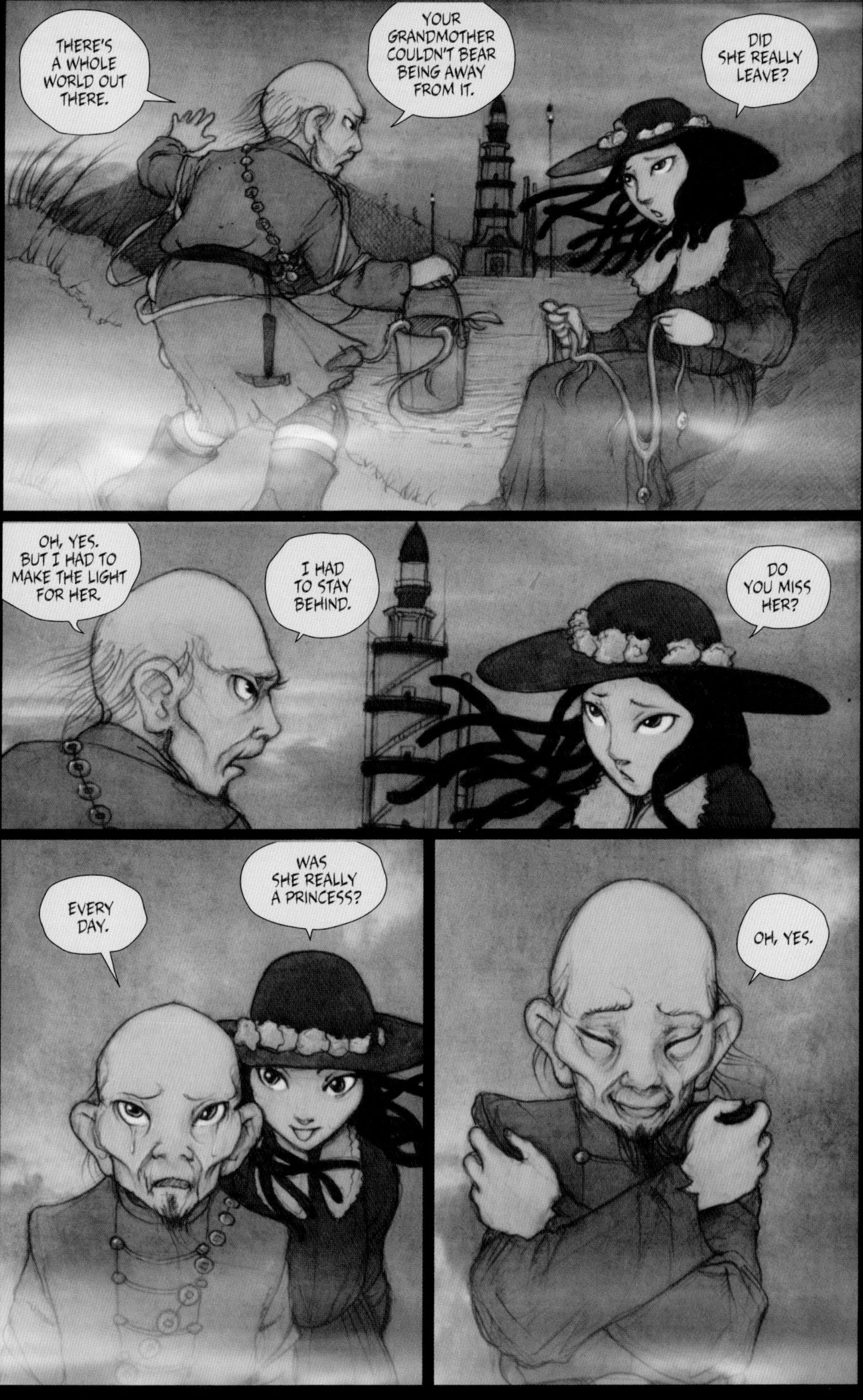
THERE'S A WHOLE WORLD OUT THERE.
YOUR GRANDMOTHER COULDN'T BEAR BEING AWAY FROM IT.
DID SHE REALLY LEAVE?
OH, YES. BUT I HAD TO MAKE THE LIGHT FOR HER.
I HAD TO STAY BEHIND.
DO YOU MISS HER?
EVERY DAY.
WAS SHE REALLY A PRINCESS?
OH, YES.

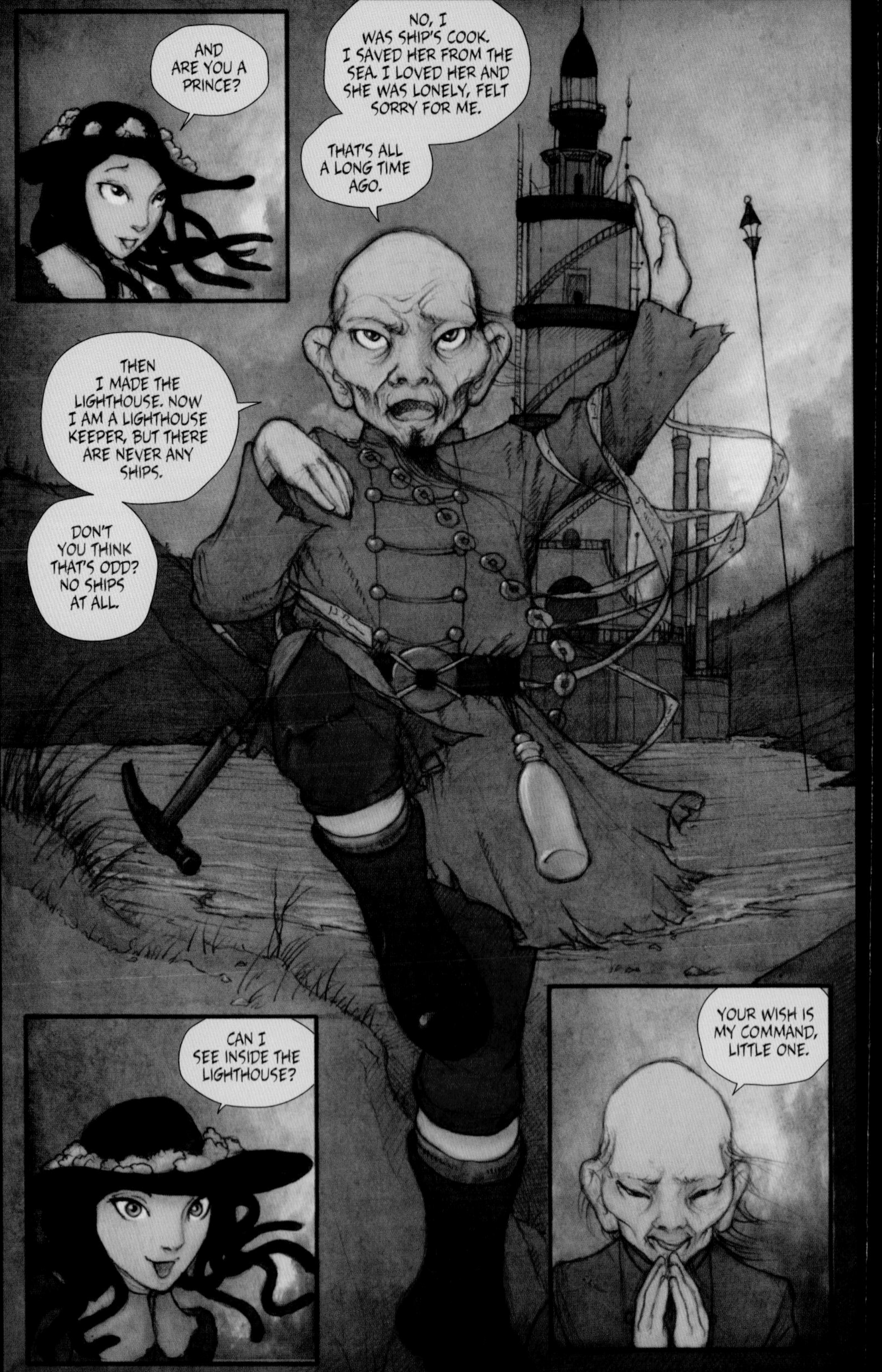
AND ARE YOU A PRINCE?
NO, I WAS SHIP'S COOK. I SAVED HER FROM THE SEA. I LOVED HER AND SHE WAS LONELY, FELT SORRY FOR ME.
THAT'S ALL A LONG TIME AGO.
THEN I MADE THE LIGHTHOUSE. NOW I AM A LIGHTHOUSE KEEPER, BUT THERE ARE NEVER ANY SHIPS.
DON'T YOU THINK THAT'S ODD? NO SHIPS AT ALL.
CAN I SEE INSIDE THE LIGHTHOUSE?
YOUR WISH IS MY COMMAND, LITTLE ONE.

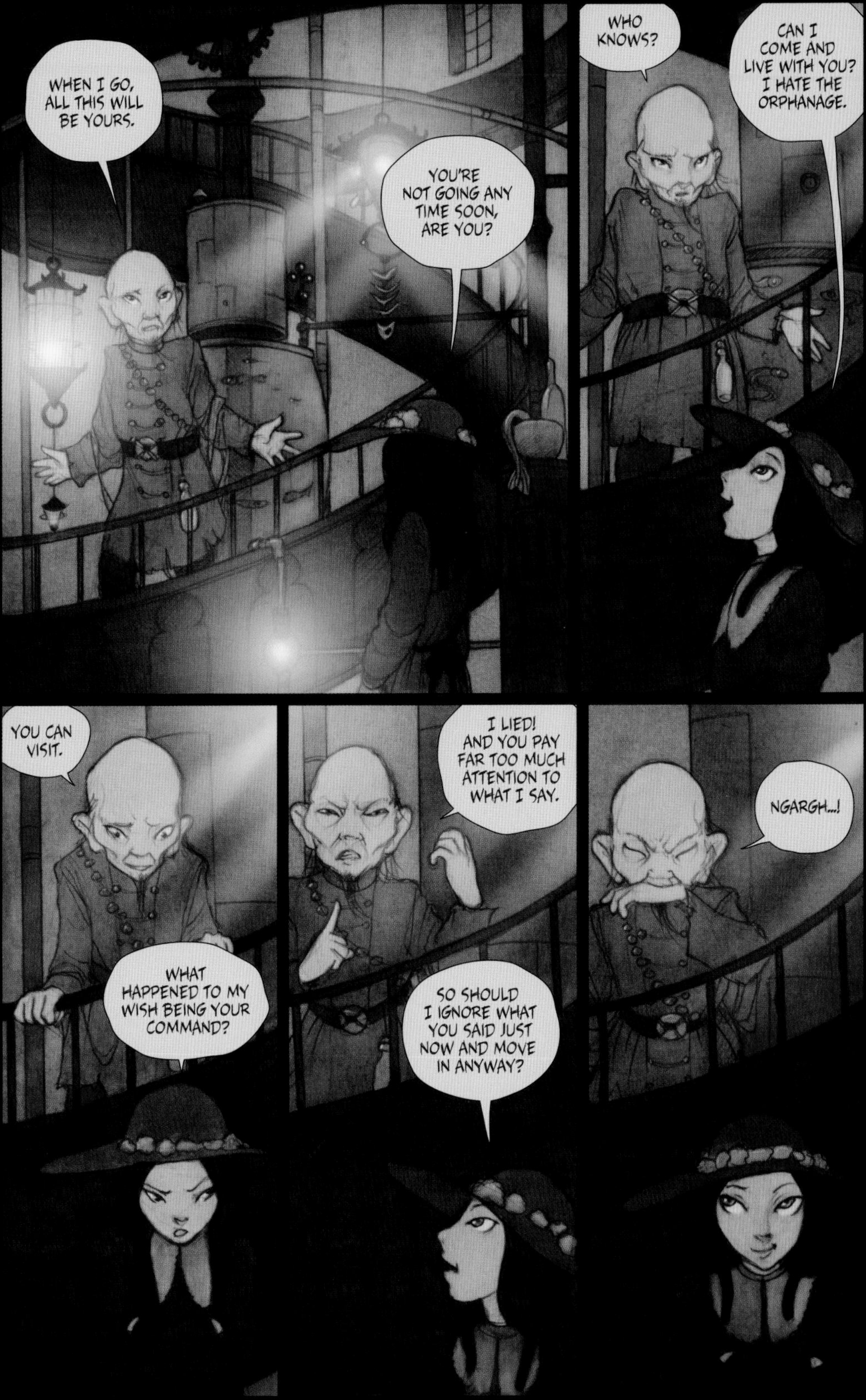
WHEN I GO, ALL THIS WILL BE YOURS.
YOU'RE NOT GOING ANY TIME SOON, ARE YOU?
WHO KNOWS?
CAN I COME AND LIVE WITH YOU? I HATE THE ORPHANAGE.
YOU CAN VISIT.
WHAT HAPPENED TO MY WISH BEING YOUR COMMAND?
I LIED! AND YOU PAY FAR TOO MUCH ATTENTION TO WHAT I SAY.
SO SHOULD I IGNORE WHAT YOU SAID JUST NOW AND MOVE IN ANYWAY?
NGARGH...!

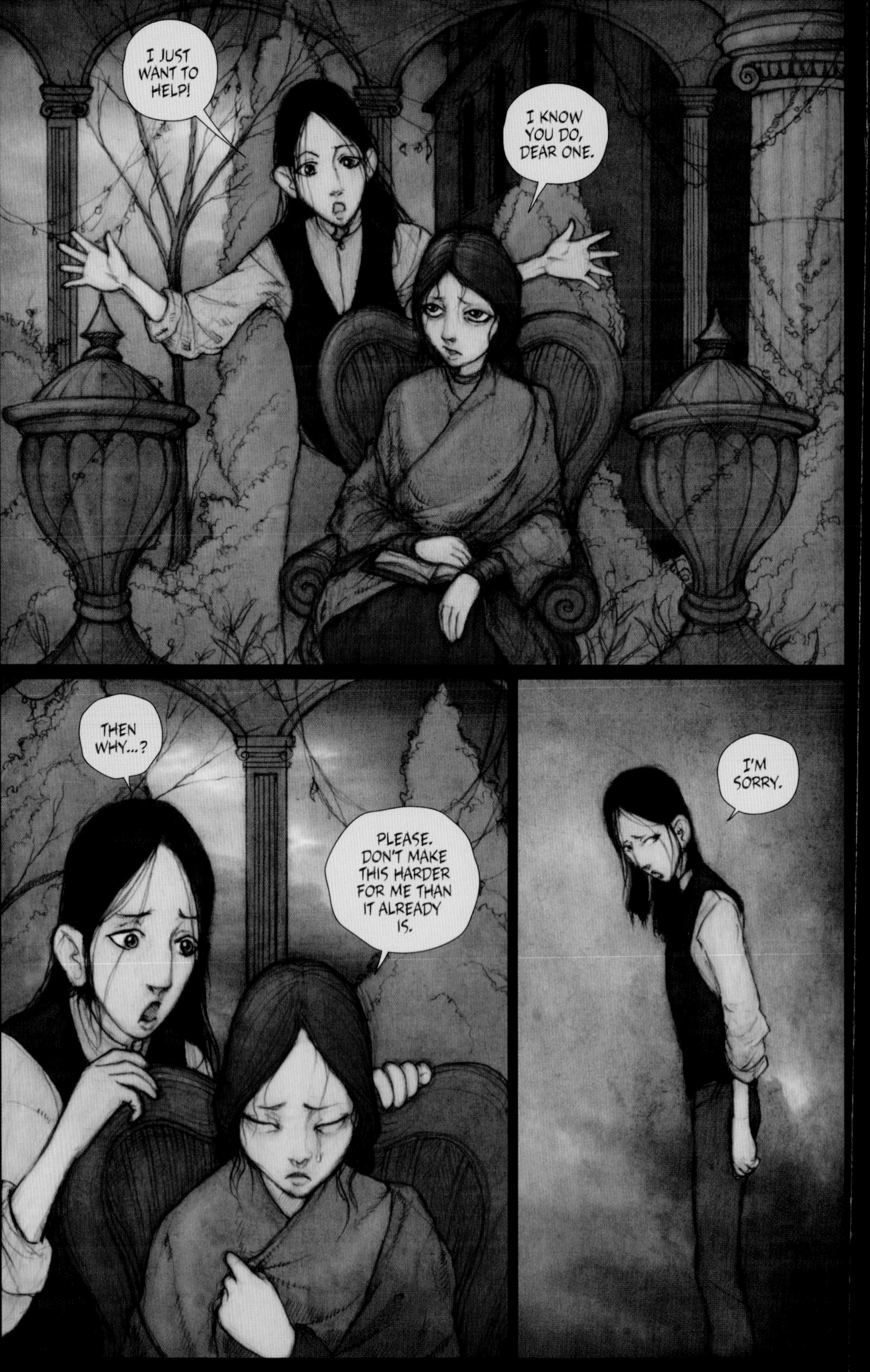
I JUST WANT TO HELP!
I KNOW YOU DO, DEAR ONE.
THEN WHY...?
PLEASE. DON'T MAKE THIS HARDER FOR ME THAN IT ALREADY IS.
I'M SORRY.

CHAPTER FOUR

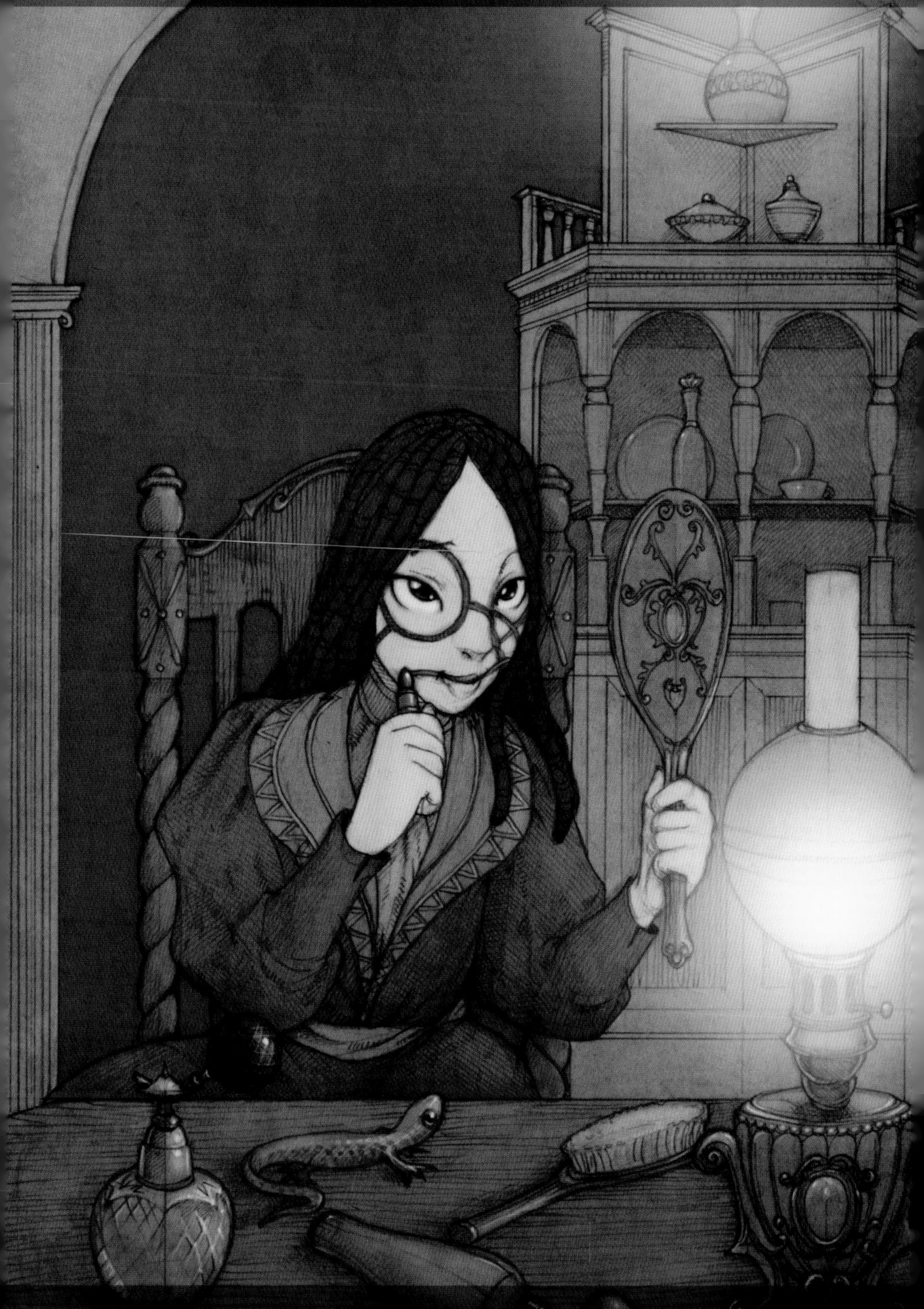

IT'LL BE REALLY UNDIGNIFIED, PROMISE

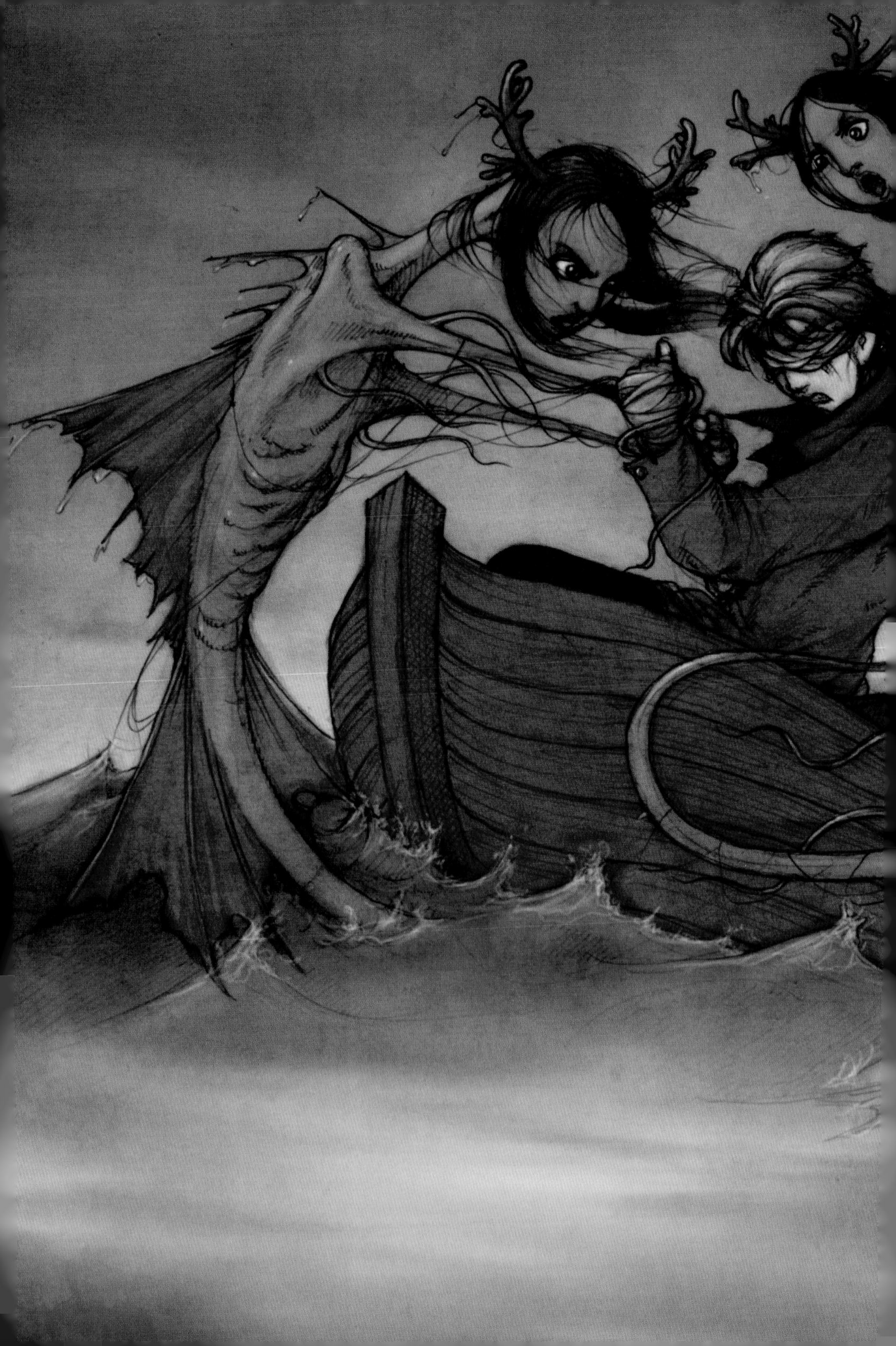

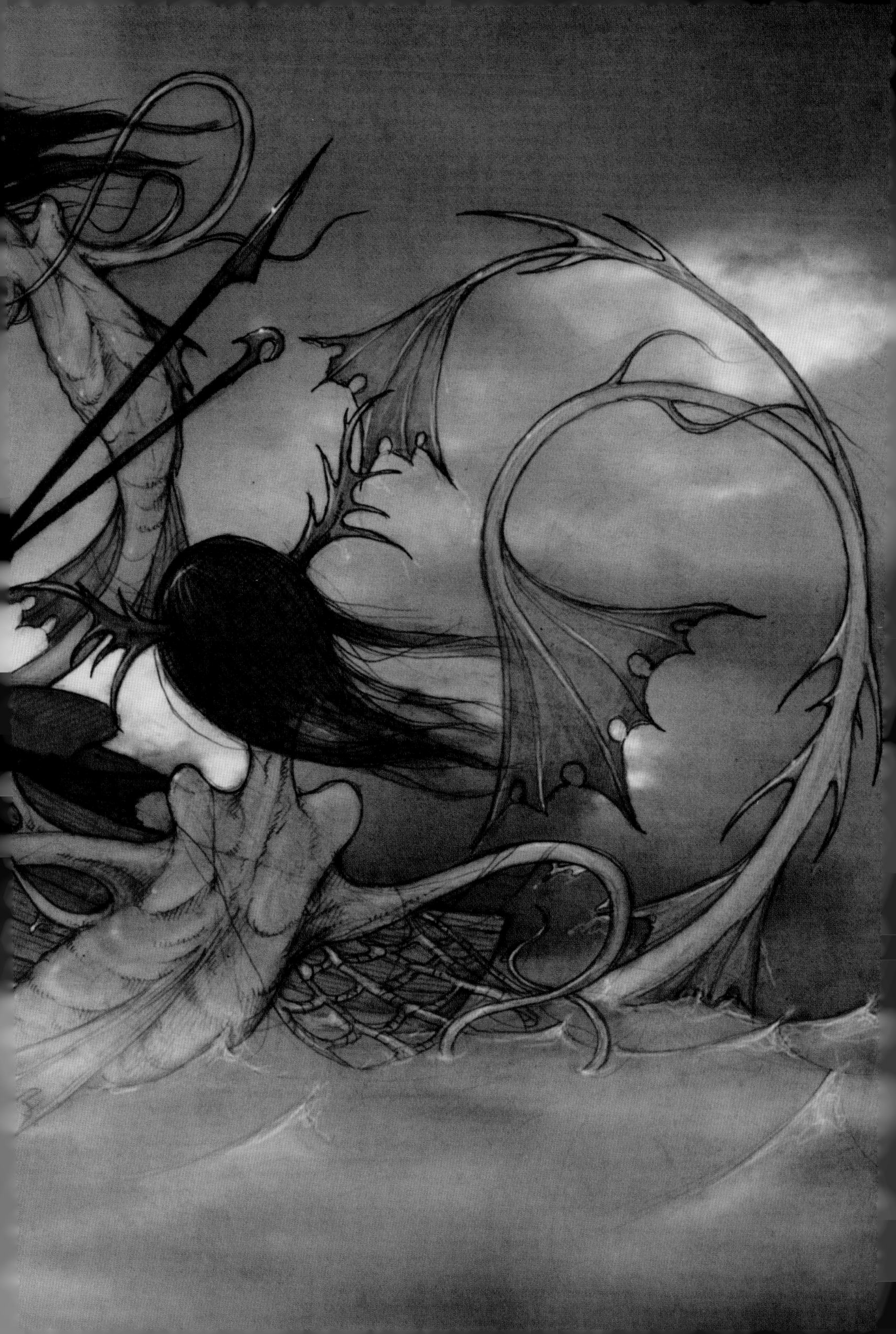

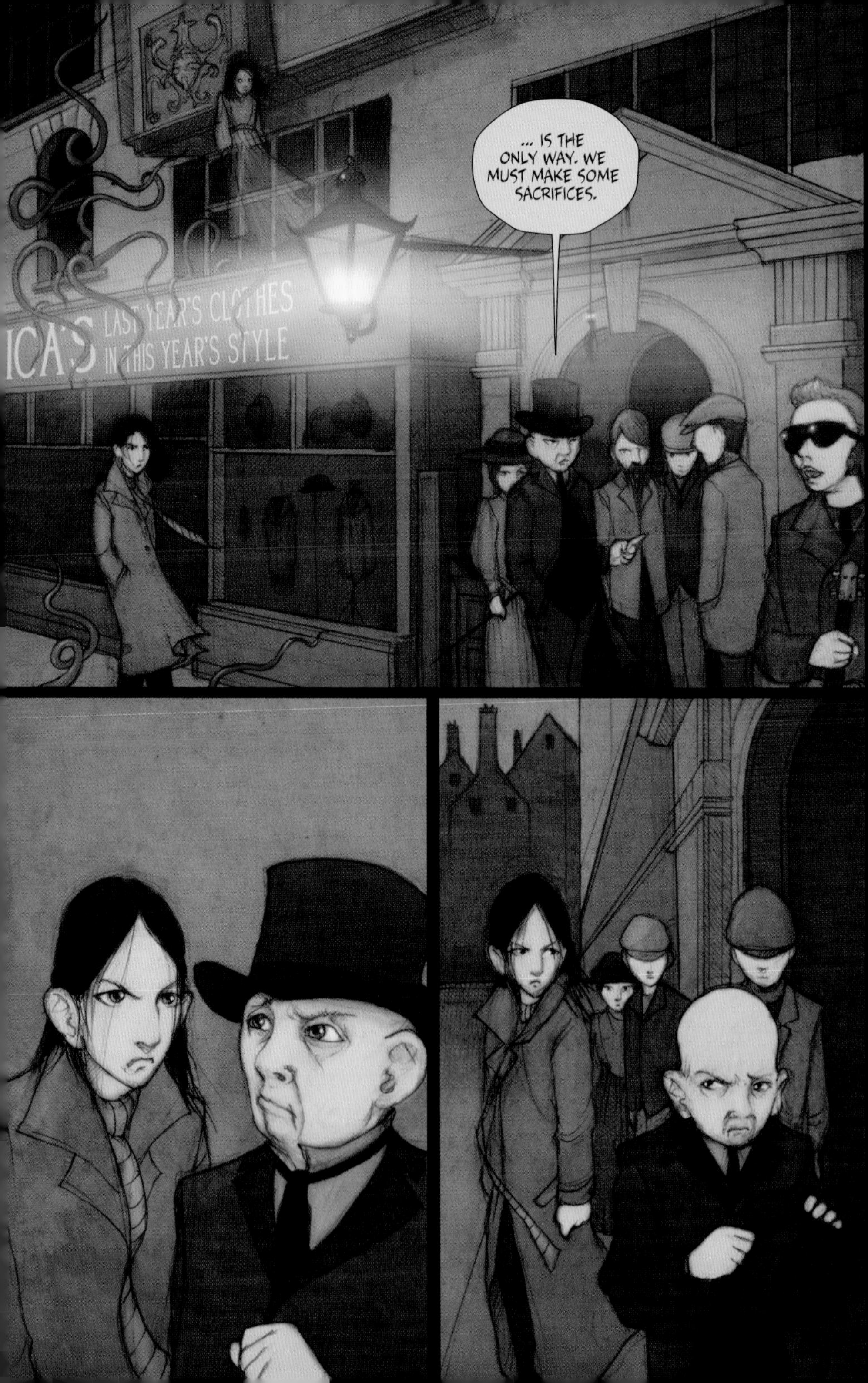
... IS THE ONLY WAY. WE MUST MAKE SOME SACRIFICES.
ICA'S LAST YEAR'S CLOTHES IN THIS YEAR'S STYLE

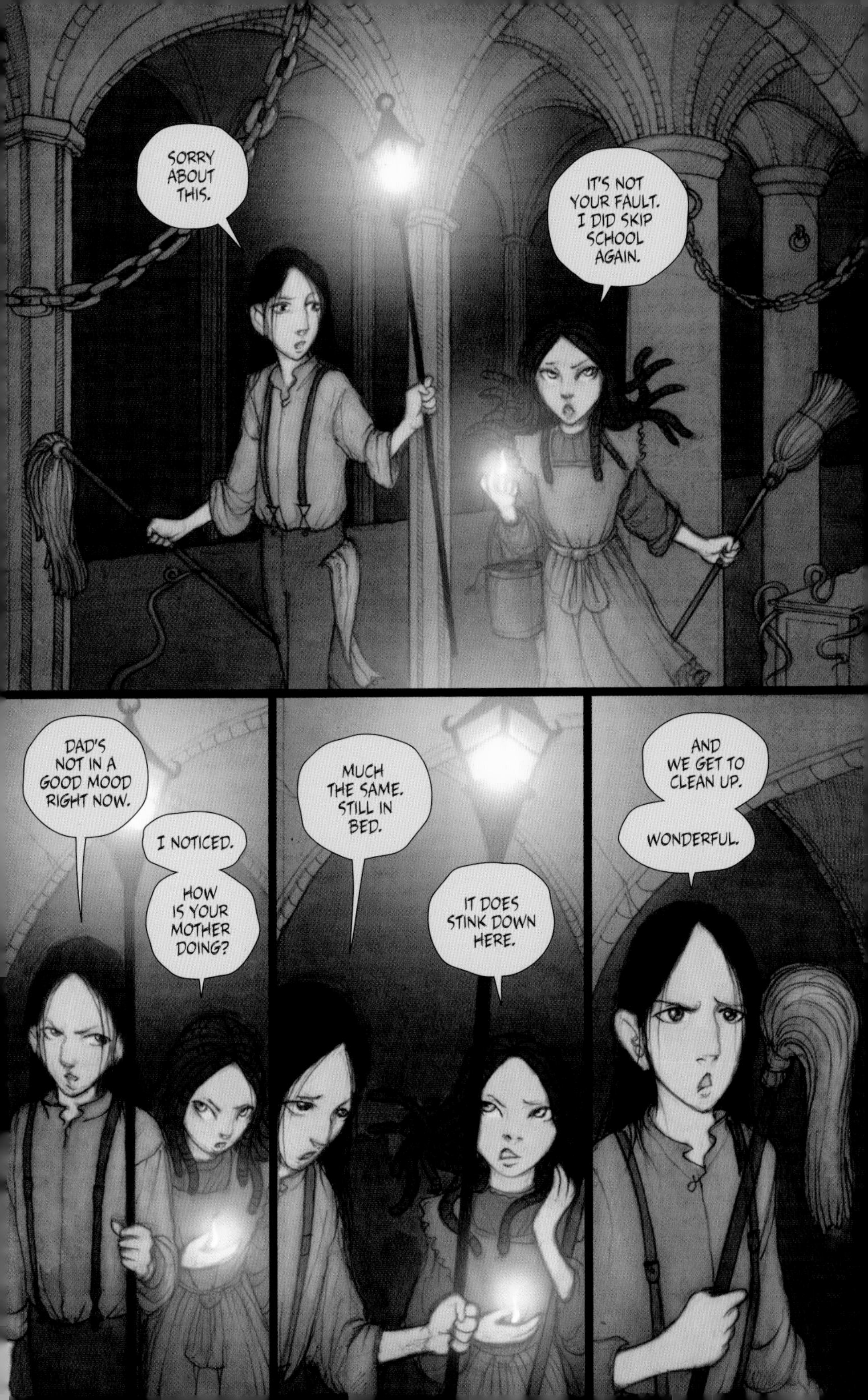
SORRY ABOUT THIS.
IT'S NOT YOUR FAULT. I DID SKIP SCHOOL AGAIN.
DAD'S NOT IN A GOOD MOOD RIGHT NOW.
I NOTICED.
HOW IS YOUR MOTHER DOING?
MUCH THE SAME. STILL IN BED.
IT DOES STINK DOWN HERE.
AND WE GET TO CLEAN UP.
WONDERFUL.

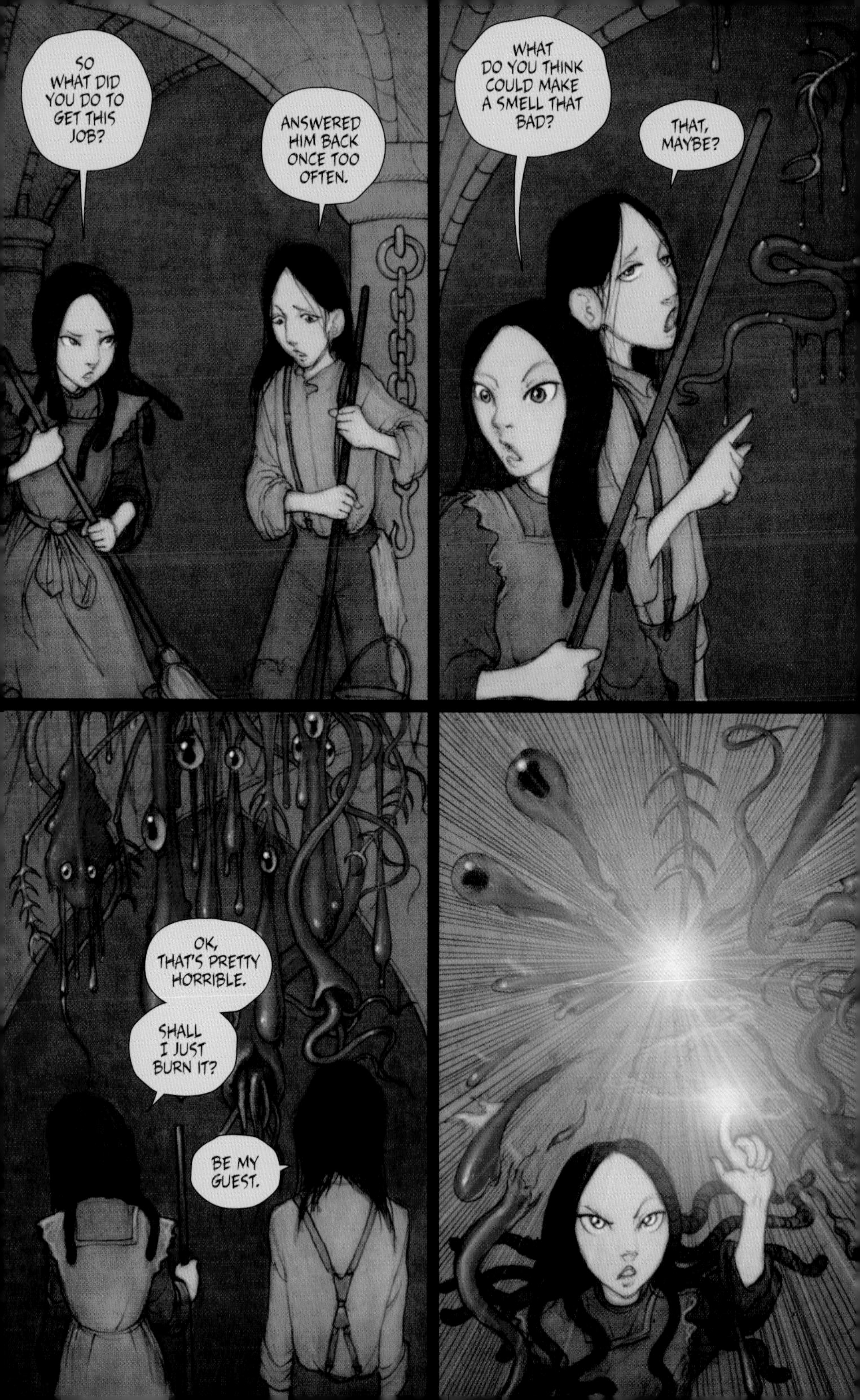
SO WHAT DID YOU DO TO GET THIS JOB?
ANSWERED HIM BACK ONCE TOO OFTEN.
WHAT DO YOU THINK COULD MAKE A SMELL THAT BAD?
THAT, MAYBE?
OK, THAT'S PRETTY HORRIBLE.
SHALL I JUST BURN IT?
BE MY GUEST.

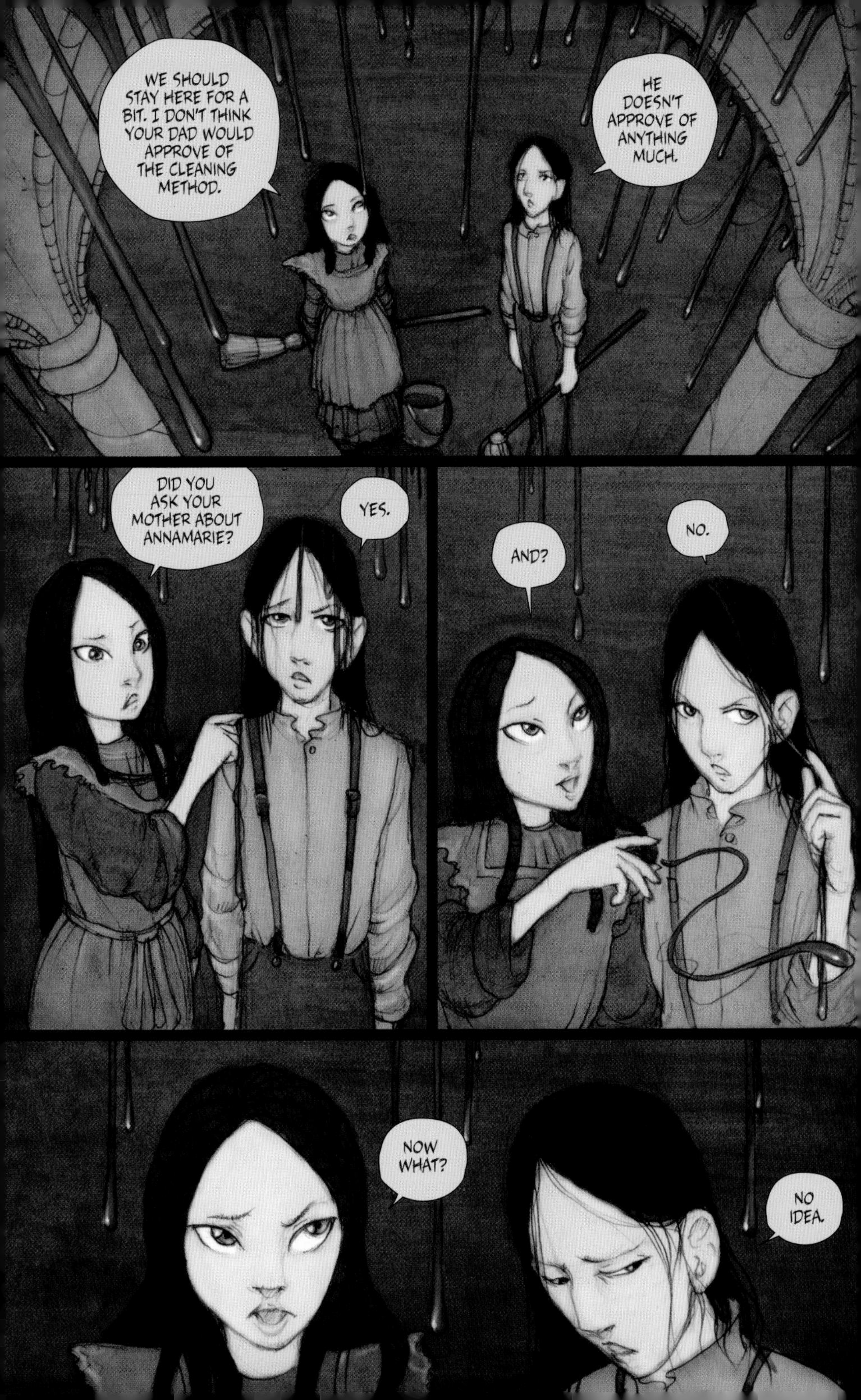
WE SHOULD STAY HERE FOR A BIT. I DON'T THINK YOUR DAD WOULD APPROVE OF THE CLEANING METHOD.
HE DOESN'T APPROVE OF ANYTHING MUCH.
DID YOU ASK YOUR MOTHER ABOUT ANNAMARIE?
YES.
AND?
NO.
NOW WHAT?
NO IDEA.

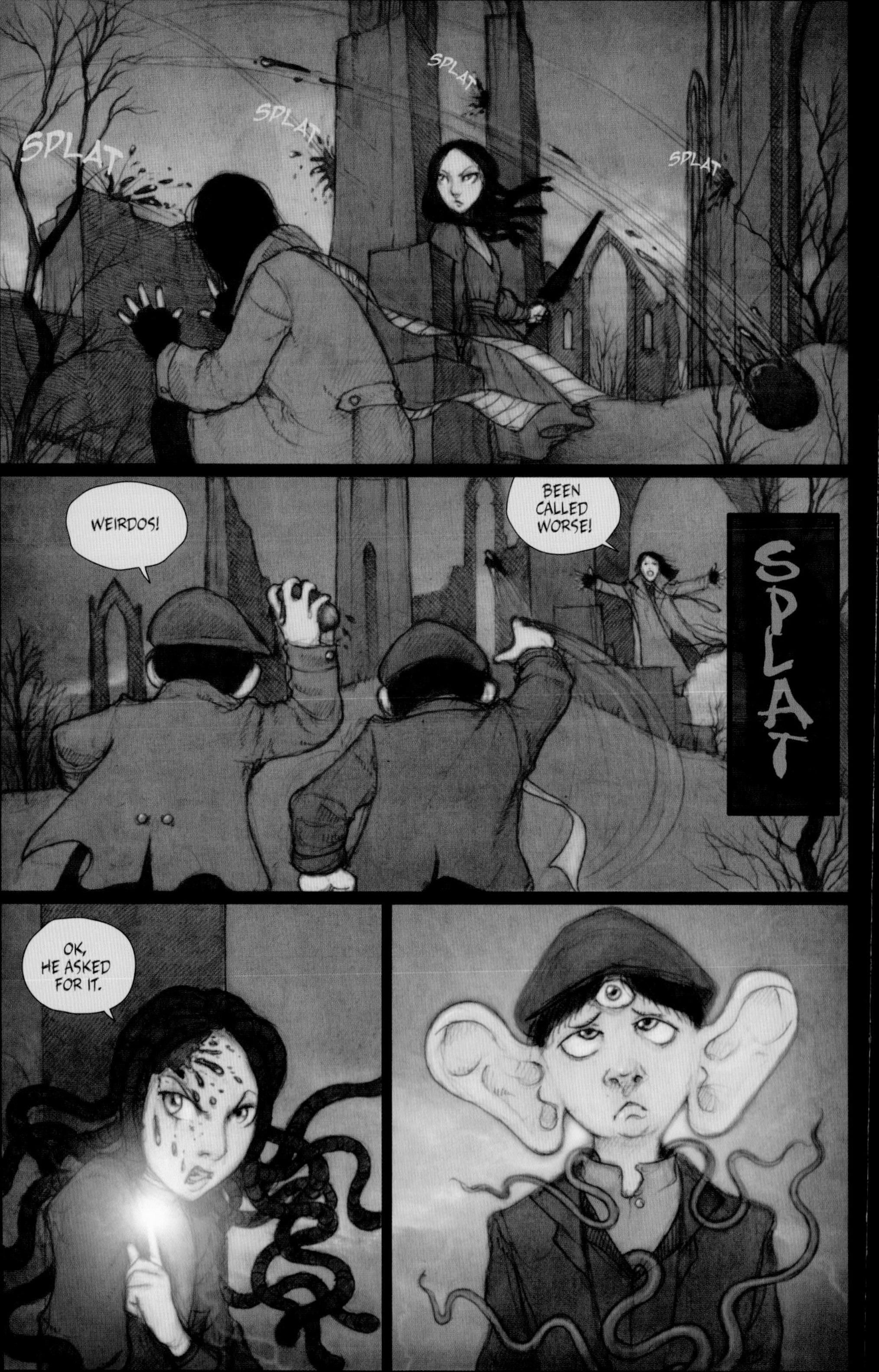
SPLAT
SPLAT
SPLAT
SPLAT
WEIRDOS!
BEEN CALLED WORSE!
SPLAT
OK, HE ASKED FOR IT.

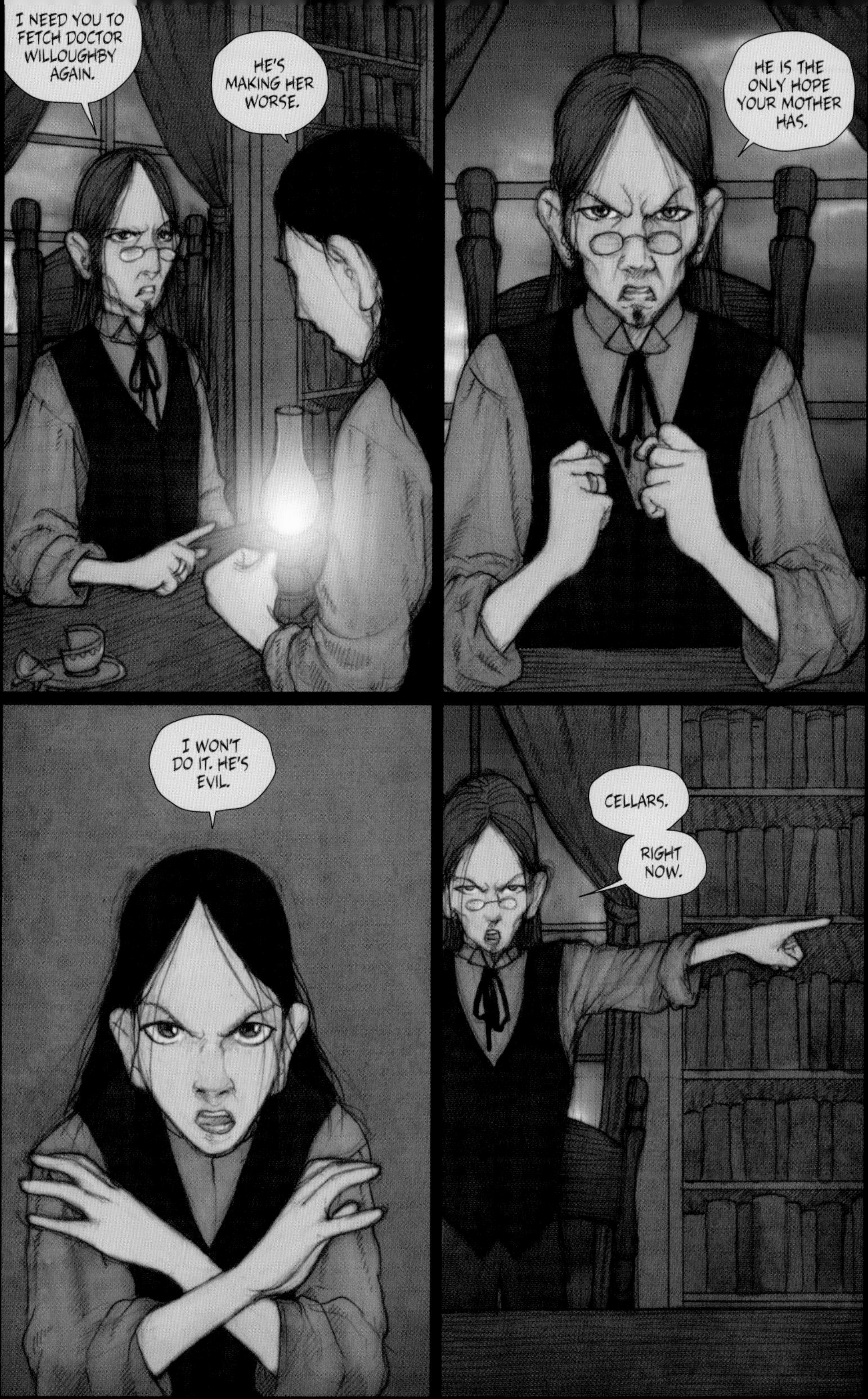
I NEED YOU TO FETCH DOCTOR WILLOUGHBY AGAIN.
HE'S MAKING HER WORSE.
HE IS THE ONLY HOPE YOUR MOTHER HAS.
I WON'T DO IT. HE'S EVIL.
CELLARS.
RIGHT NOW.

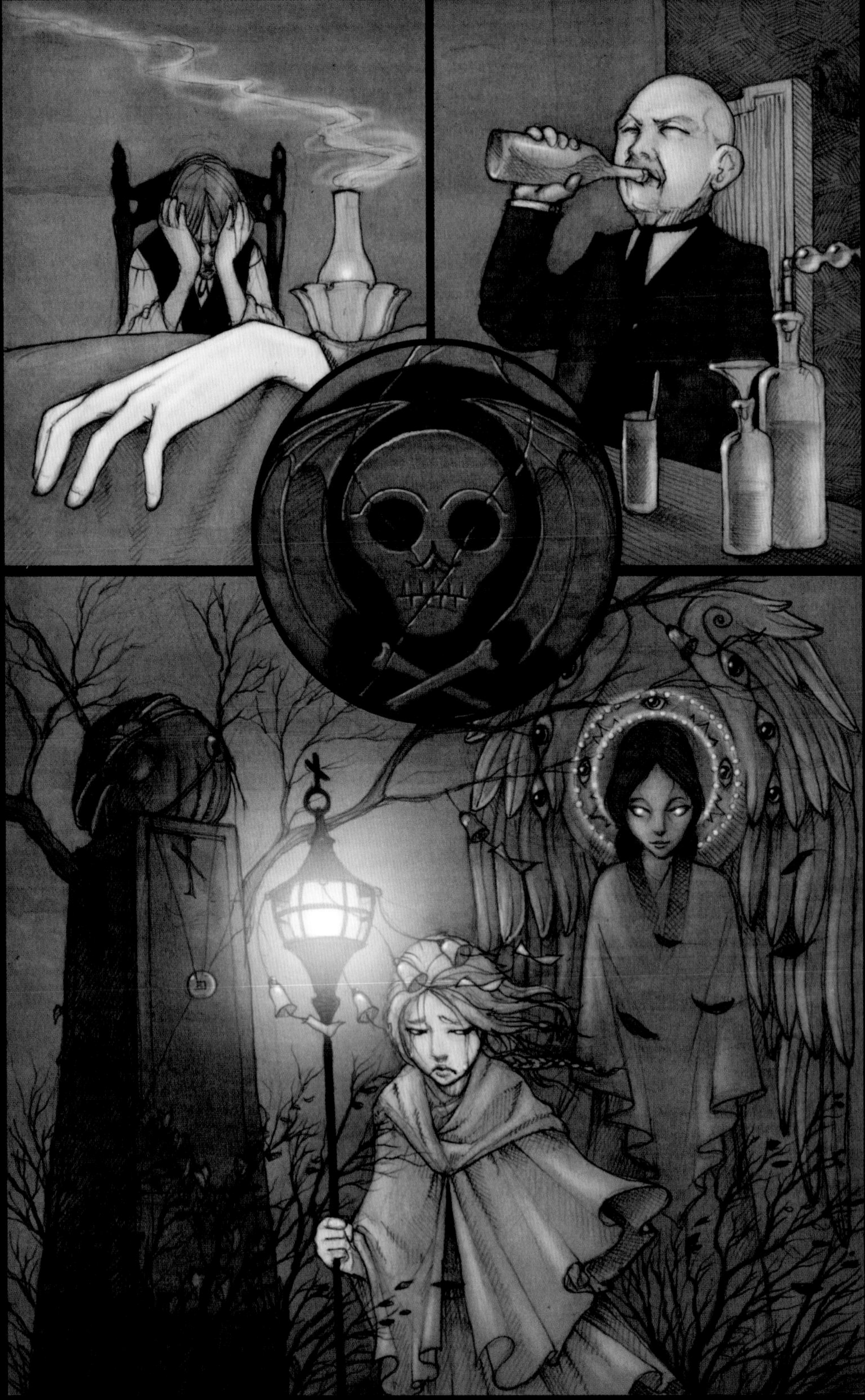

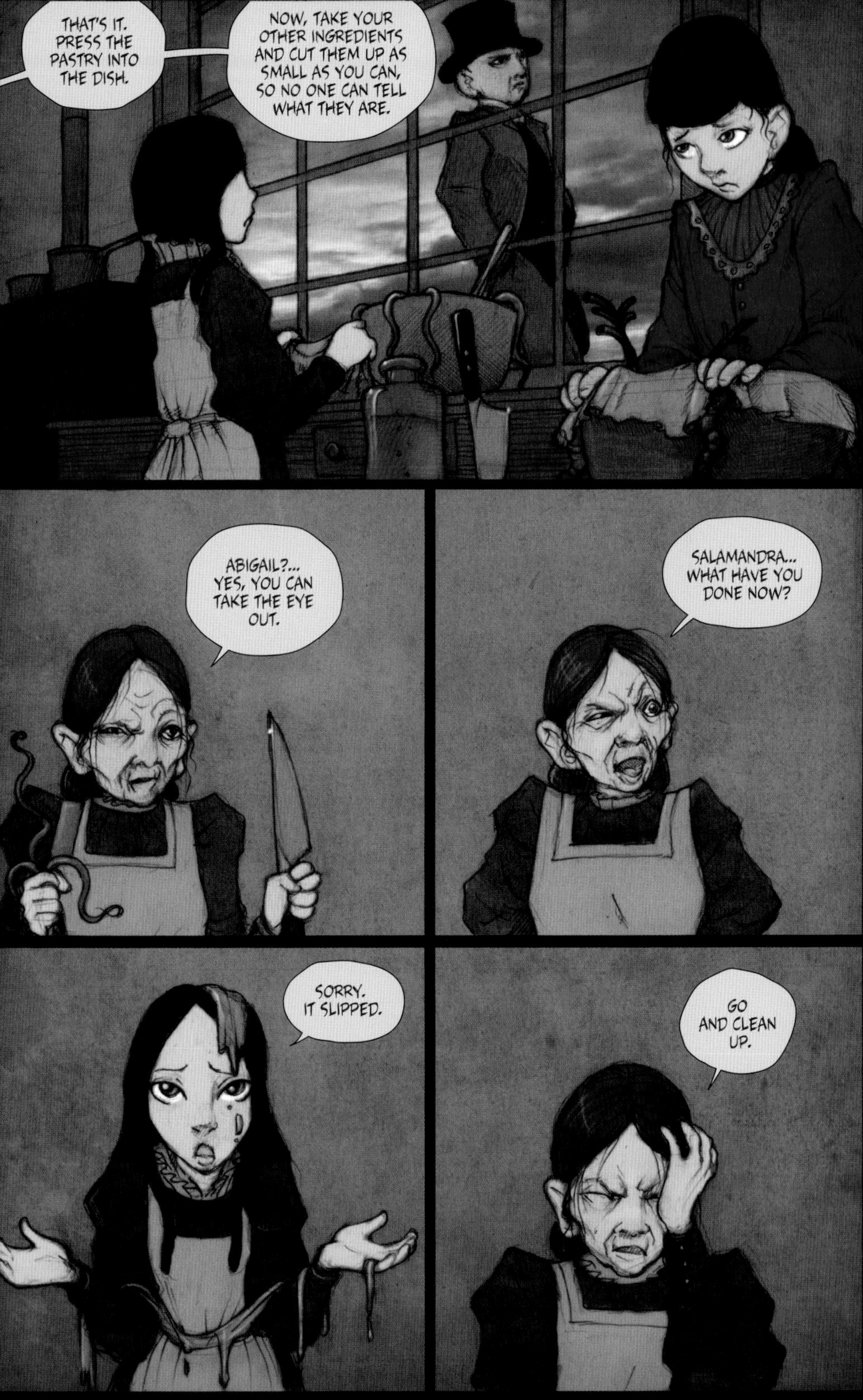
THAT'S IT. PRESS THE PASTRY INTO THE DISH.
NOW, TAKE YOUR OTHER INGREDIENTS AND CUT THEM UP AS SMALL AS YOU CAN, SO NO ONE CAN TELL WHAT THEY ARE.
ABIGAIL?... YES, YOU CAN TAKE THE EYE OUT.
SALAMANDRA... WHAT HAVE YOU DONE NOW?
SORRY. IT SLIPPED.
GO AND CLEAN UP.

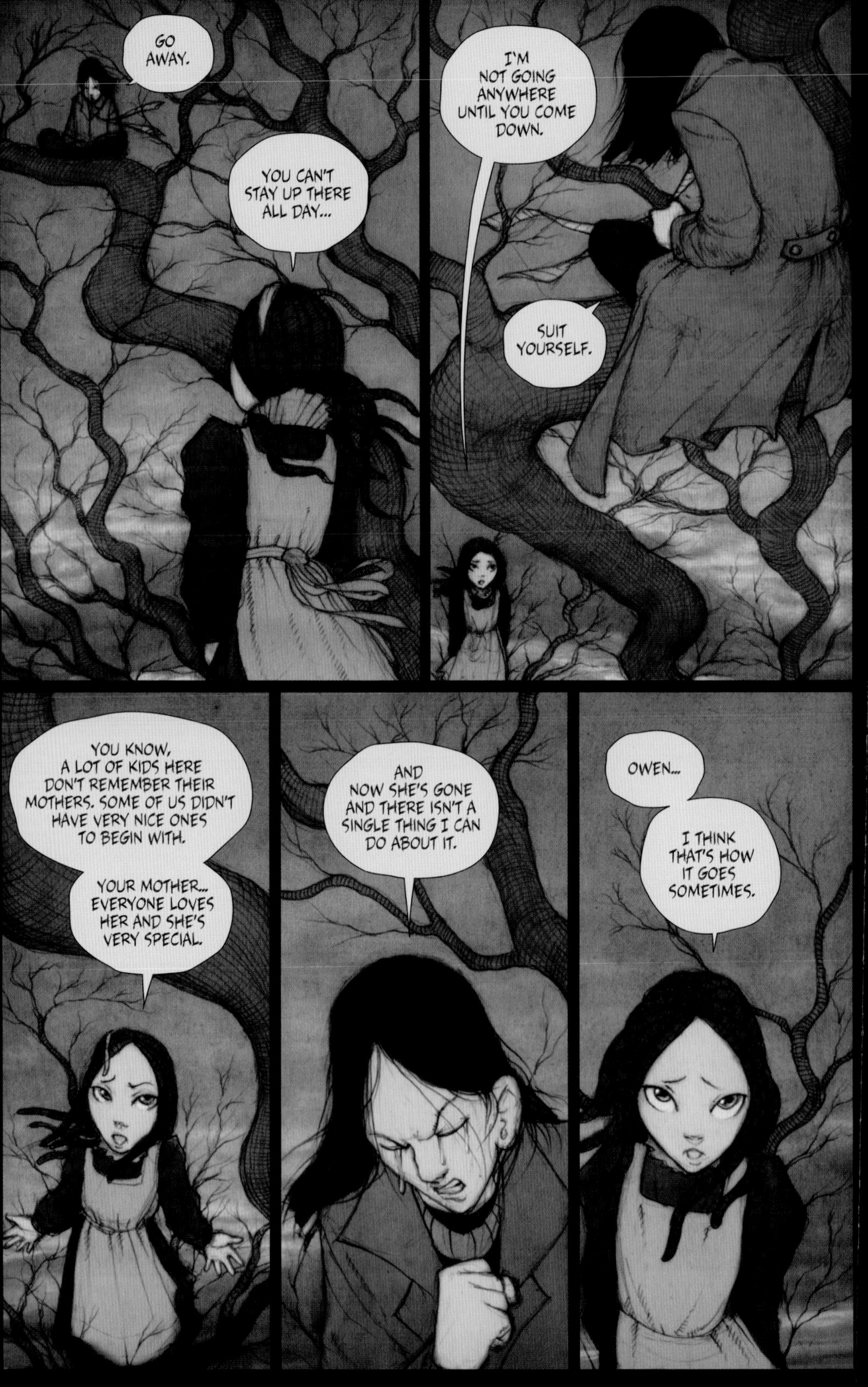
GO AWAY.
YOU CAN'T STAY UP THERE ALL DAY...
I'M NOT GOING ANYWHERE UNTIL YOU COME DOWN.
SUIT YOURSELF.
YOU KNOW, A LOT OF KIDS HERE DON'T REMEMBER THEIR MOTHERS. SOME OF US DIDN'T HAVE VERY NICE ONES TO BEGIN WITH.
YOUR MOTHER... EVERYONE LOVES HER AND SHE'S VERY SPECIAL.
AND NOW SHE'S GONE AND THERE ISN'T A SINGLE THING I CAN DO ABOUT IT.
OWEN...
I THINK THAT'S HOW IT GOES SOMETIMES.

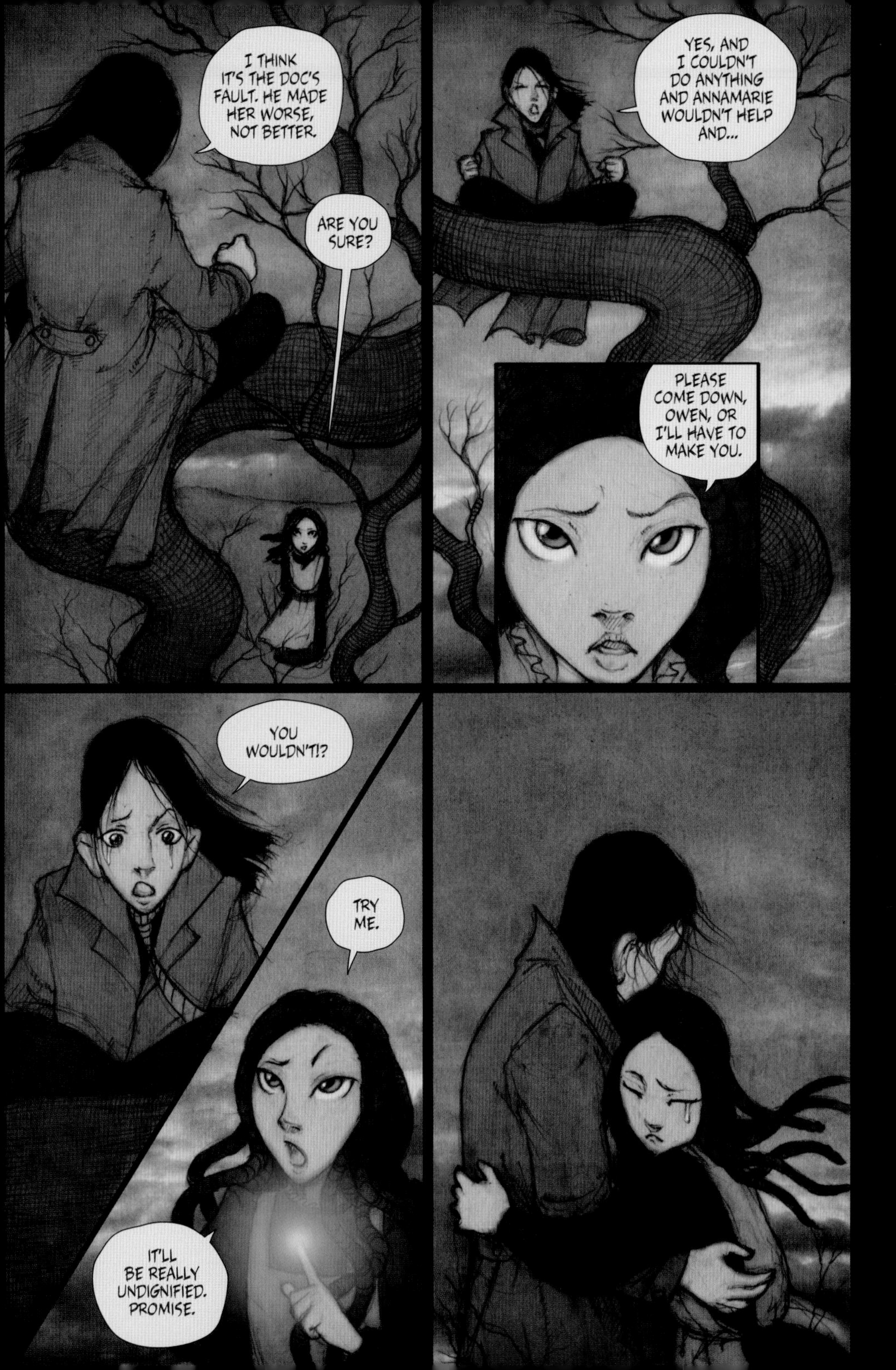
I THINK IT'S THE DOC'S FAULT. HE MADE HER WORSE, NOT BETTER.
ARE YOU SURE?
YES, AND I COULDN'T DO ANYTHING AND ANNAMARIE WOULDN'T HELP AND...
PLEASE COME DOWN, OWEN, OR I'LL HAVE TO MAKE YOU.
YOU WOULDN'T!?
TRY ME.
IT'LL BE REALLY UNDIGNIFIED. PROMISE.

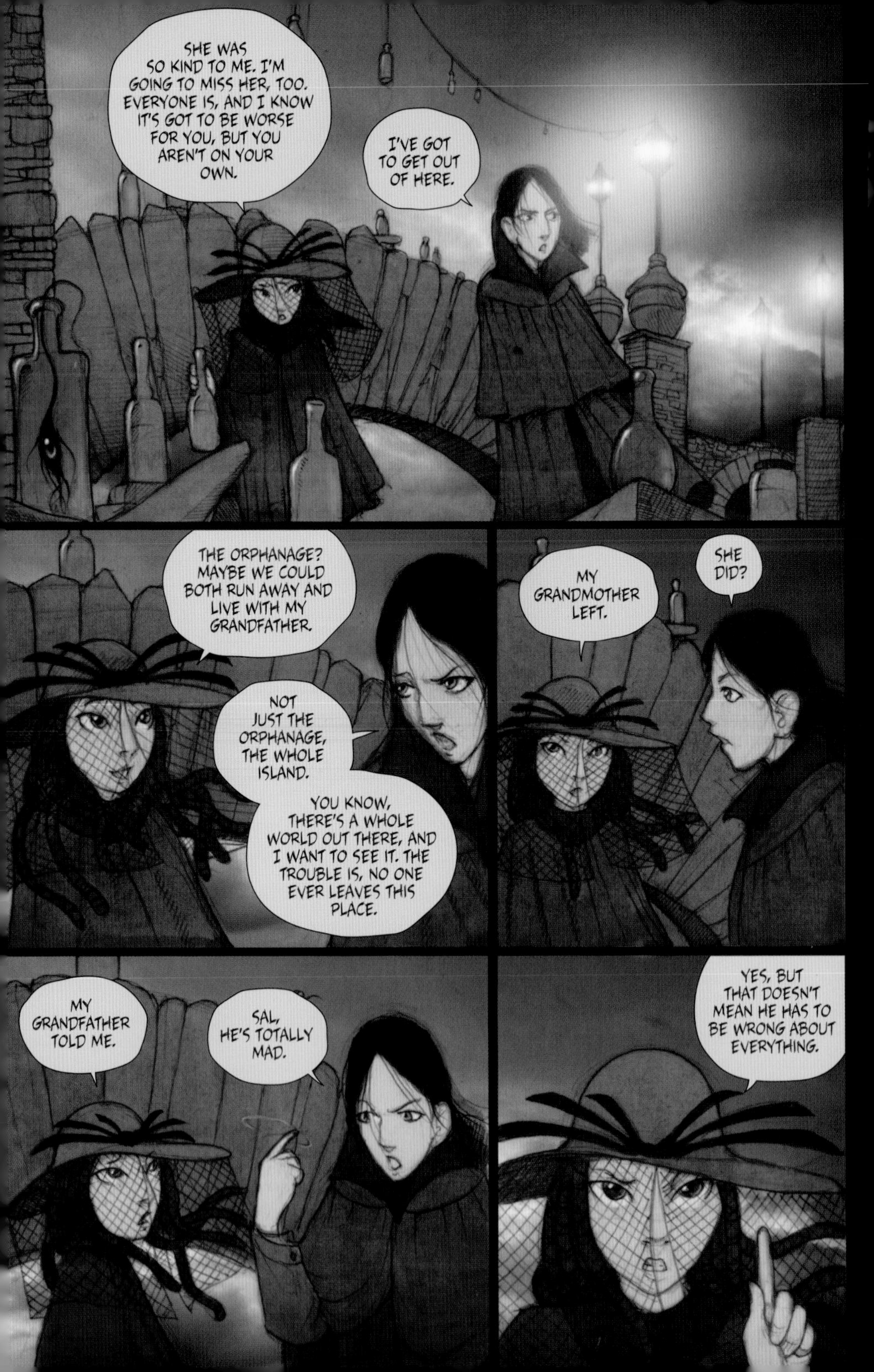
SHE WAS SO KIND TO ME. I'M GOING TO MISS HER, TOO. EVERYONE IS, AND I KNOW IT'S GOT TO BE WORSE FOR YOU, BUT YOU AREN'T ON YOUR OWN.
I'VE GOT TO GET OUT OF HERE.
THE ORPHANAGE? MAYBE WE COULD BOTH RUN AWAY AND LIVE WITH MY GRANDFATHER.
NOT JUST THE ORPHANAGE, THE WHOLE ISLAND.
YOU KNOW, THERE'S A WHOLE WORLD OUT THERE, AND I WANT TO SEE IT. THE TROUBLE IS, NO ONE EVER LEAVES THIS PLACE.
MY GRANDMOTHER LEFT.
SHE DID?
MY GRANDFATHER TOLD ME.
SAL, HE'S TOTALLY MAD.
YES, BUT THAT DOESN'T MEAN HE HAS TO BE WRONG ABOUT EVERYTHING.

CHAPTER FIVE

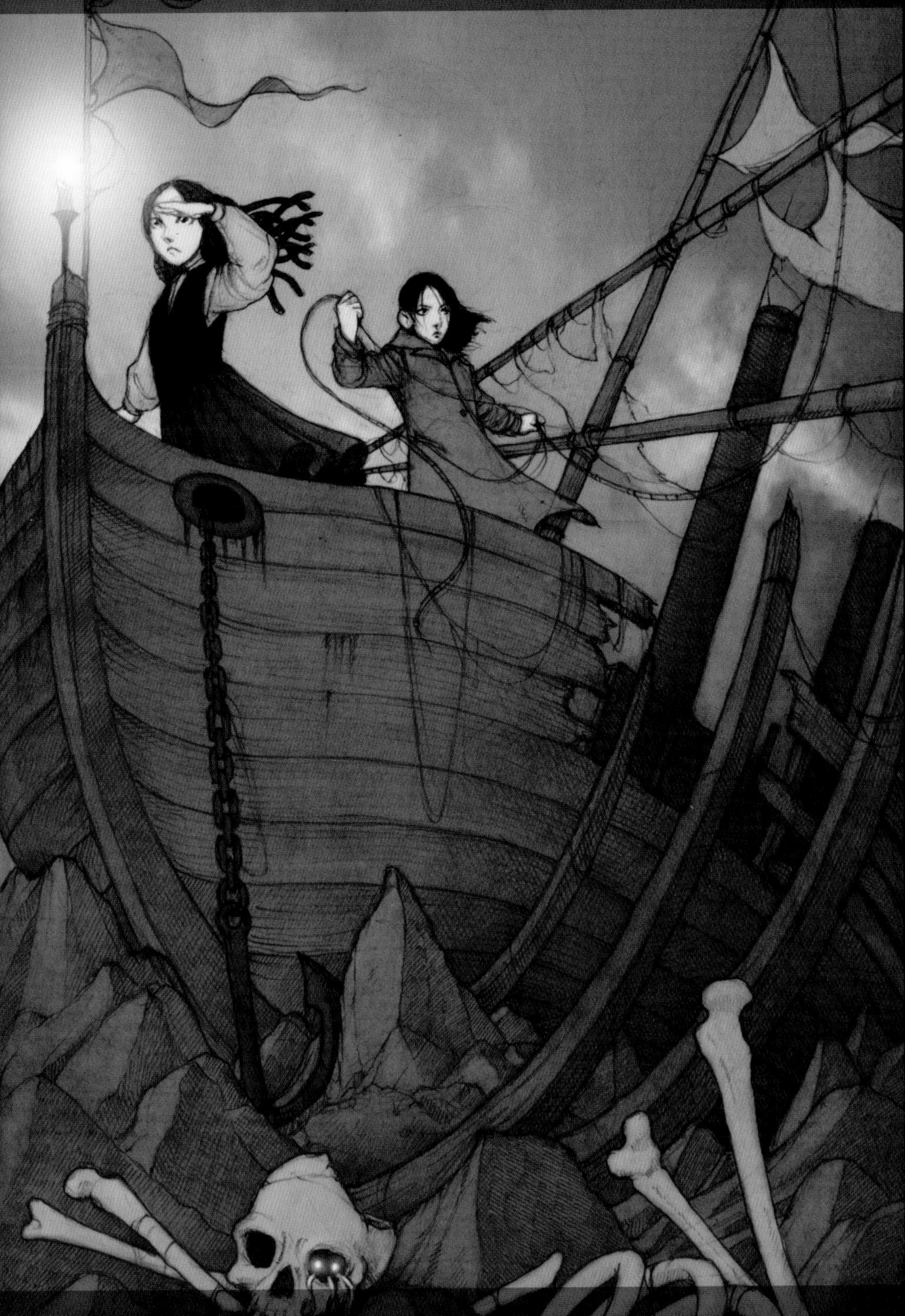

WE ARE NO MORE THAN CLAY

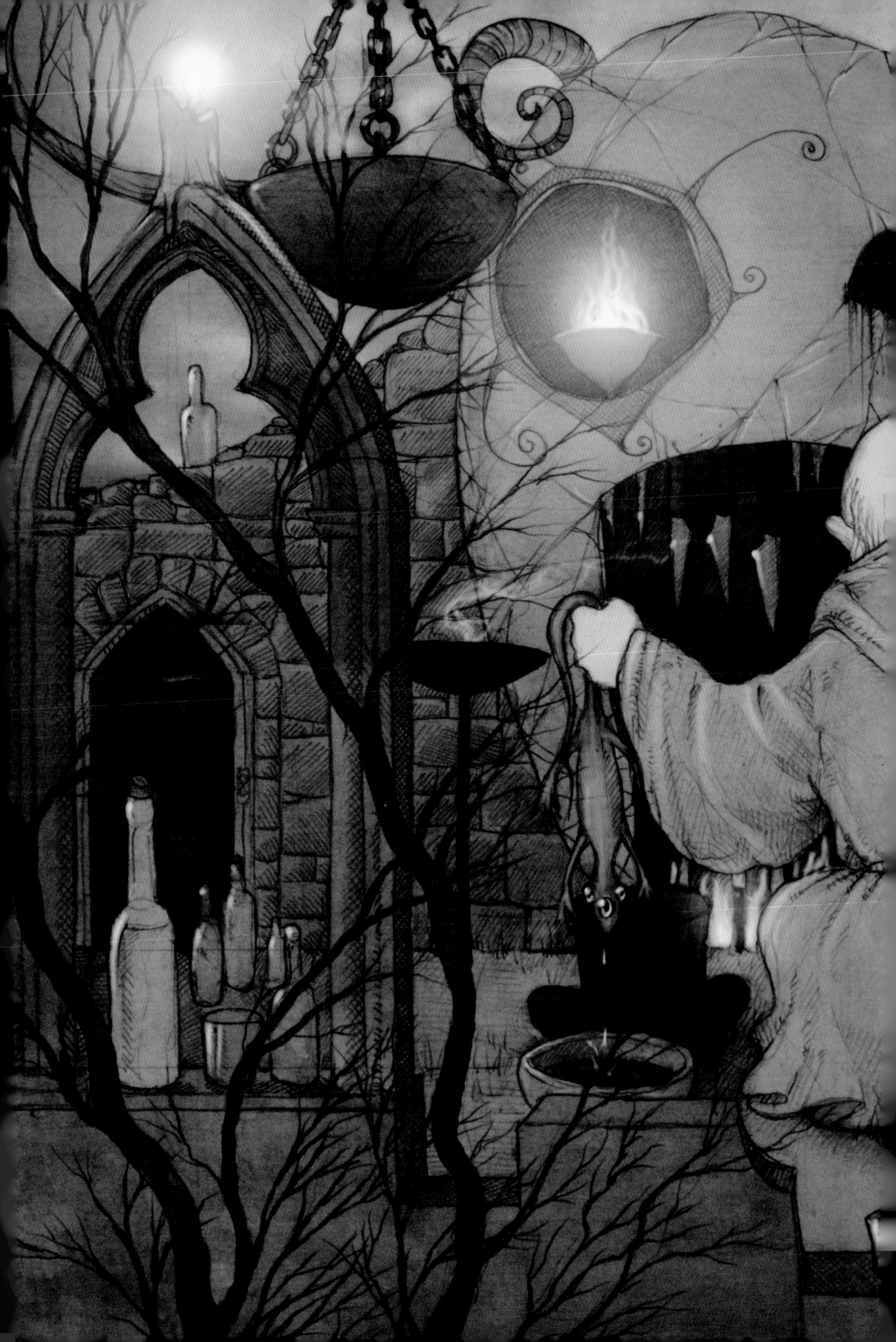

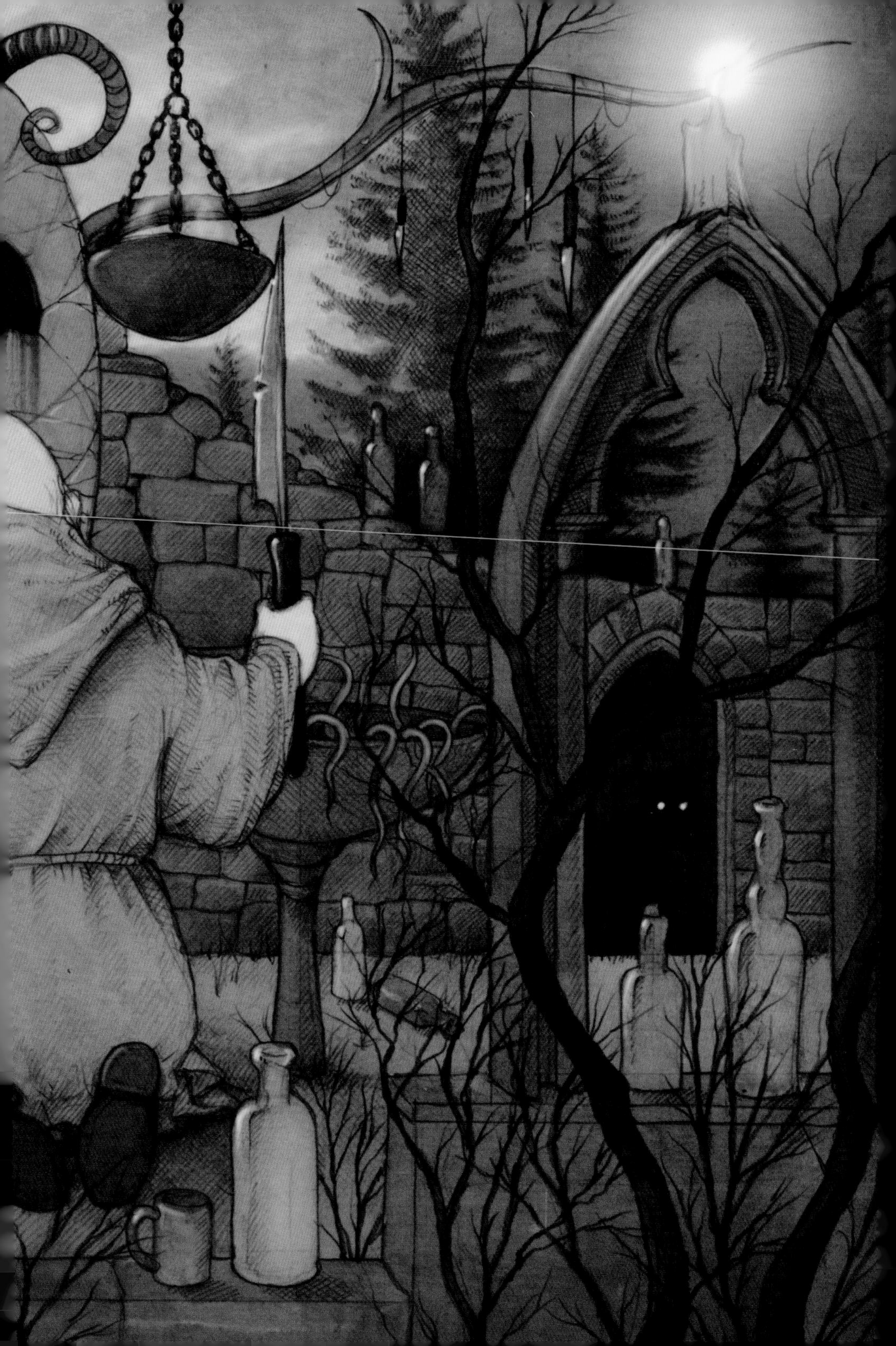

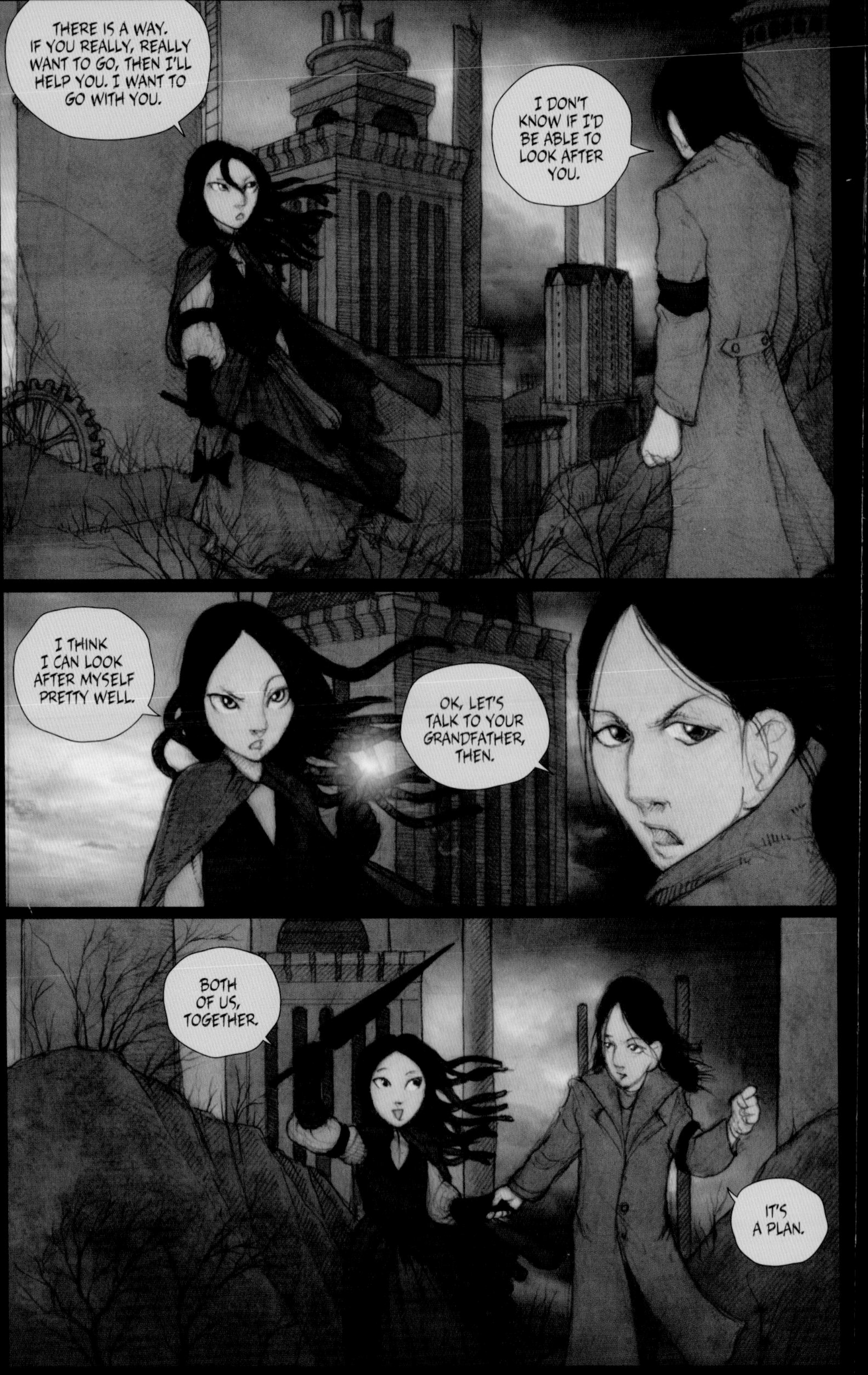
THERE IS A WAY. IF YOU REALLY, REALLY WANT TO GO, THEN I'LL HELP YOU. I WANT TO GO WITH YOU.
I DON'T KNOW IF I'D BE ABLE TO LOOK AFTER YOU.
I THINK I CAN LOOK AFTER MYSELF PRETTY WELL.
OK, LET'S TALK TO YOUR GRANDFATHER, THEN.
BOTH OF US, TOGETHER.
IT'S A PLAN.

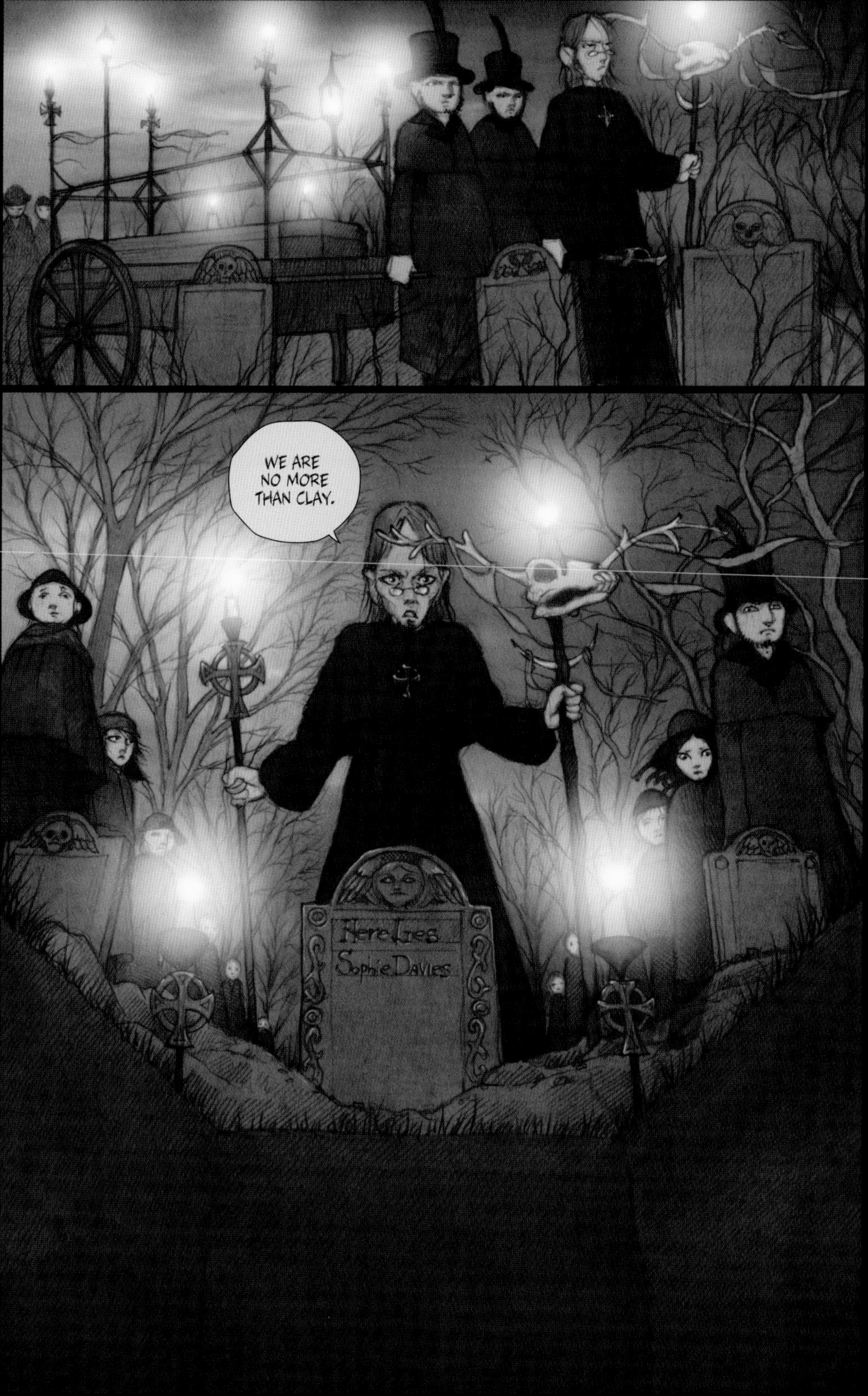
WE ARE NO MORE THAN CLAY.
Here Lies
Sophie Davies

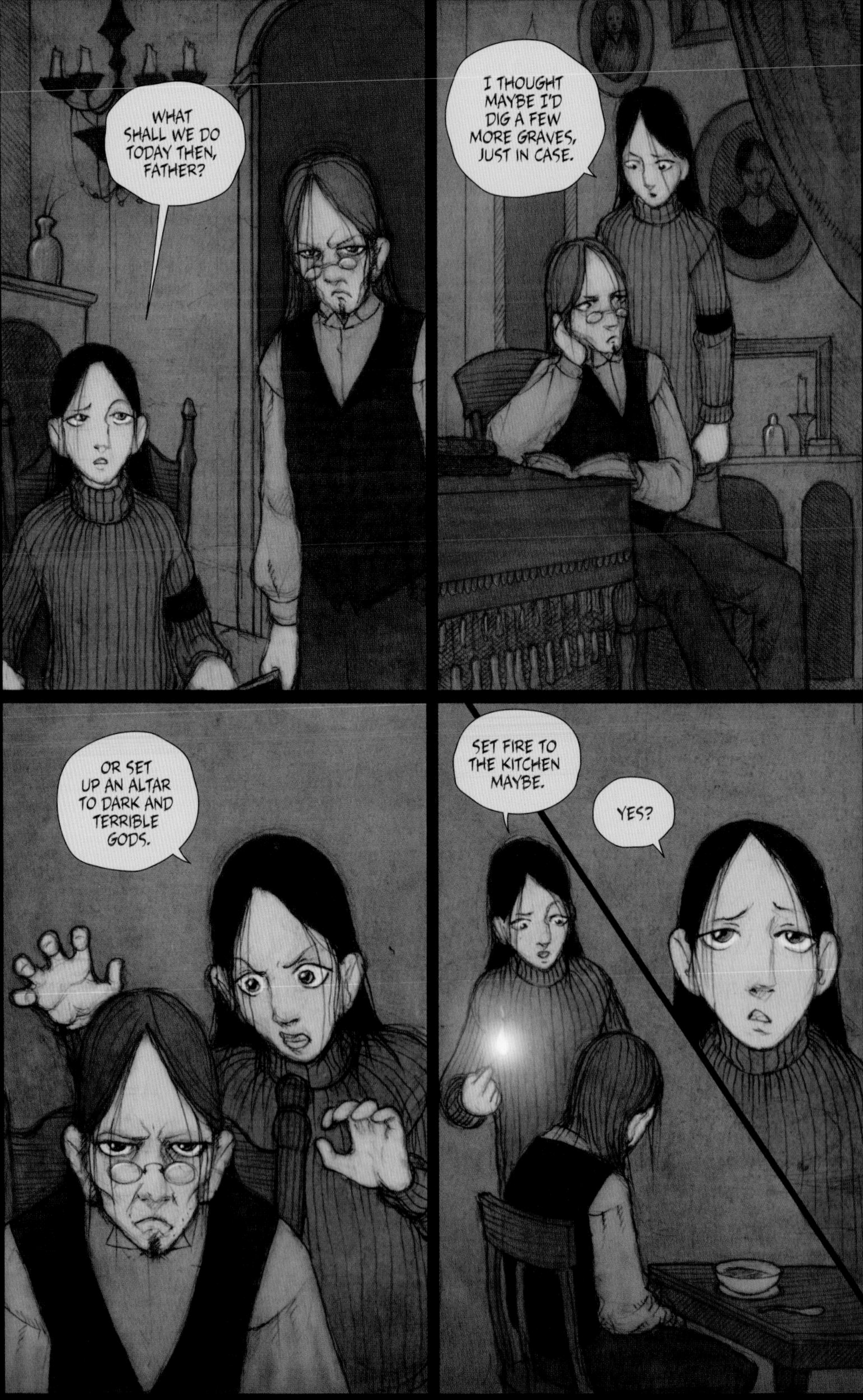
WHAT SHALL WE DO TODAY THEN, FATHER?
I THOUGHT MAYBE I'D DIG A FEW MORE GRAVES, JUST IN CASE.
OR SET UP AN ALTAR TO DARK AND TERRIBLE GODS.
SET FIRE TO THE KITCHEN MAYBE.
YES?

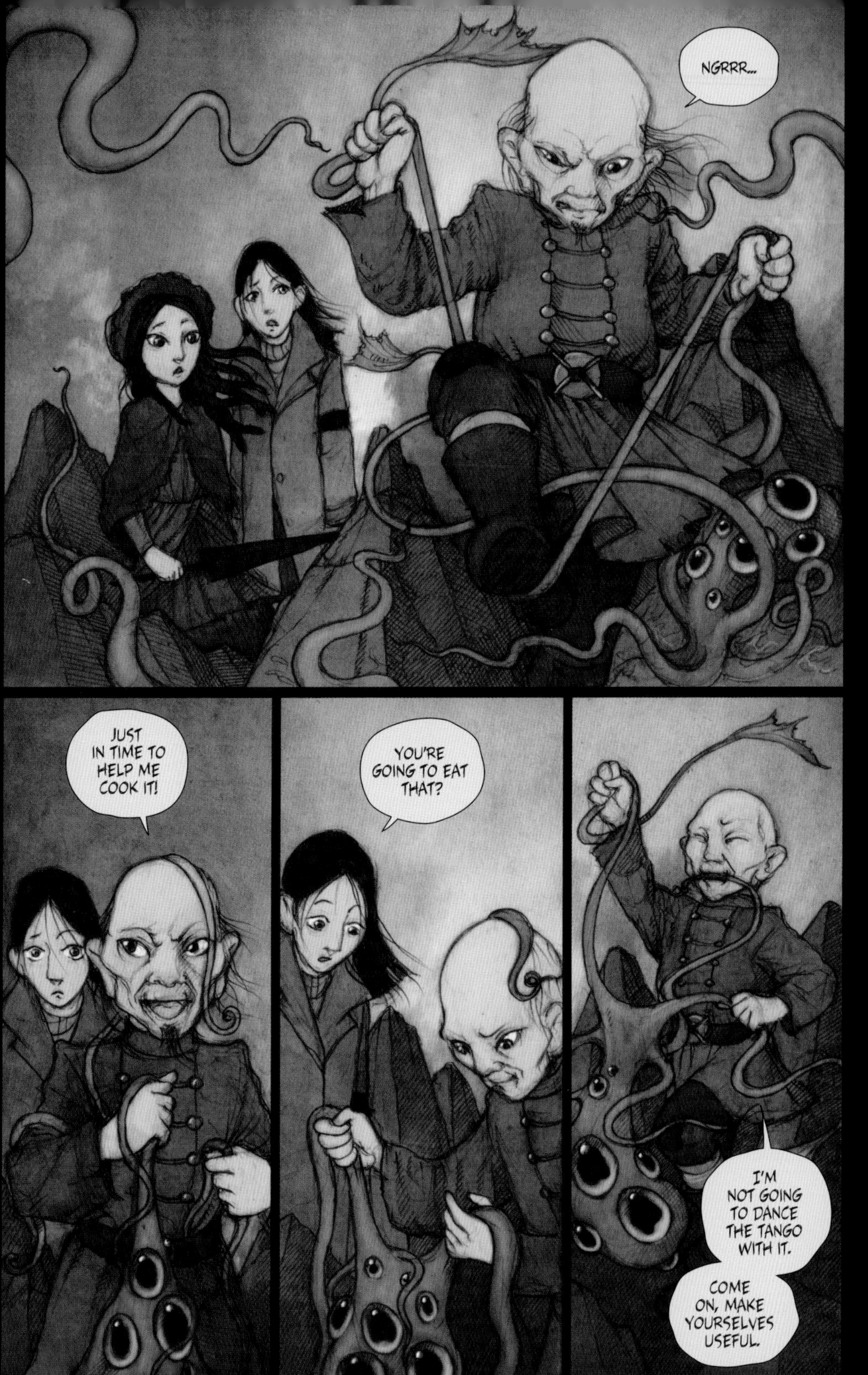
NGRRR...
JUST IN TIME TO HELP ME COOK IT!
YOU'RE GOING TO EAT THAT?
I'M NOT GOING TO DANCE THE TANGO WITH IT.
COME ON, MAKE YOURSELVES USEFUL.

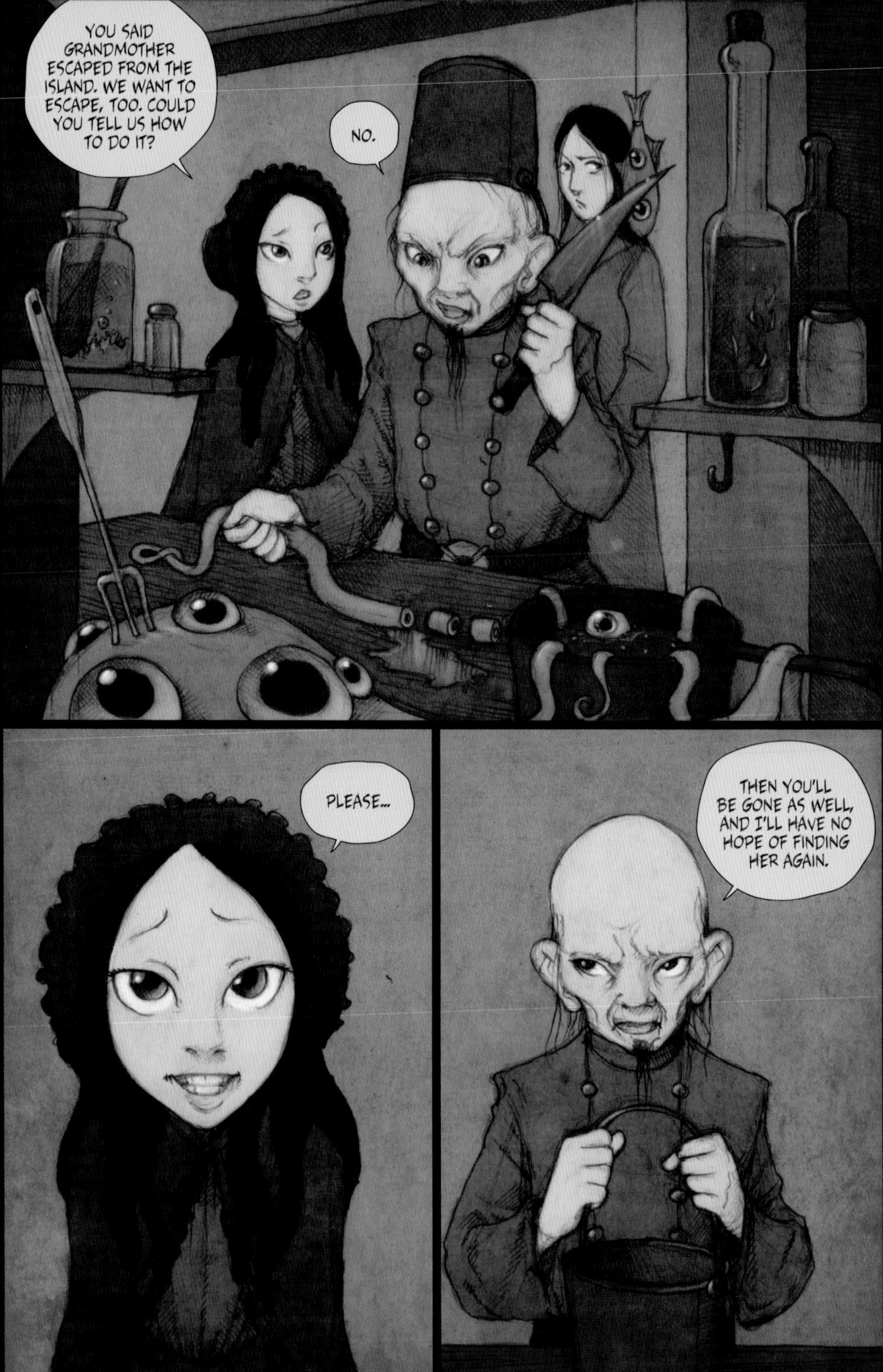
YOU SAID GRANDMOTHER ESCAPED FROM THE ISLAND. WE WANT TO ESCAPE, TOO. COULD YOU TELL US HOW TO DO IT?
NO.
PLEASE...
THEN YOU'LL BE GONE AS WELL, AND I'LL HAVE NO HOPE OF FINDING HER AGAIN.

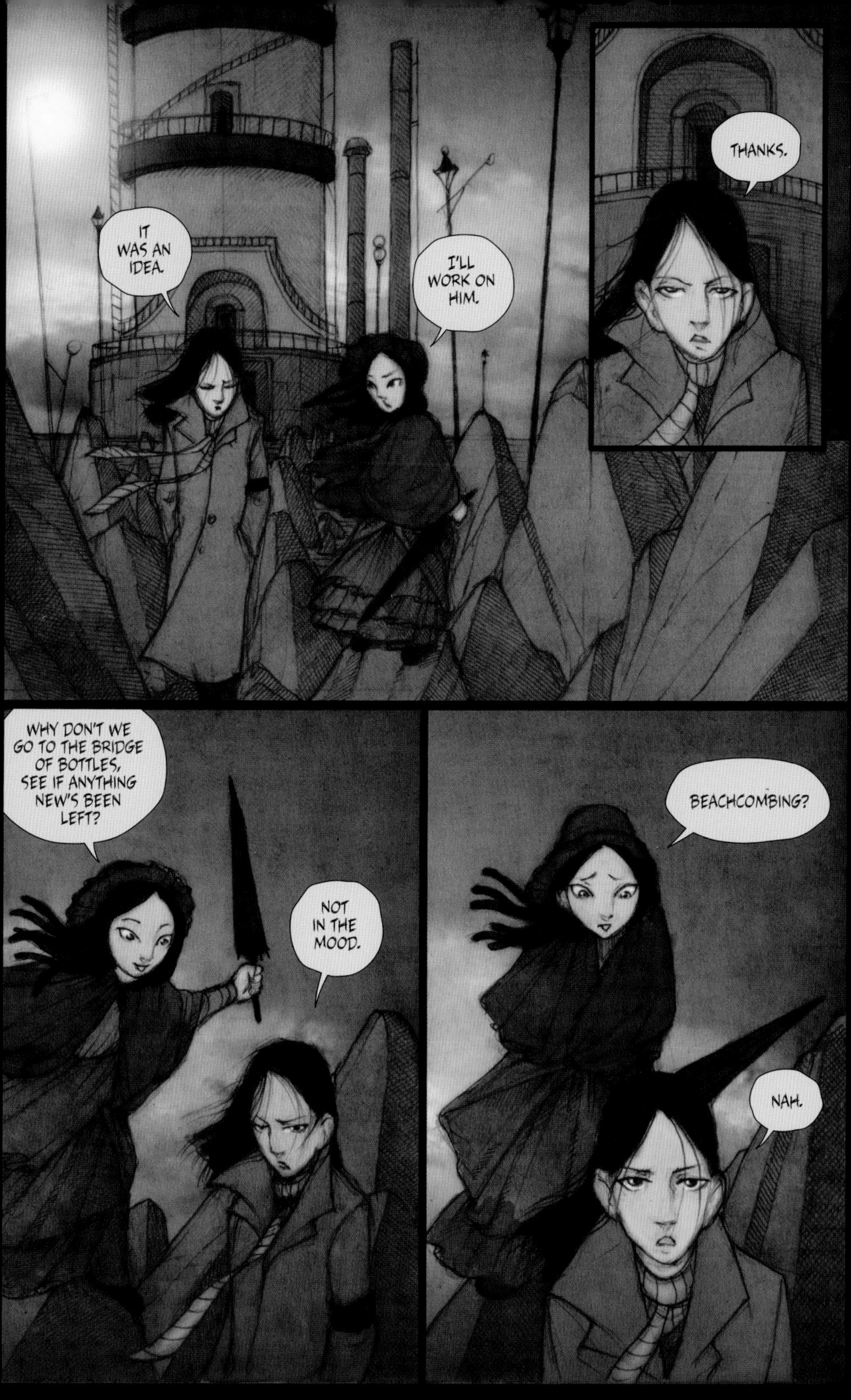
IT WAS AN IDEA.
I'LL WORK ON HIM.
THANKS.
WHY DON'T WE GO TO THE BRIDGE OF BOTTLES, SEE IF ANYTHING NEW'S BEEN LEFT?
NOT IN THE MOOD.
BEACHCOMBING?
NAH.

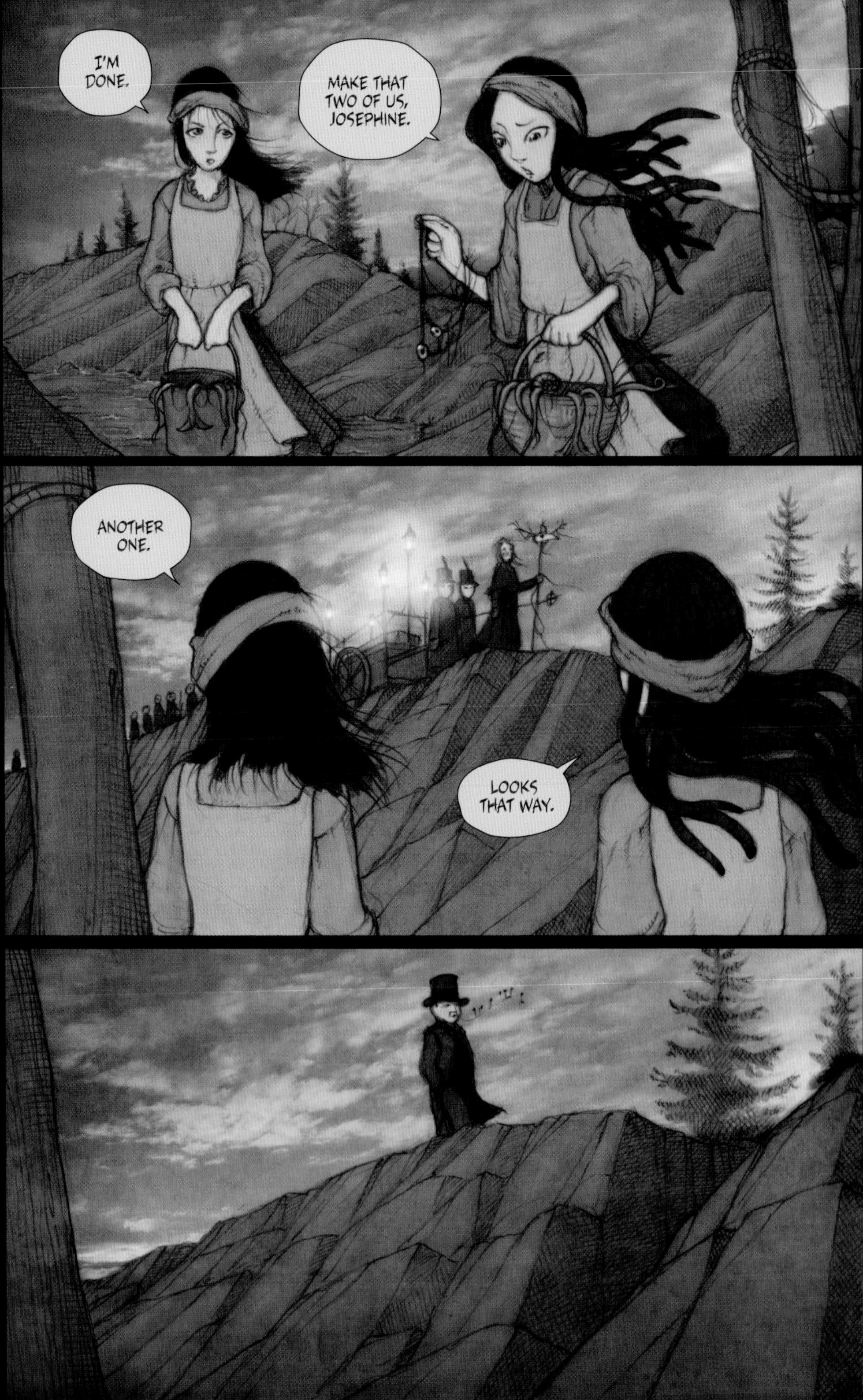
I'M DONE.
MAKE THAT TWO OF US, JOSEPHINE.
ANOTHER ONE.
LOOKS THAT WAY.

CHAPTER SIX

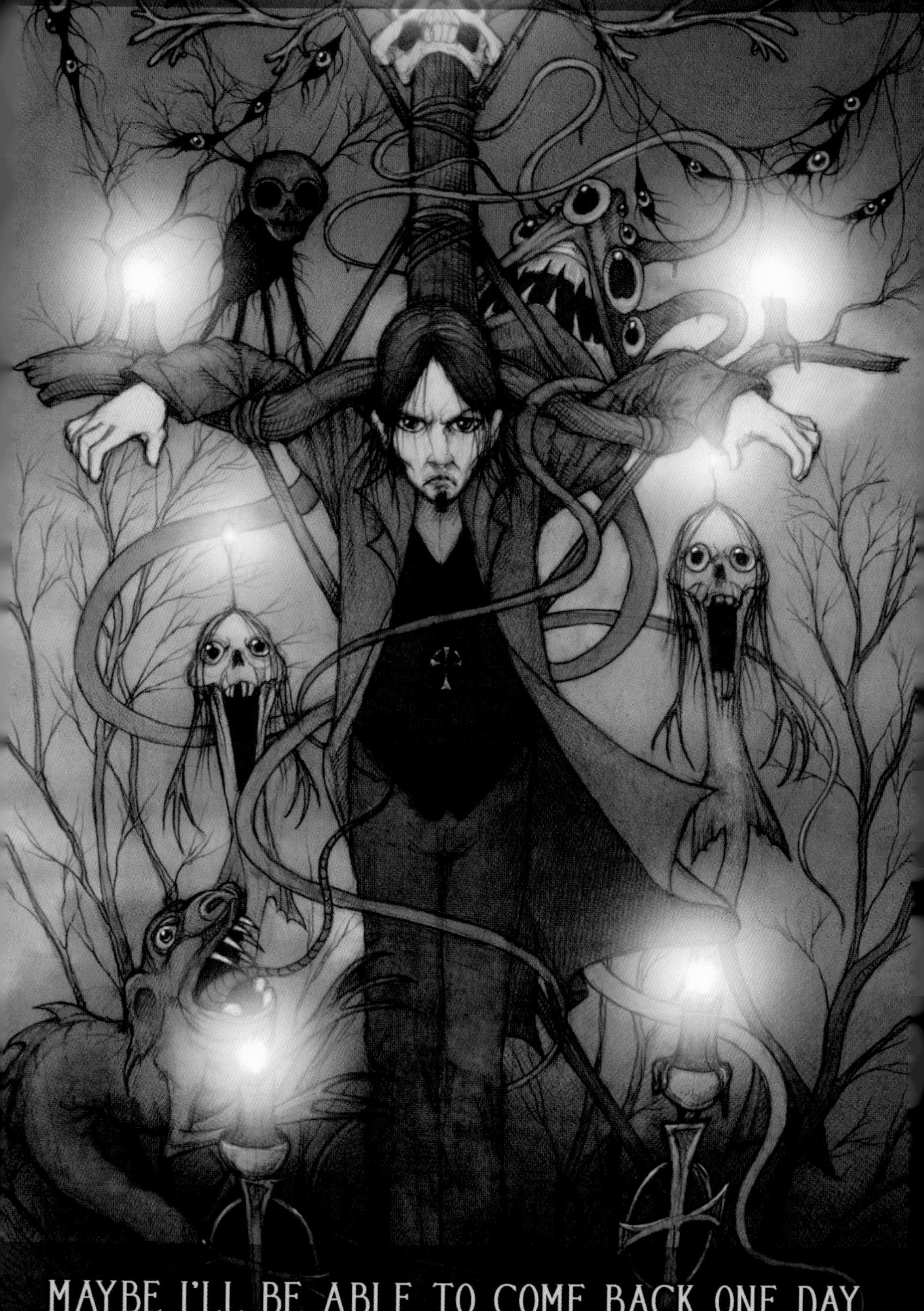

MAYBE I'LL BE ABLE TO COME BACK ONE DAY
AND MAKE THINGS BETTER HERE

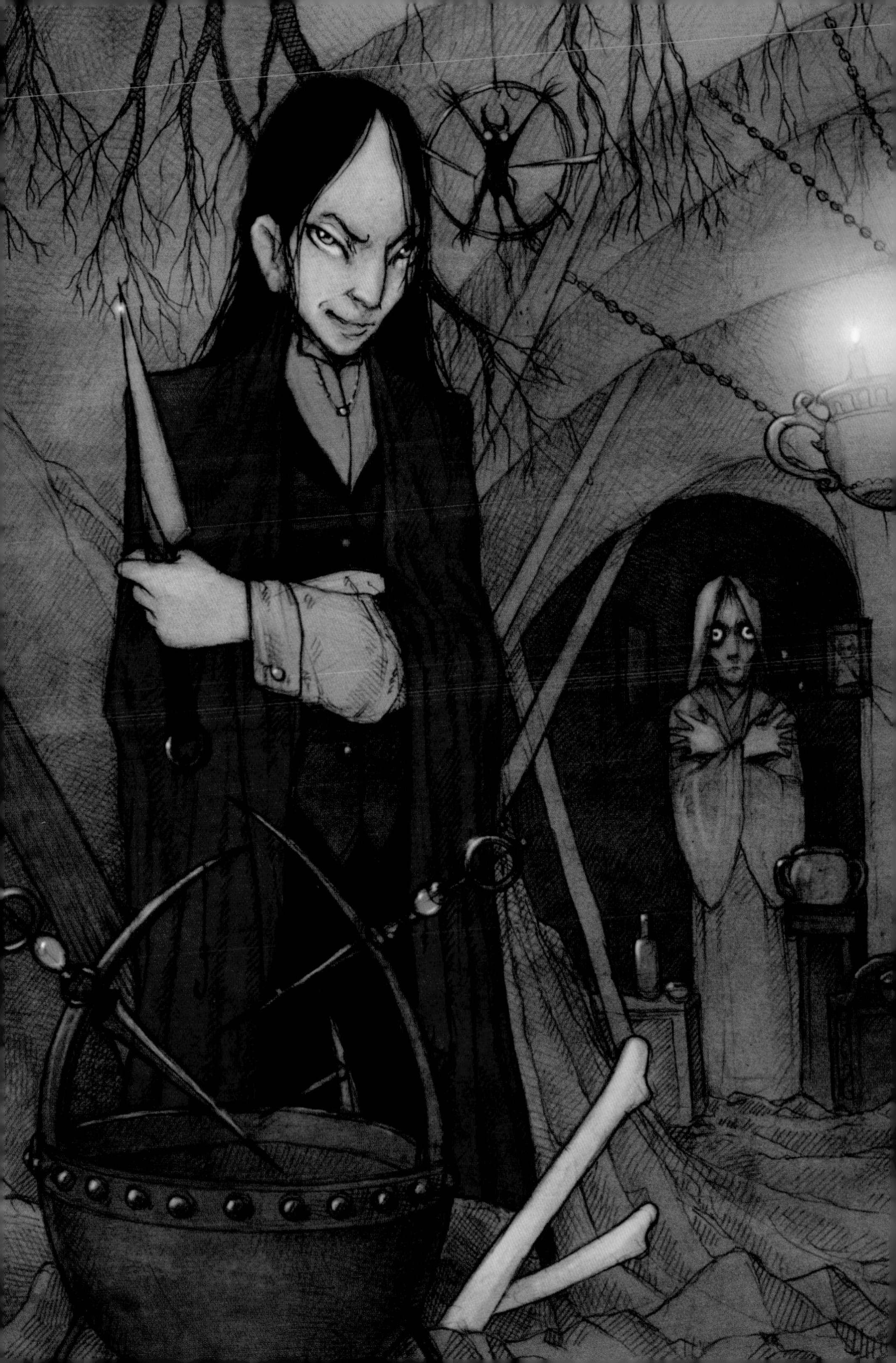

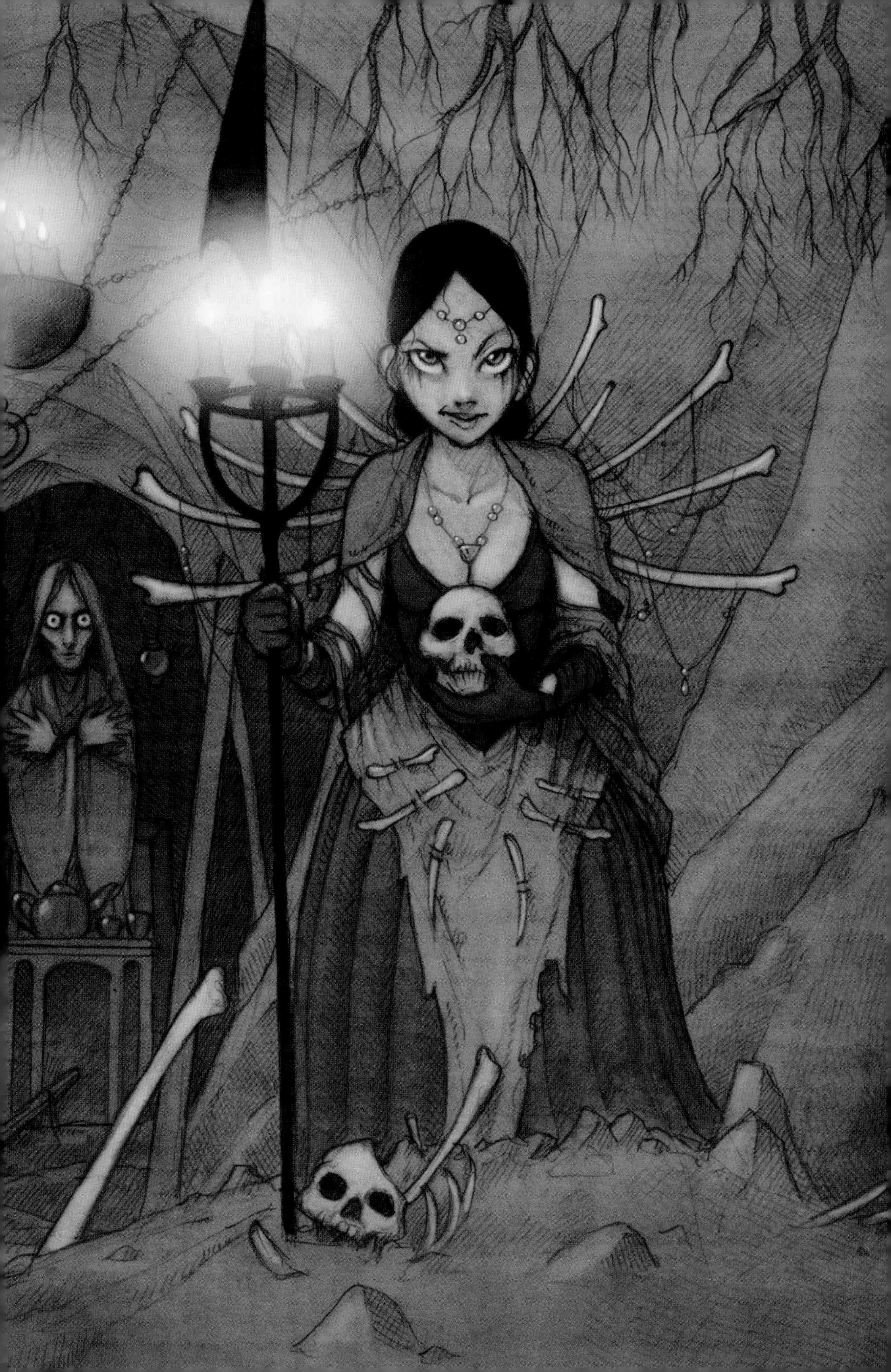

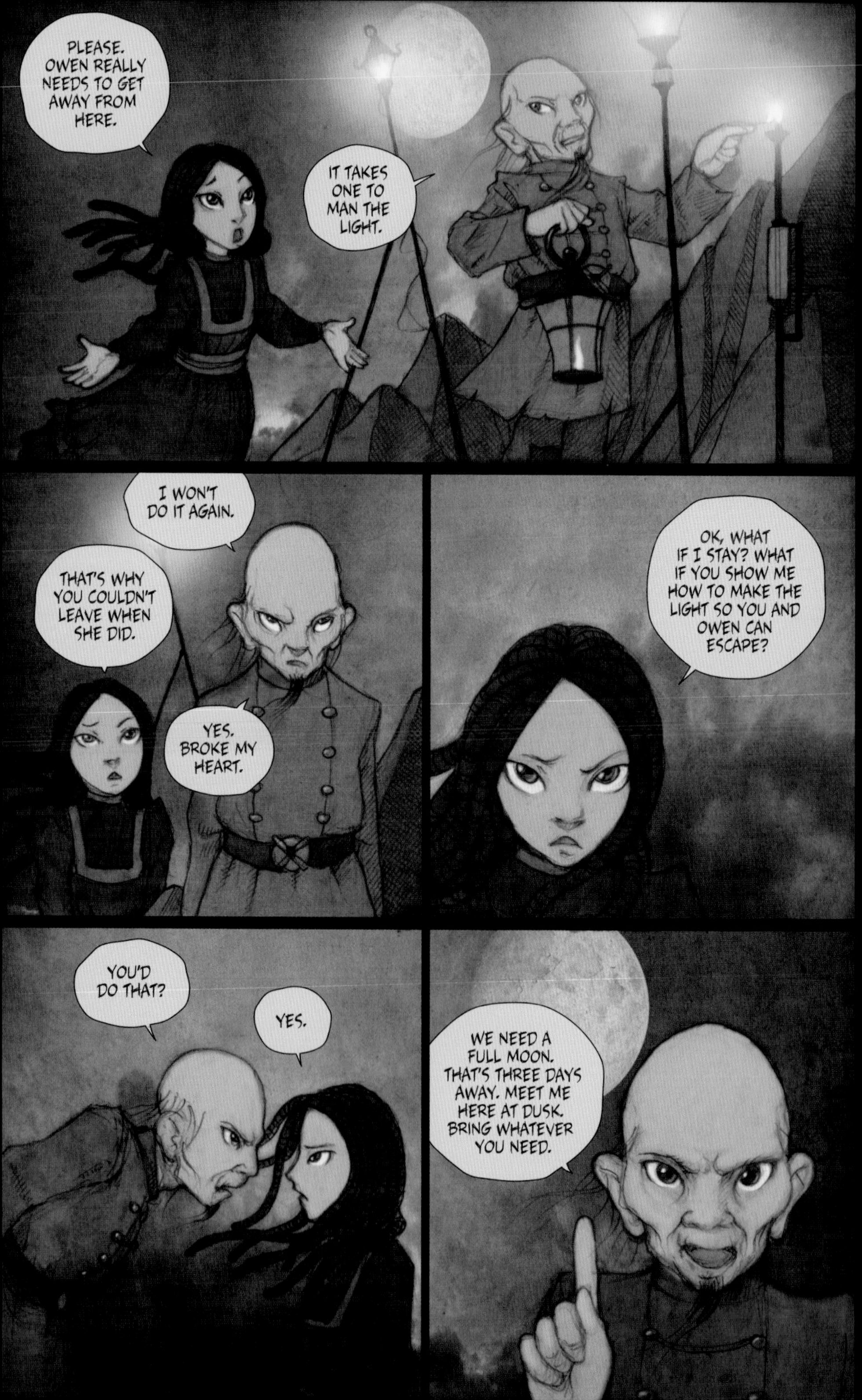
PLEASE. OWEN REALLY NEEDS TO GET AWAY FROM HERE.
IT TAKES ONE TO MAN THE LIGHT.
I WON'T DO IT AGAIN.
THAT'S WHY YOU COULDN'T LEAVE WHEN SHE DID.
YES. BROKE MY HEART.
OK, WHAT IF I STAY? WHAT IF YOU SHOW ME HOW TO MAKE THE LIGHT SO YOU AND OWEN CAN ESCAPE?
YOU'D DO THAT?
YES.
WE NEED A FULL MOON. THAT'S THREE DAYS AWAY. MEET ME HERE AT DUSK. BRING WHATEVER YOU NEED.

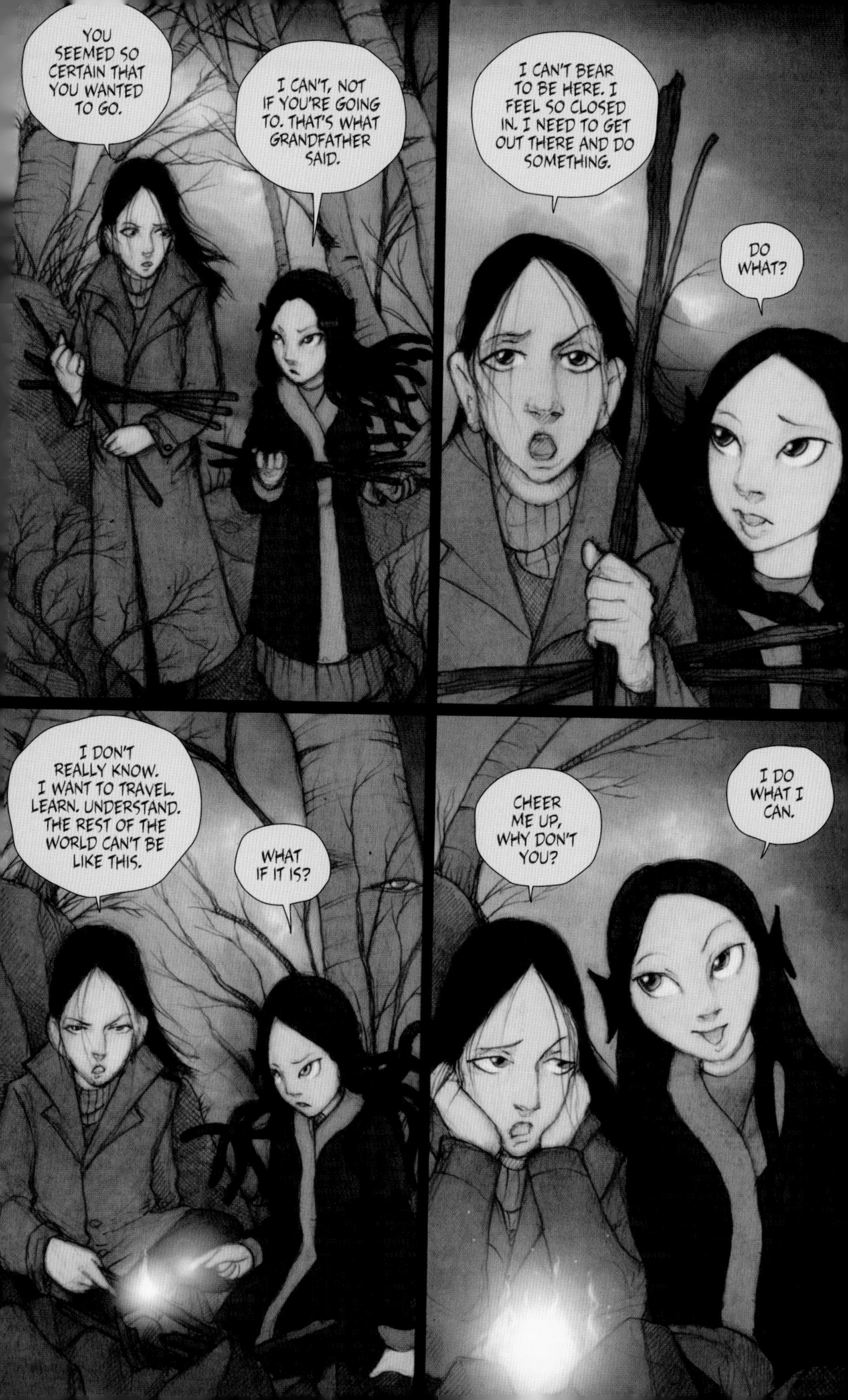
YOU SEEMED SO CERTAIN THAT YOU WANTED TO GO.
I CAN'T, NOT IF YOU'RE GOING TO. THAT'S WHAT GRANDFATHER SAID.
I CAN'T BEAR TO BE HERE. I FEEL SO CLOSED IN. I NEED TO GET OUT THERE AND DO SOMETHING.
DO WHAT?
I DON'T REALLY KNOW. I WANT TO TRAVEL. LEARN. UNDERSTAND. THE REST OF THE WORLD CAN'T BE LIKE THIS.
WHAT IF IT IS?
CHEER ME UP, WHY DON'T YOU?
I DO WHAT I CAN.

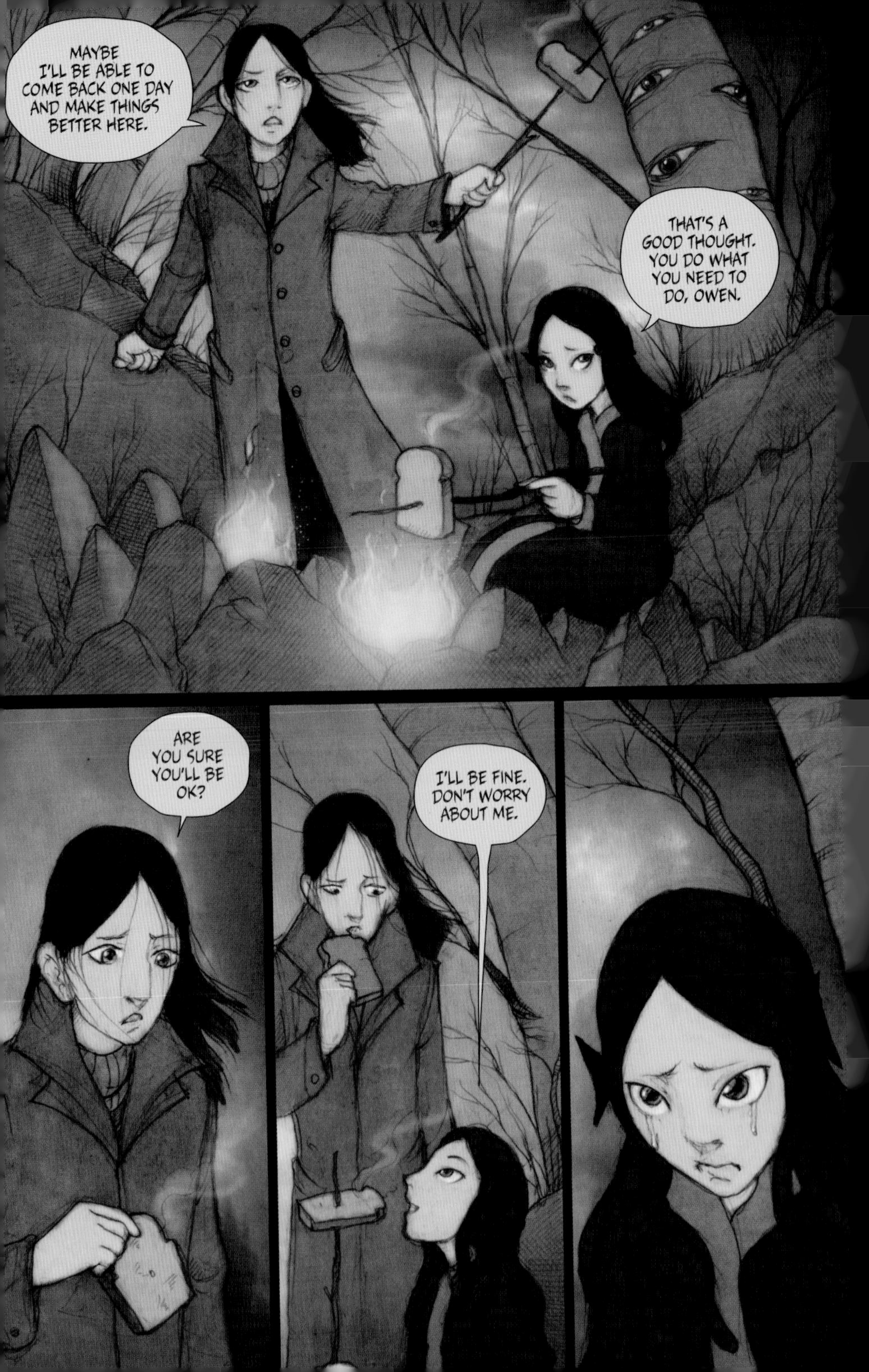
MAYBE I'LL BE ABLE TO COME BACK ONE DAY AND MAKE THINGS BETTER HERE.
THAT'S A GOOD THOUGHT. YOU DO WHAT YOU NEED TO DO, OWEN.
ARE YOU SURE YOU'LL BE OK?
I'LL BE FINE. DON'T WORRY ABOUT ME.

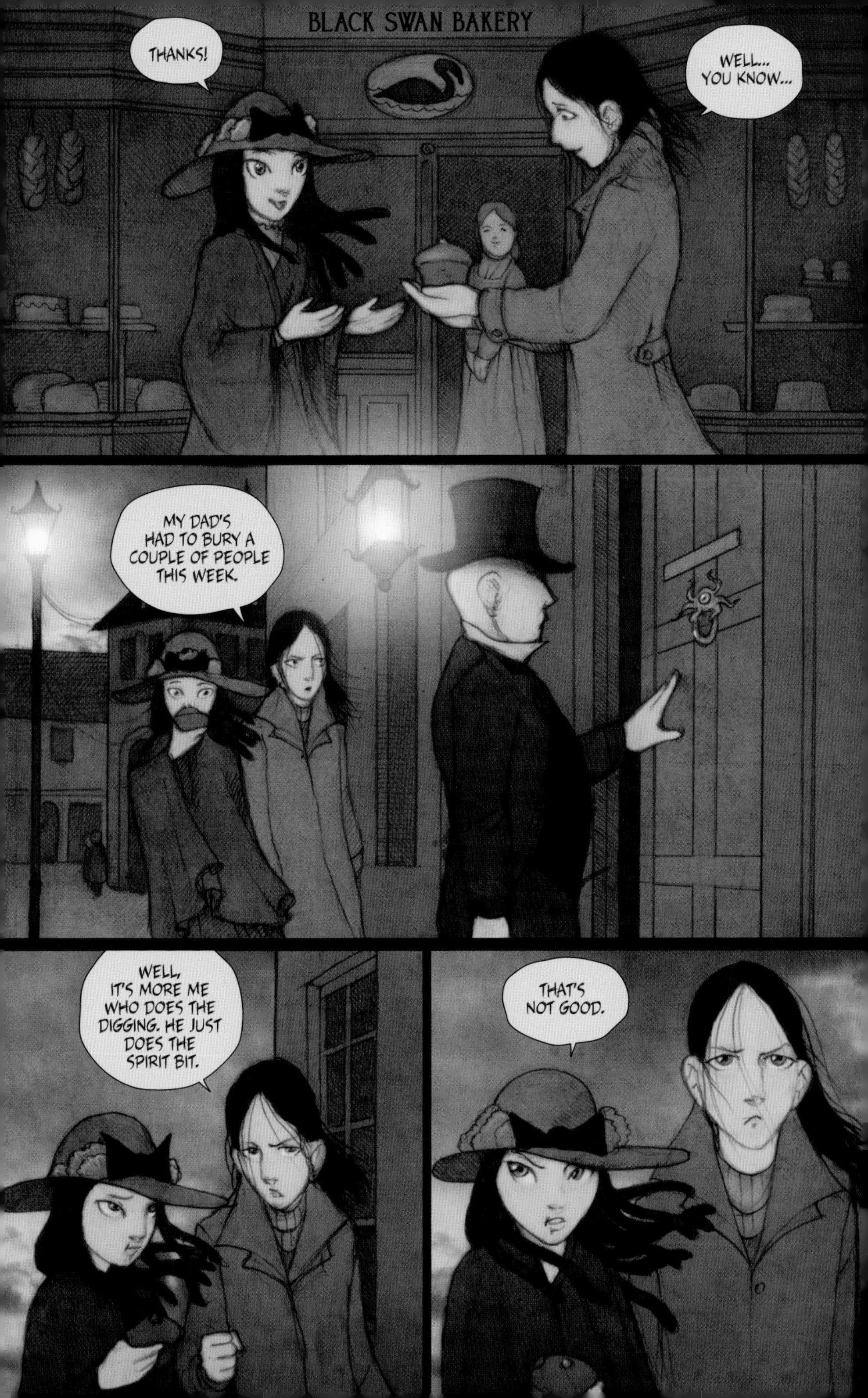
BLACK SWAN BAKERY
THANKS!
WELL... YOU KNOW...
MY DAD'S HAD TO BURY A COUPLE OF PEOPLE THIS WEEK.
WELL, IT'S MORE ME WHO DOES THE DIGGING. HE JUST DOES THE SPIRIT BIT.
THAT'S NOT GOOD.

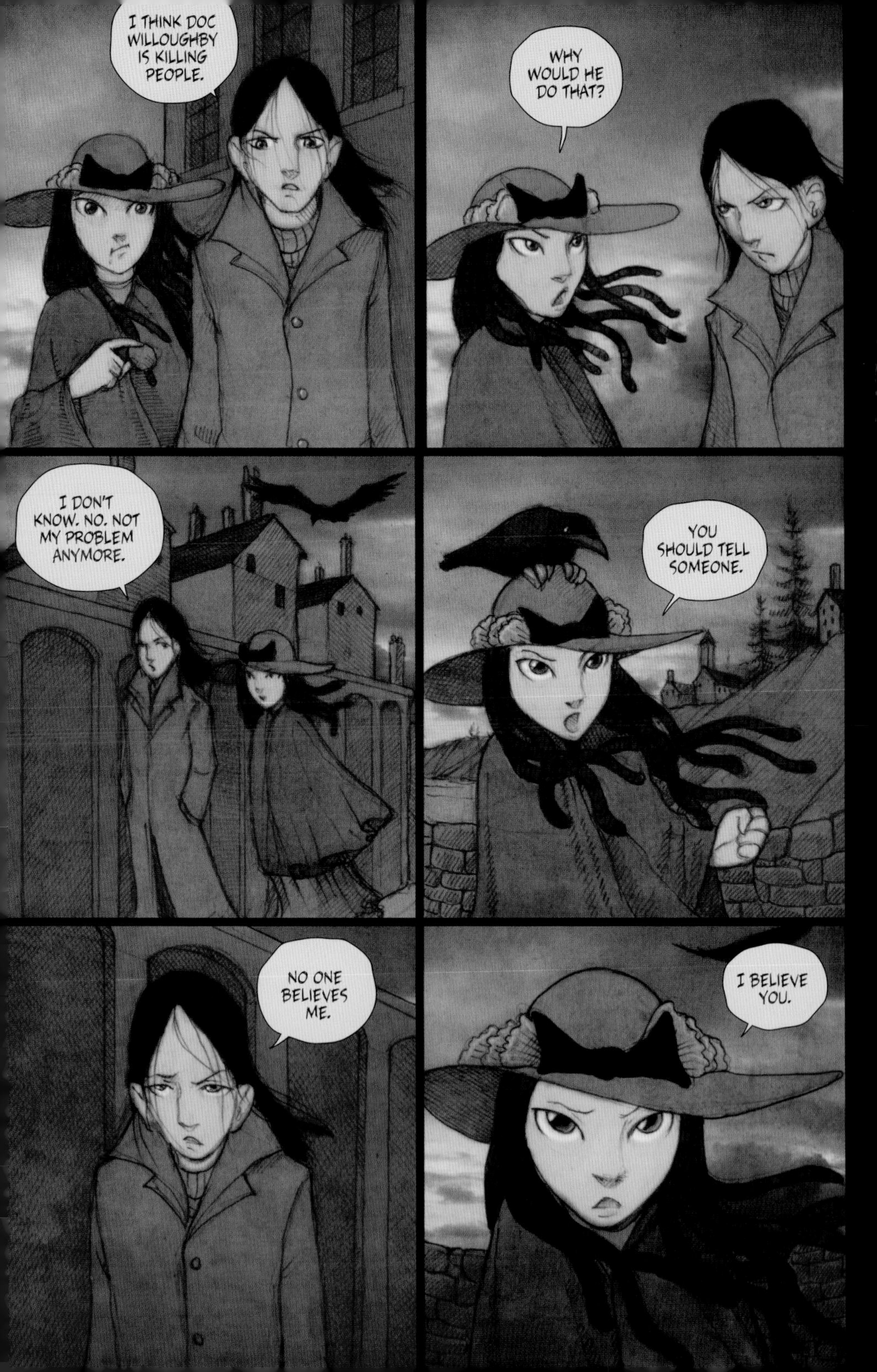
I THINK DOC WILLOUGHBY IS KILLING PEOPLE.
WHY WOULD HE DO THAT?
I DON'T KNOW. NO. NOT MY PROBLEM ANYMORE.
YOU SHOULD TELL SOMEONE.
NO ONE BELIEVES ME.
I BELIEVE YOU.

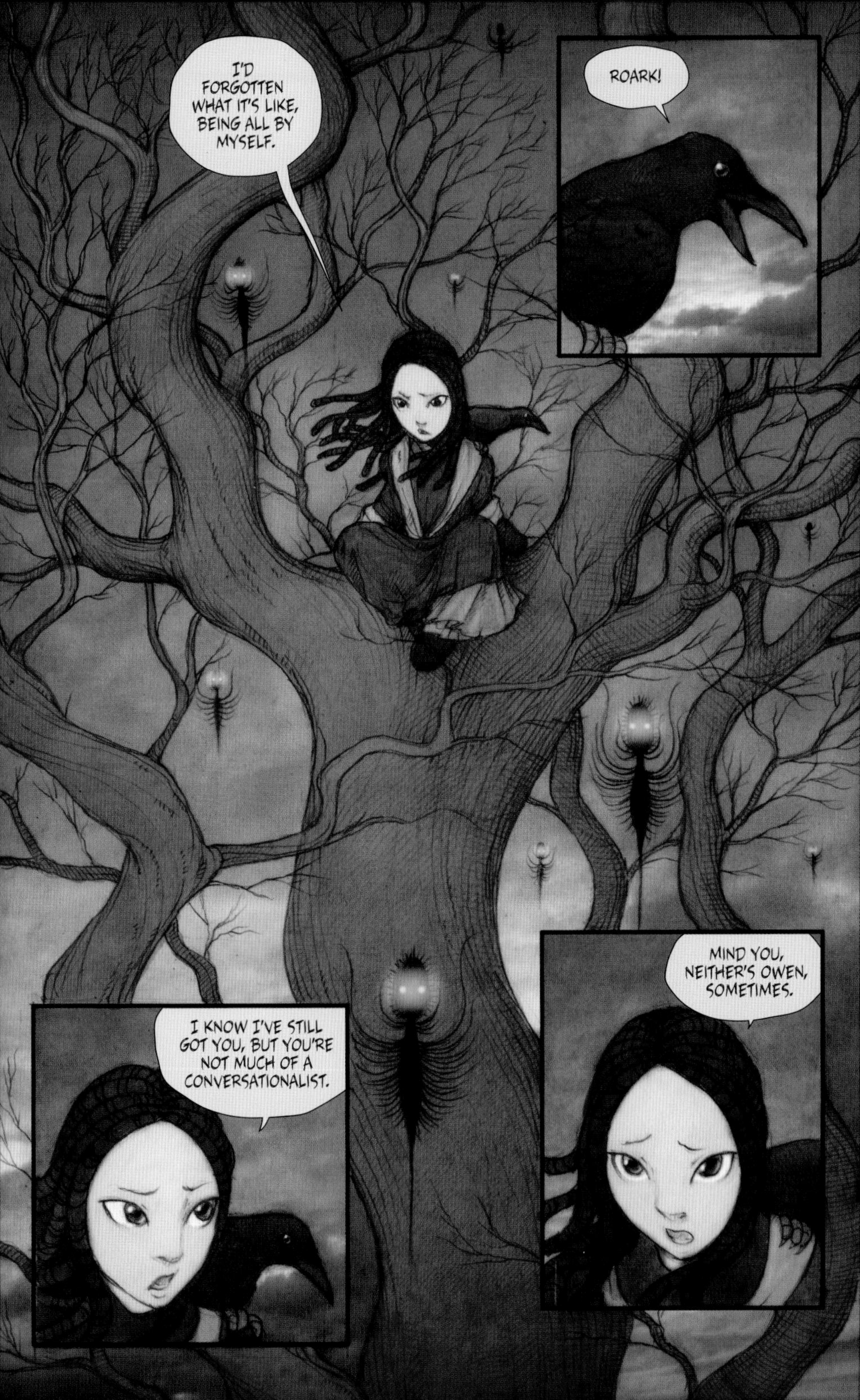

I'D FORGOTTEN WHAT IT'S LIKE, BEING ALL BY MYSELF.
ROARK!
I KNOW I'VE STILL GOT YOU, BUT YOU'RE NOT MUCH OF A CONVERSATIONALIST.
MIND YOU, NEITHER'S OWEN, SOMETIMES.

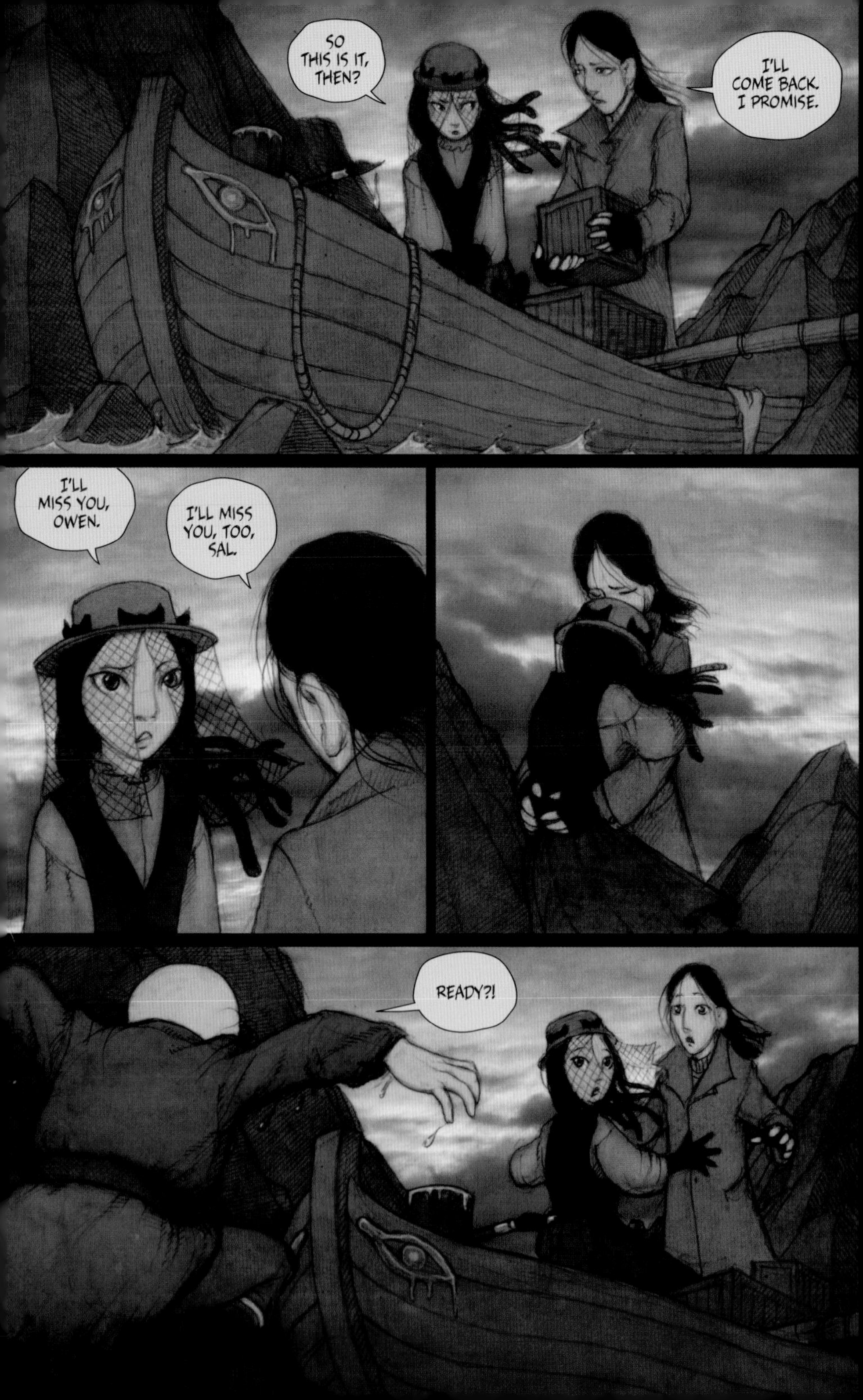
SO THIS IS IT, THEN?
I'LL COME BACK. I PROMISE.
I'LL MISS YOU, OWEN.
I'LL MISS YOU, TOO, SAL.
READY?!

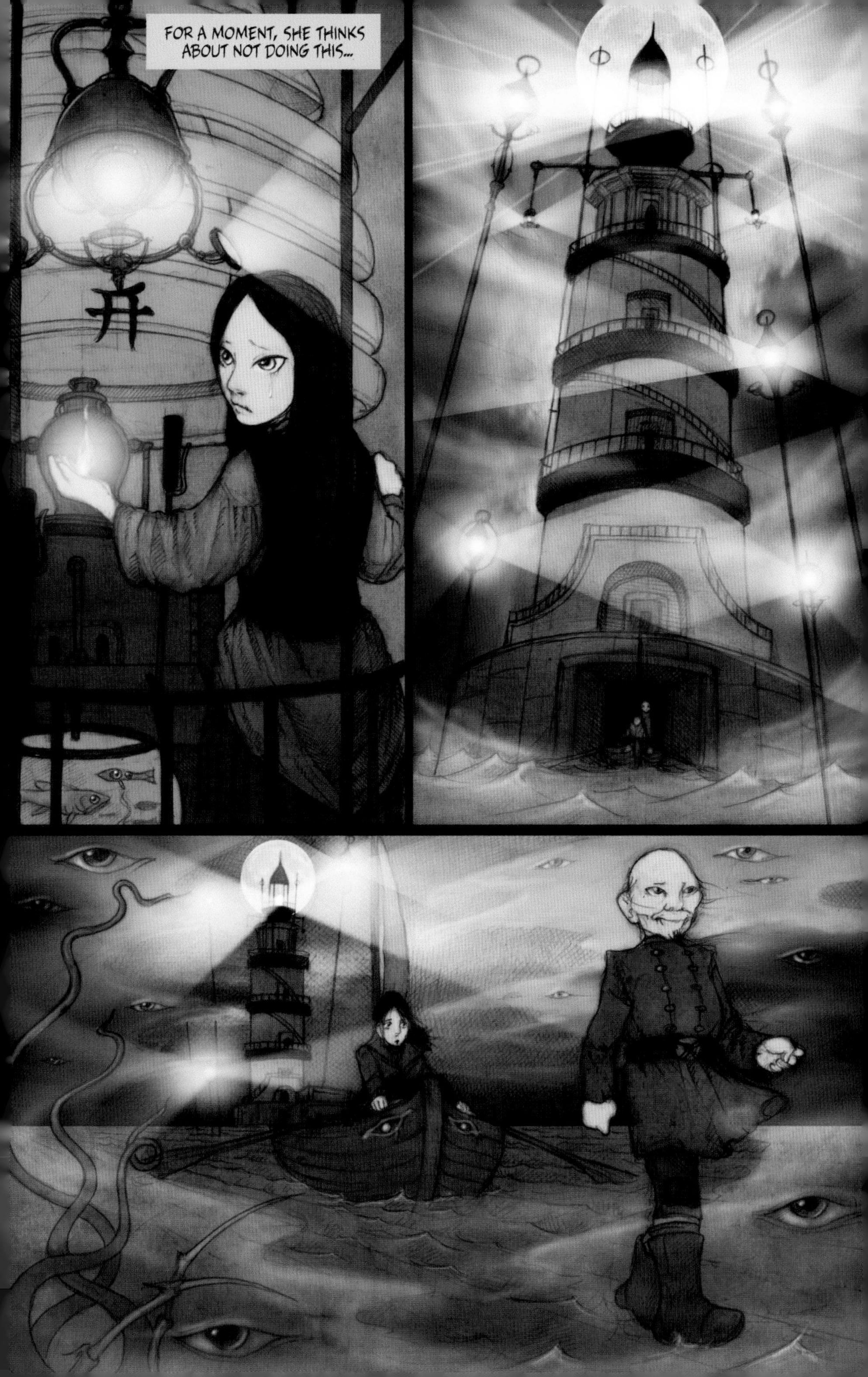
FOR A MOMENT, SHE THINKS ABOUT NOT DOING THIS...

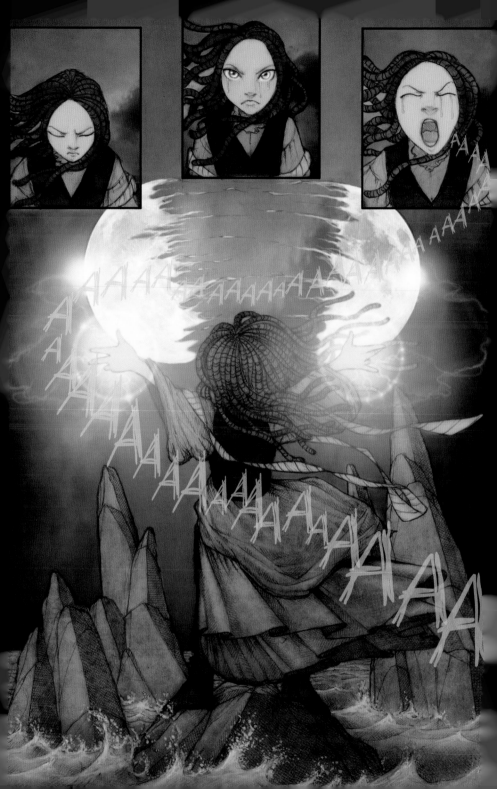

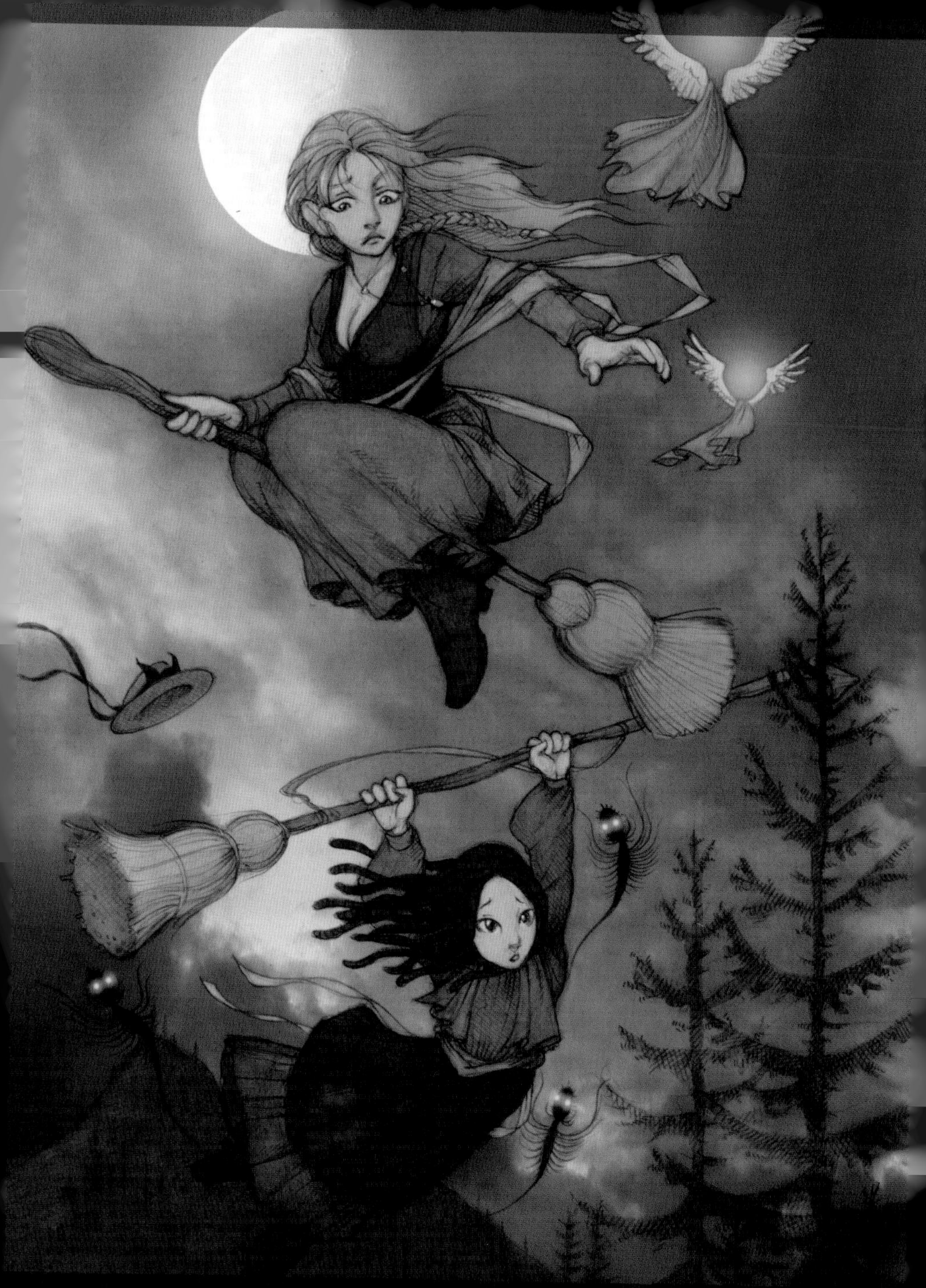

AND I'M PRETTY SURE LUNCH HAD BLOOD IN IT

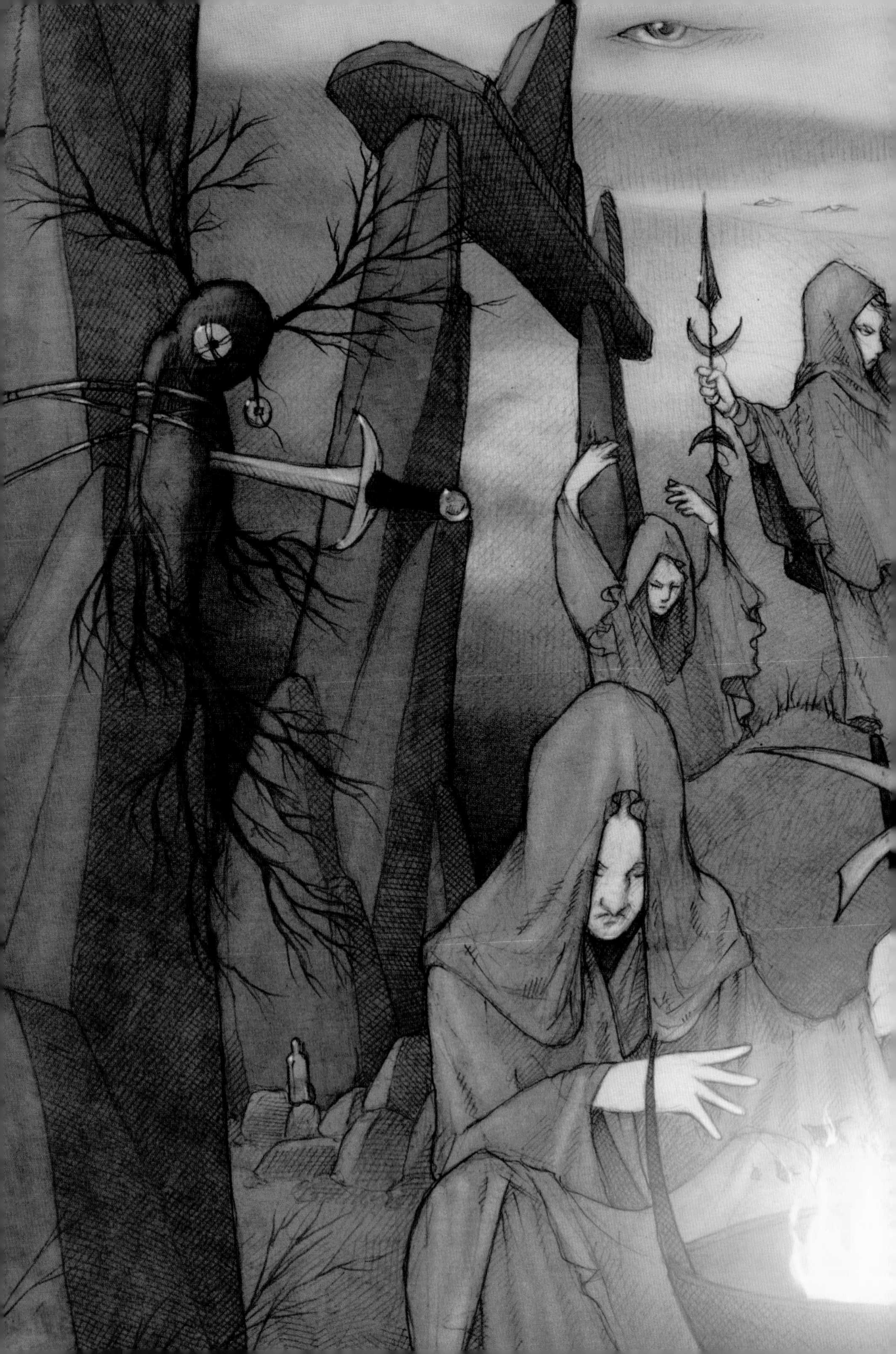

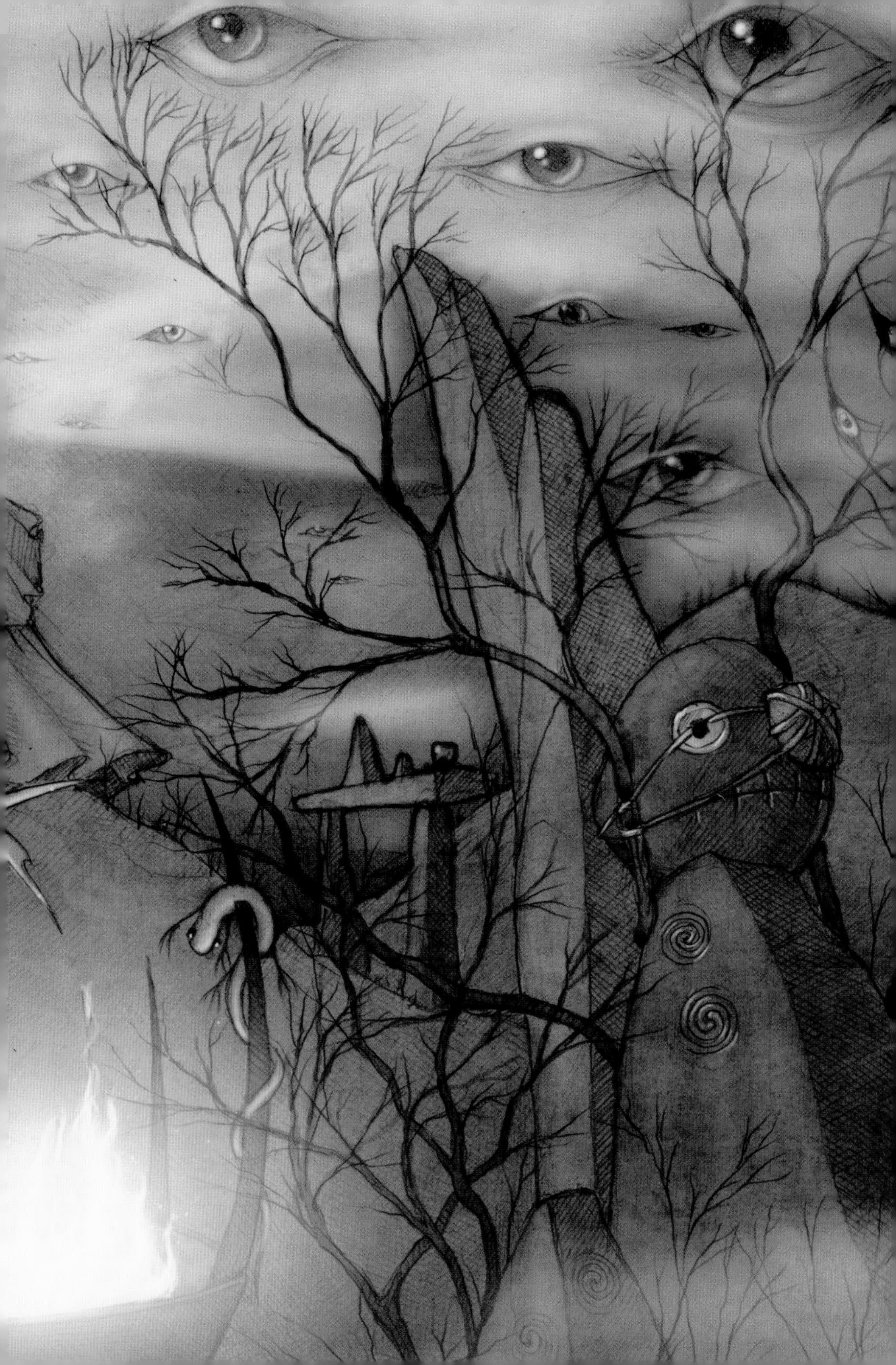

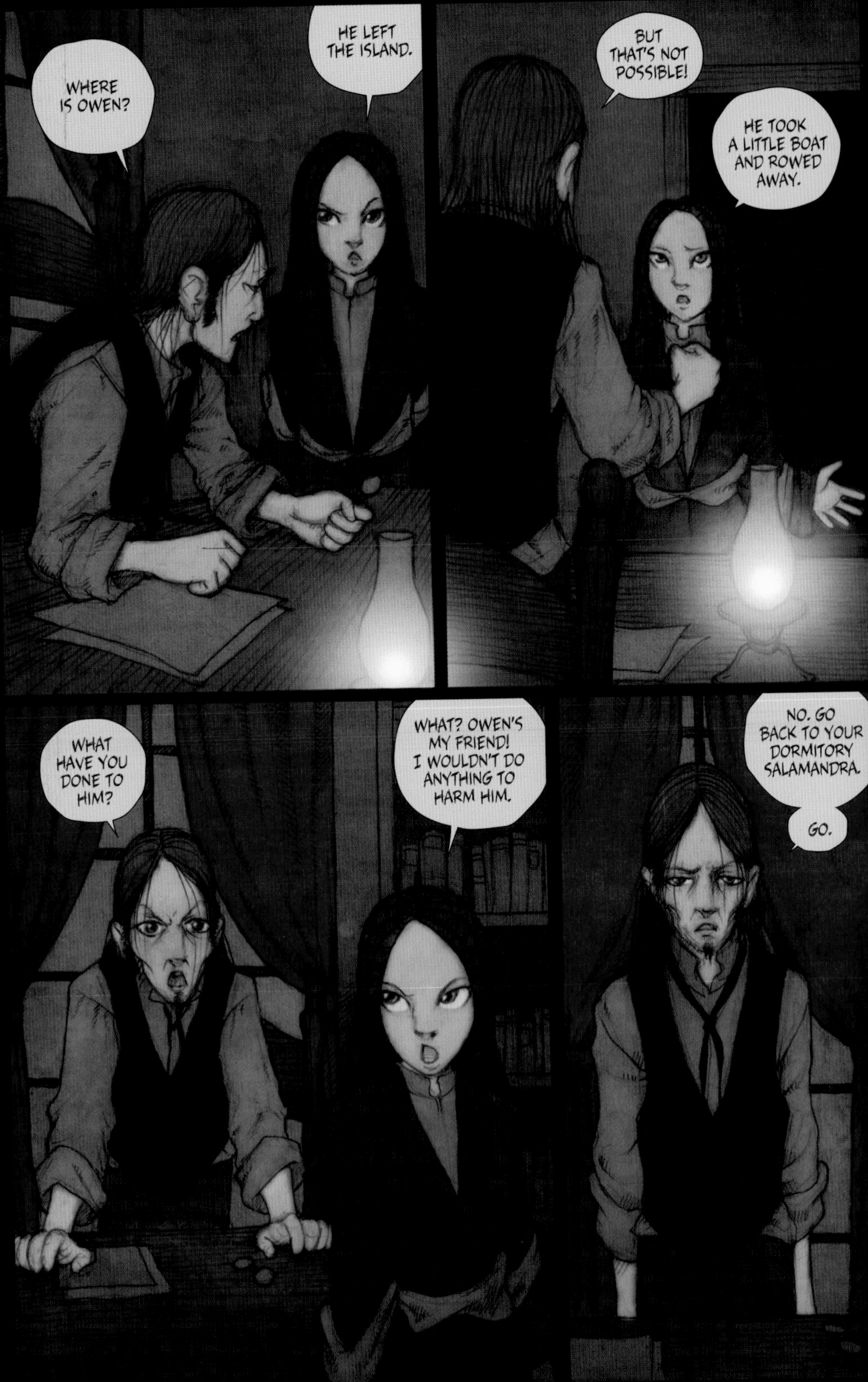
WHERE IS OWEN?
HE LEFT THE ISLAND.
BUT THAT'S NOT POSSIBLE!
HE TOOK A LITTLE BOAT AND ROWED AWAY.
WHAT HAVE YOU DONE TO HIM?
WHAT? OWEN'S MY FRIEND! I WOULDN'T DO ANYTHING TO HARM HIM.
NO. GO BACK TO YOUR DORMITORY SALAMANDRA.
GO.

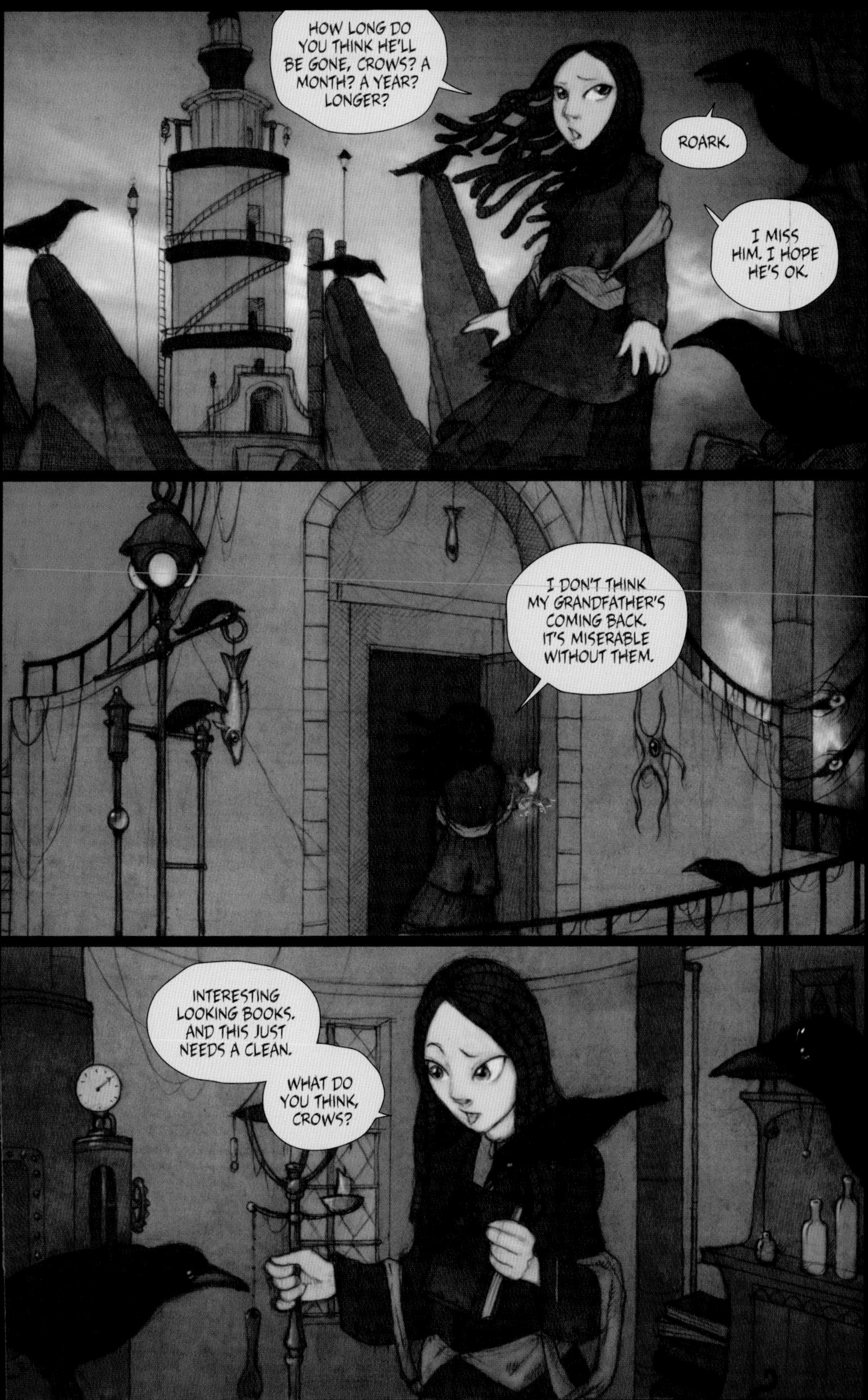
HOW LONG DO YOU THINK HE'LL BE GONE, CROWS? A MONTH? A YEAR? LONGER?
ROARK.
I MISS HIM. I HOPE HE'S OK.
I DON'T THINK MY GRANDFATHER'S COMING BACK. IT'S MISERABLE WITHOUT THEM.
INTERESTING LOOKING BOOKS. AND THIS JUST NEEDS A CLEAN.
WHAT DO YOU THINK, CROWS?

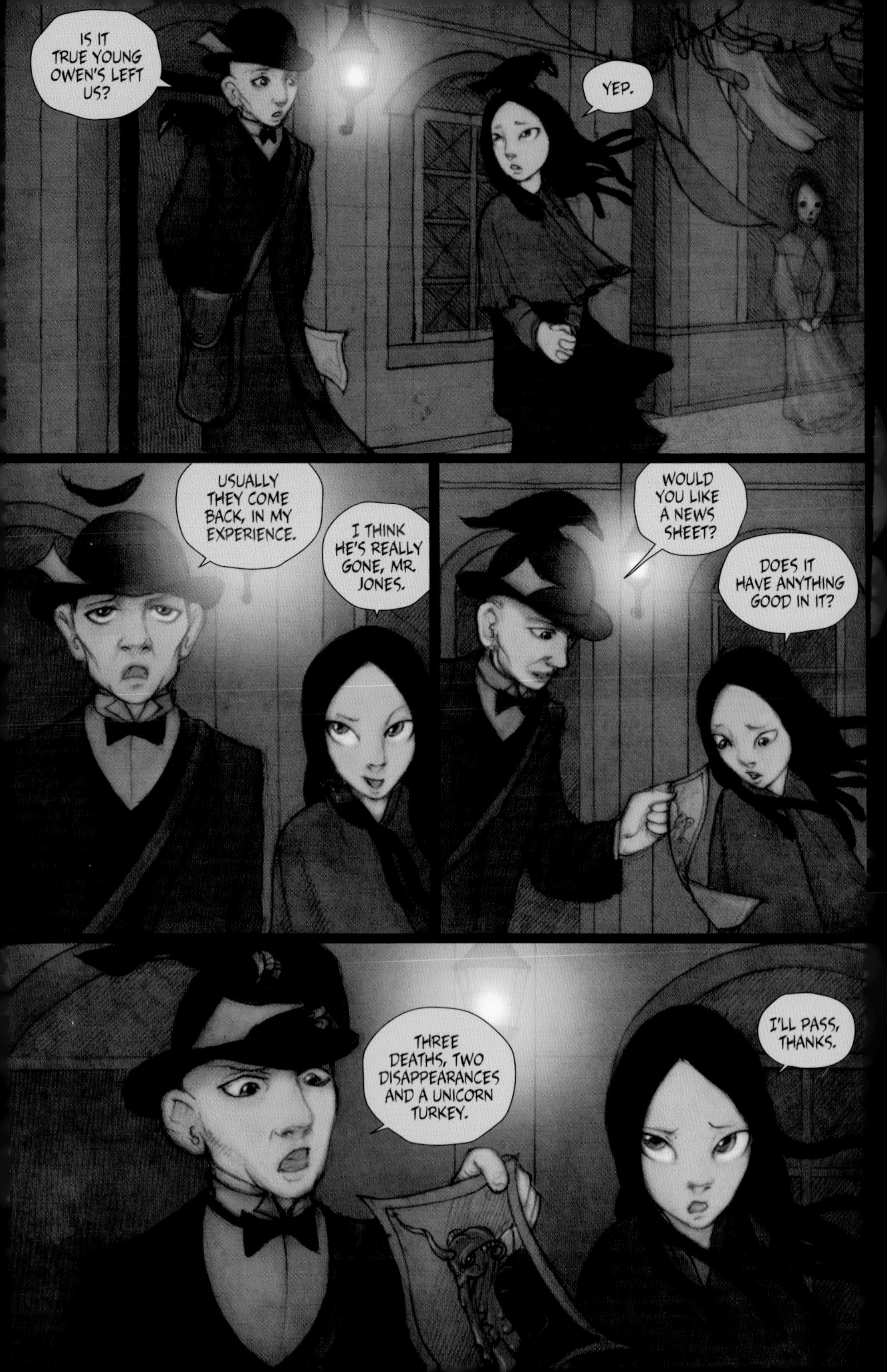

IS IT TRUE YOUNG OWEN'S LEFT US?
YEP.
USUALLY THEY COME BACK, IN MY EXPERIENCE.
I THINK HE'S REALLY GONE, MR. JONES.
WOULD YOU LIKE A NEWS SHEET?
DOES IT HAVE ANYTHING GOOD IN IT?
THREE DEATHS, TWO DISAPPEARANCES AND A UNICORN TURKEY.
I'LL PASS, THANKS.

The waves are bigger than anything imaginable. Whole worlds within themselves.

Not dying is a source of constant surprise.

Every new breath unexpected.

Wetness is pretty much a given. Skin soaked, bone chilled, wet beyond
all previous measures of water saturation. We could wring my skin out to good effect.

And somehow the boat is still the right way up.

Moving.

All the things from beneath the waves that might eat me have so far chosen
Not to.

There are some things it pays not to question.
I do not want any of them to change their minds.

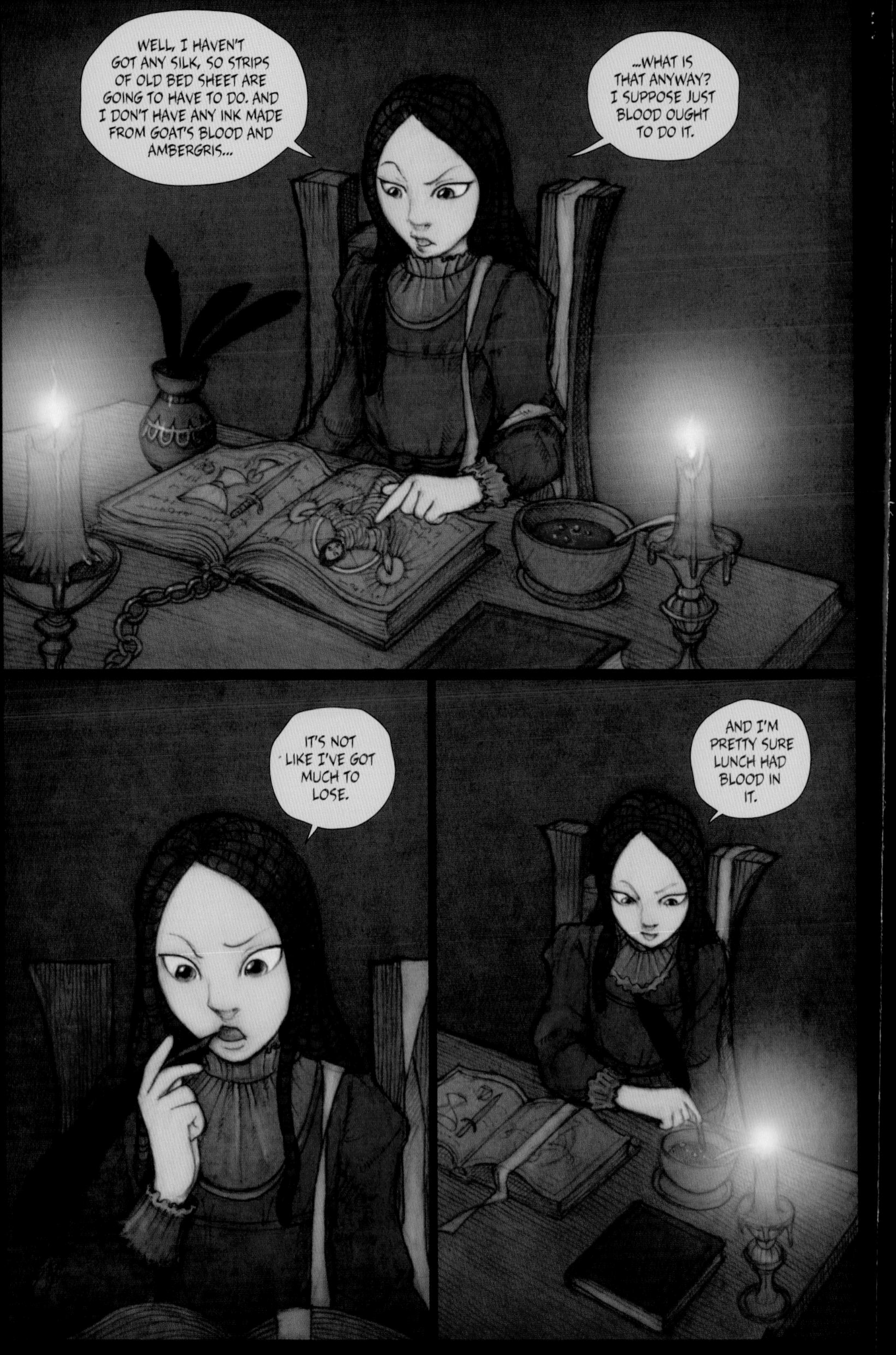
WELL, I HAVEN'T GOT ANY SILK, SO STRIPS OF OLD BED SHEET ARE GOING TO HAVE TO DO. AND I DON'T HAVE ANY INK MADE FROM GOAT'S BLOOD AND AMBERGRIS...
...WHAT IS THAT ANYWAY? I SUPPOSE JUST BLOOD OUGHT TO DO IT.
IT'S NOT LIKE I'VE GOT MUCH TO LOSE.
AND I'M PRETTY SURE LUNCH HAD BLOOD IN IT.

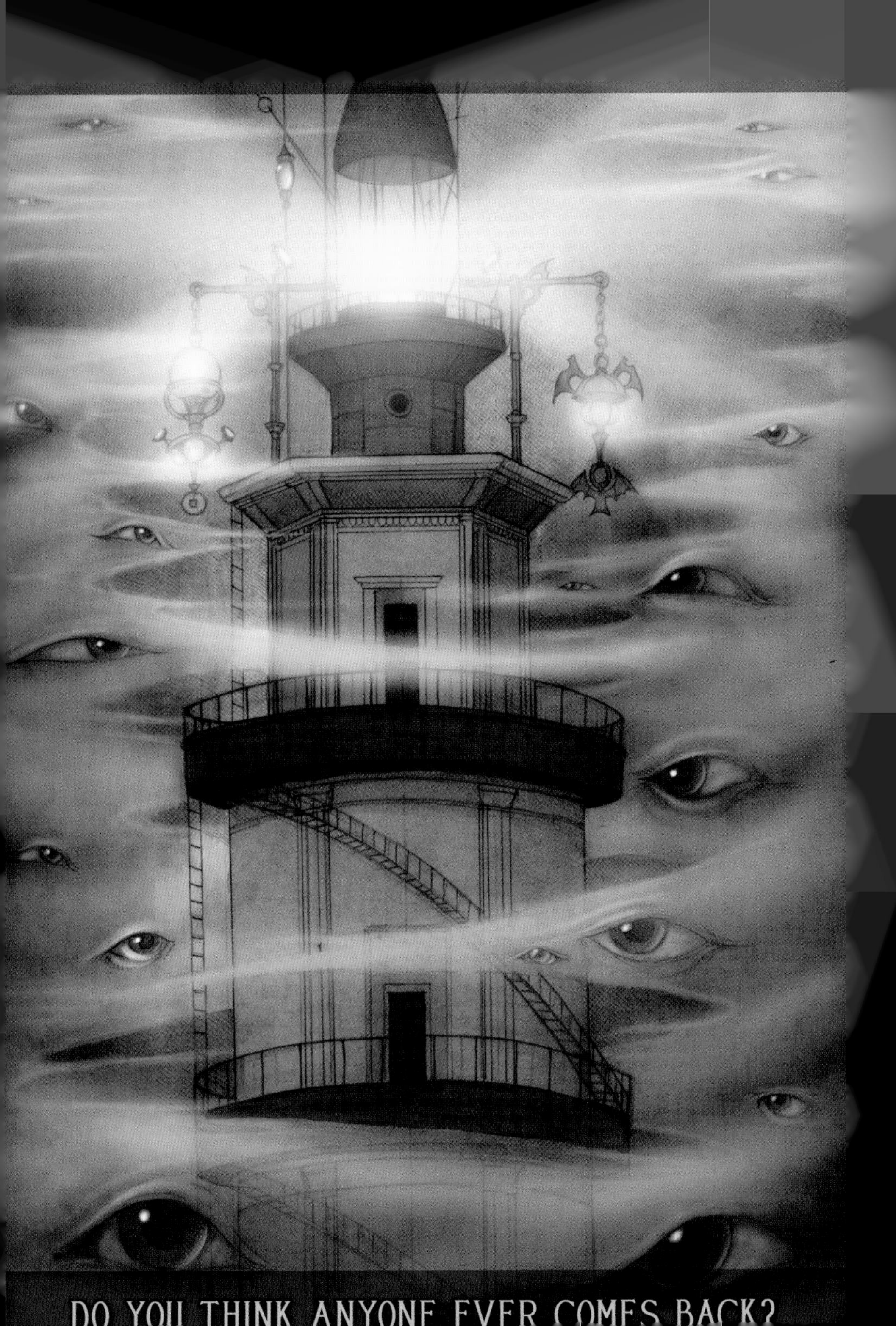

DO YOU THINK ANYONE EVER COMES BACK?

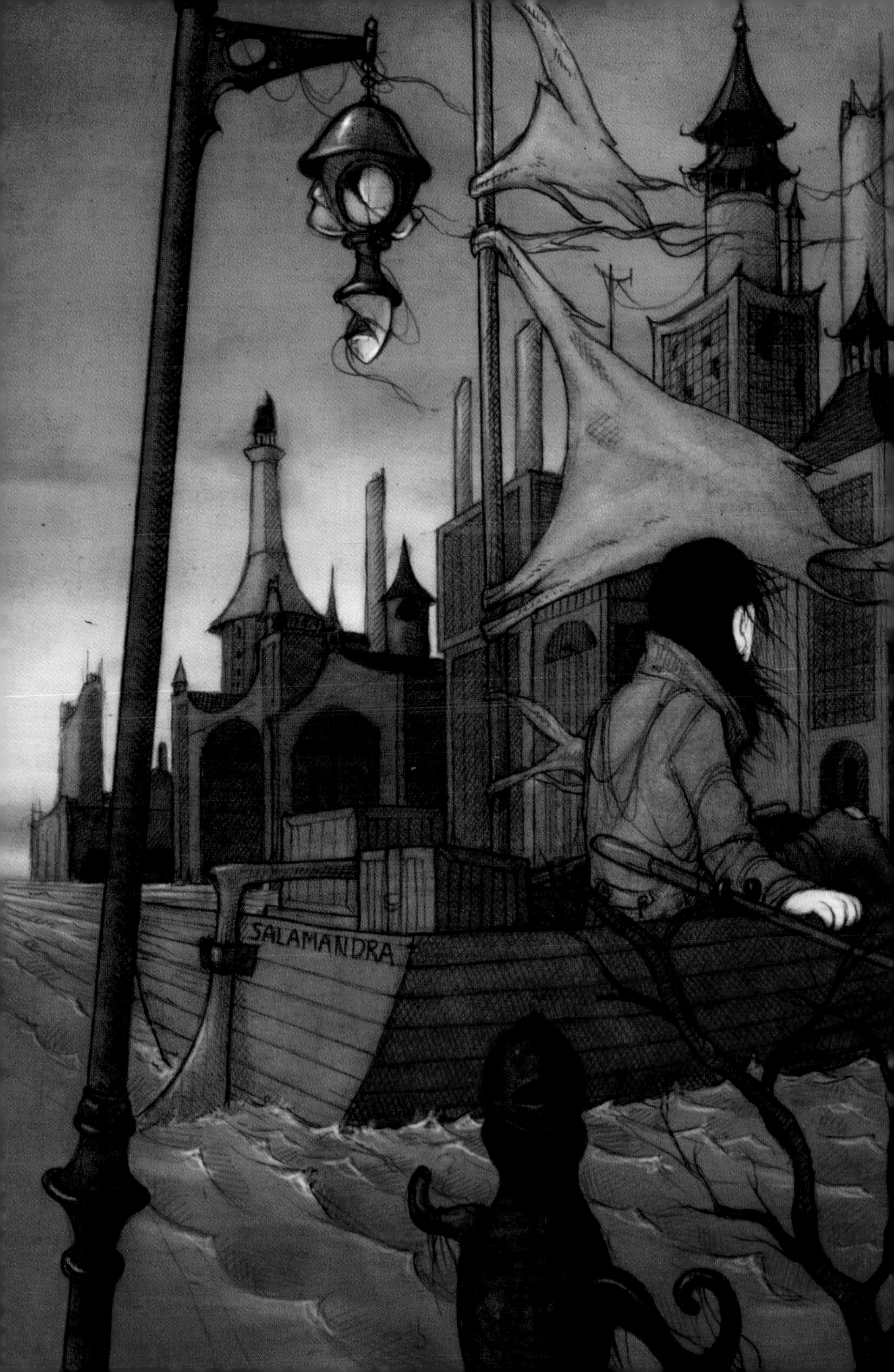
SALAMANDRA

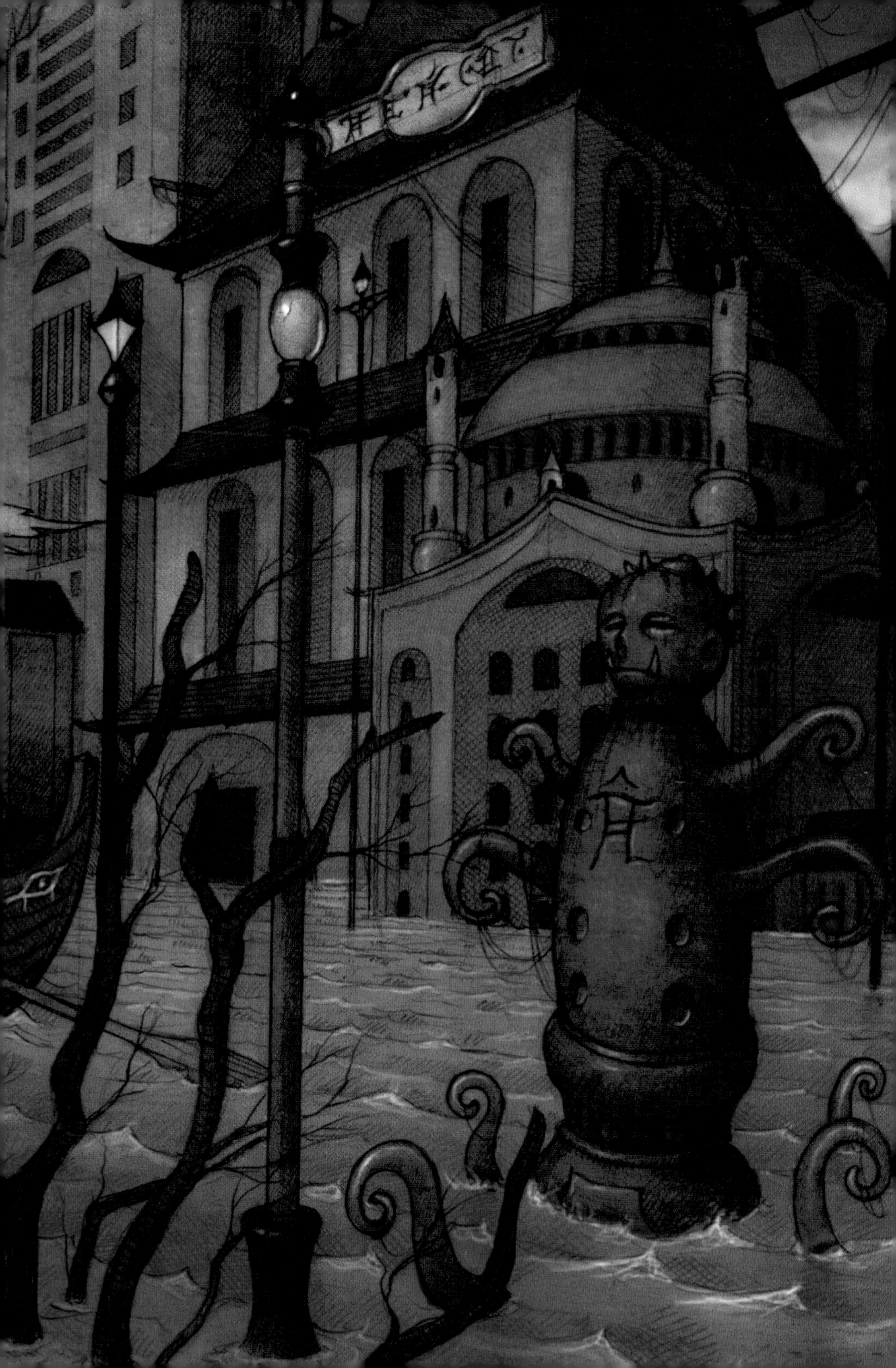

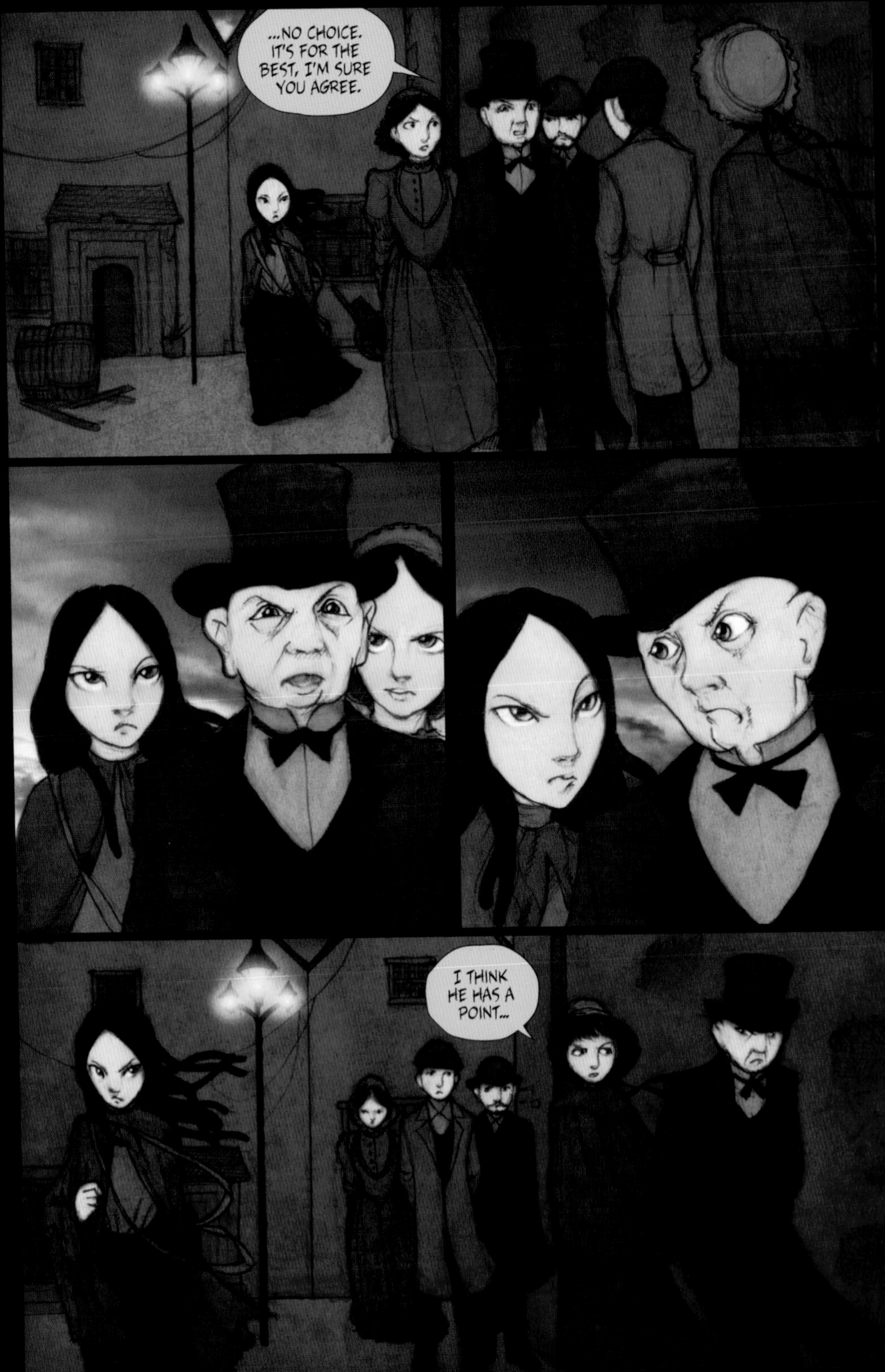
...NO CHOICE. IT'S FOR THE BEST, I'M SURE YOU AGREE.
I THINK HE HAS A POINT...

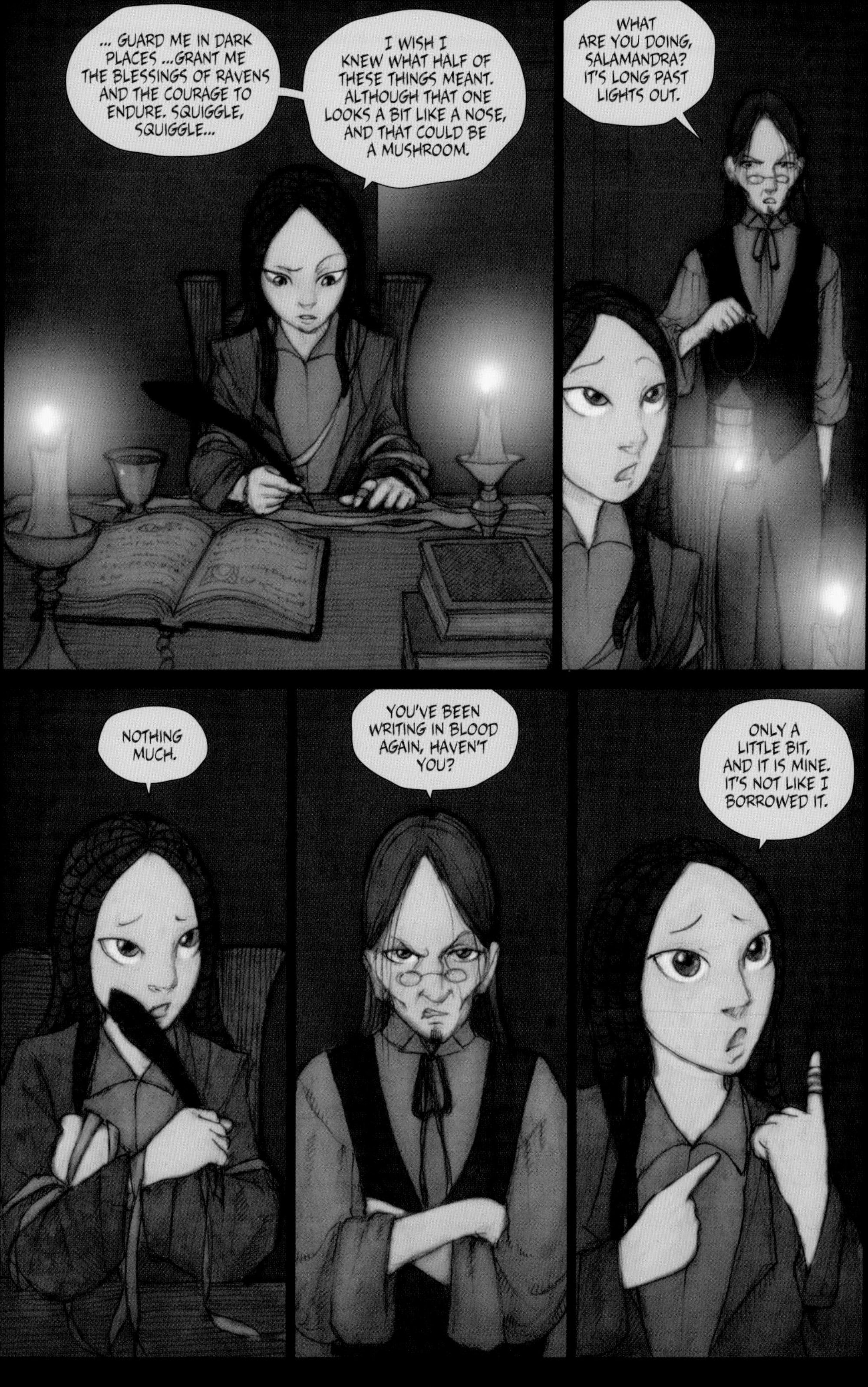
... GUARD ME IN DARK PLACES ...GRANT ME THE BLESSINGS OF RAVENS AND THE COURAGE TO ENDURE. SQUIGGLE, SQUIGGLE...
I WISH I KNEW WHAT HALF OF THESE THINGS MEANT. ALTHOUGH THAT ONE LOOKS A BIT LIKE A NOSE, AND THAT COULD BE A MUSHROOM.
WHAT ARE YOU DOING, SALAMANDRA? IT'S LONG PAST LIGHTS OUT.
NOTHING MUCH.
YOU'VE BEEN WRITING IN BLOOD AGAIN, HAVEN'T YOU?
ONLY A LITTLE BIT, AND IT IS MINE. IT'S NOT LIKE I BORROWED IT.

THAT REALLY ISN'T THE POINT. WE CAN'T GO ON LIKE THIS, SALAMANDRA.
I KNOW. IT'S TIME FOR ME TO MOVE ON, ISN'T IT? THANKS FOR GIVING ME THIS LONG. I KNOW IT'S BEEN HARD FOR YOU.
I DON'T WANT TO THROW YOU OUT. YOU'RE SO YOUNG STILL, AND I DO HAVE A DUTY TO LOOK AFTER YOU. BUT ALL THIS NASTY OCCULTISH NONSENSE...I CAN'T HAVE IT IN THIS HOUSE. COULDN'T YOU JUST GIVE IT UP?
NO. IT'S WHO I AM. I'M DOING IT BECAUSE I HAVE TO. I THINK THERE ARE MUCH WORSE THINGS THAN ME 'ROUND HERE.

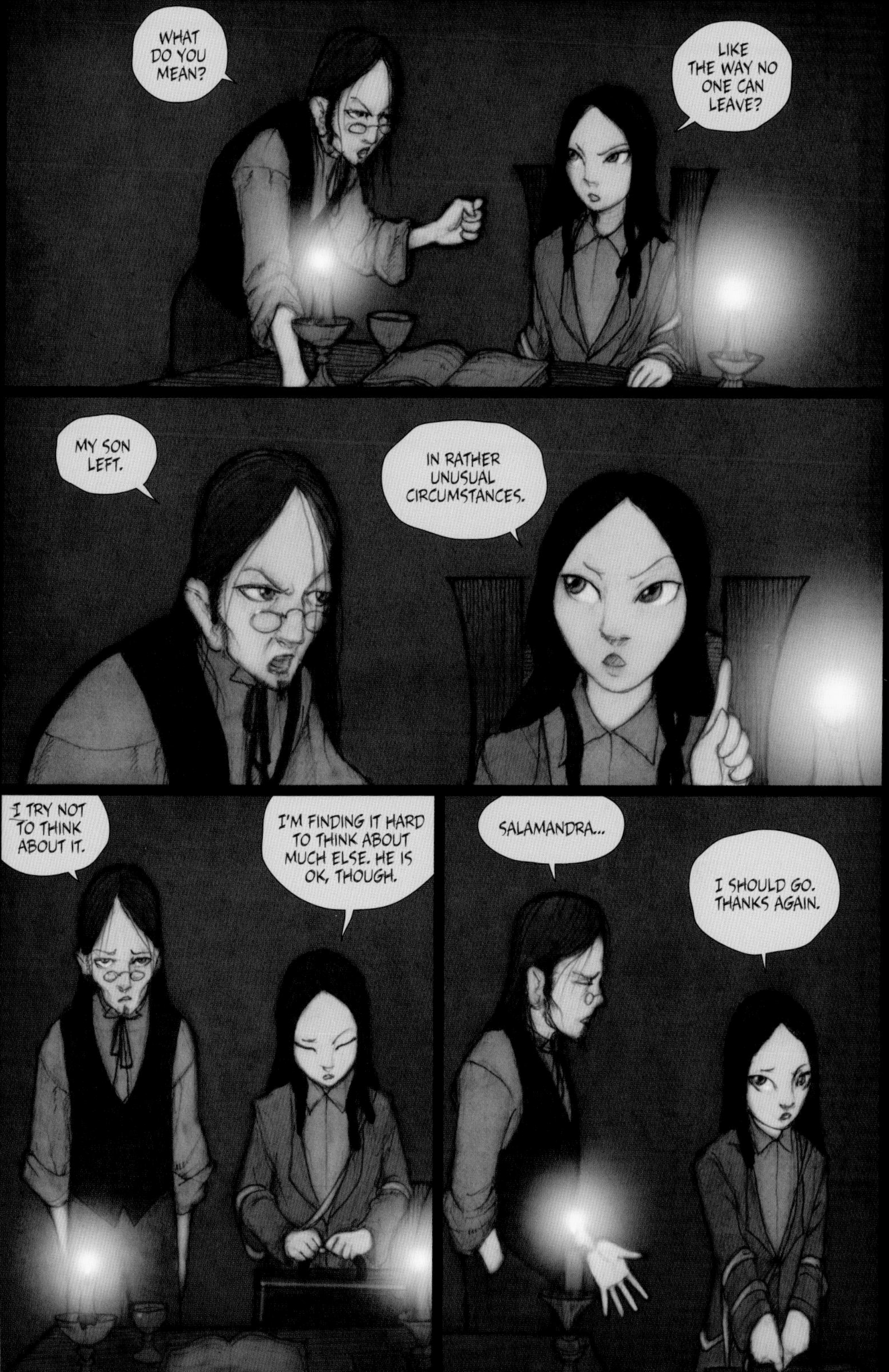
WHAT DO YOU MEAN?
LIKE THE WAY NO ONE CAN LEAVE?
MY SON LEFT.
IN RATHER UNUSUAL CIRCUMSTANCES.
I TRY NOT TO THINK ABOUT IT.
I'M FINDING IT HARD TO THINK ABOUT MUCH ELSE. HE IS OK, THOUGH.
SALAMANDRA...
I SHOULD GO. THANKS AGAIN.

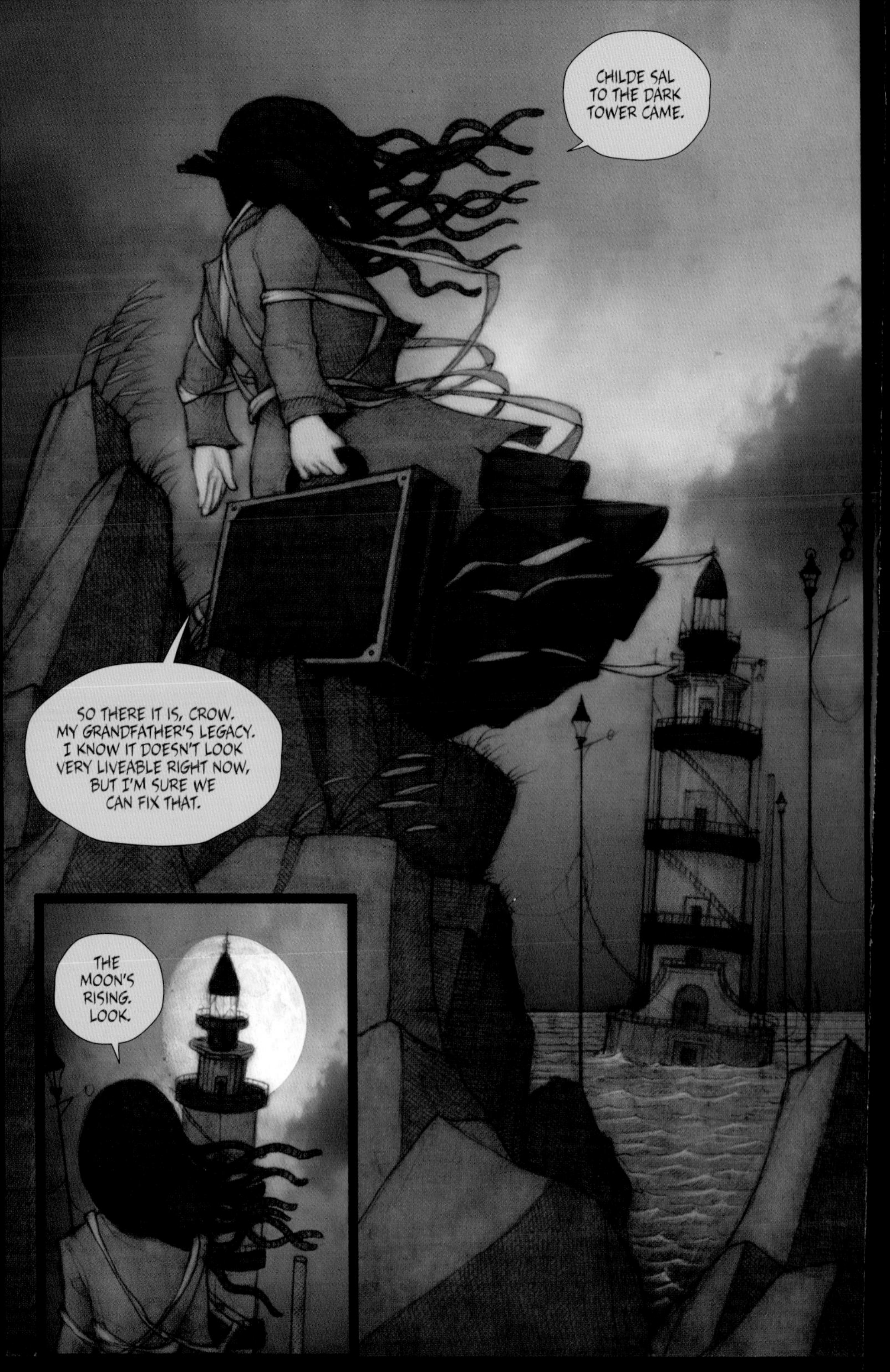
CHILDE SAL TO THE DARK TOWER CAME.
SO THERE IT IS, CROW. MY GRANDFATHER'S LEGACY. I KNOW IT DOESN'T LOOK VERY LIVEABLE RIGHT NOW, BUT I'M SURE WE CAN FIX THAT.
THE MOON'S RISING. LOOK.

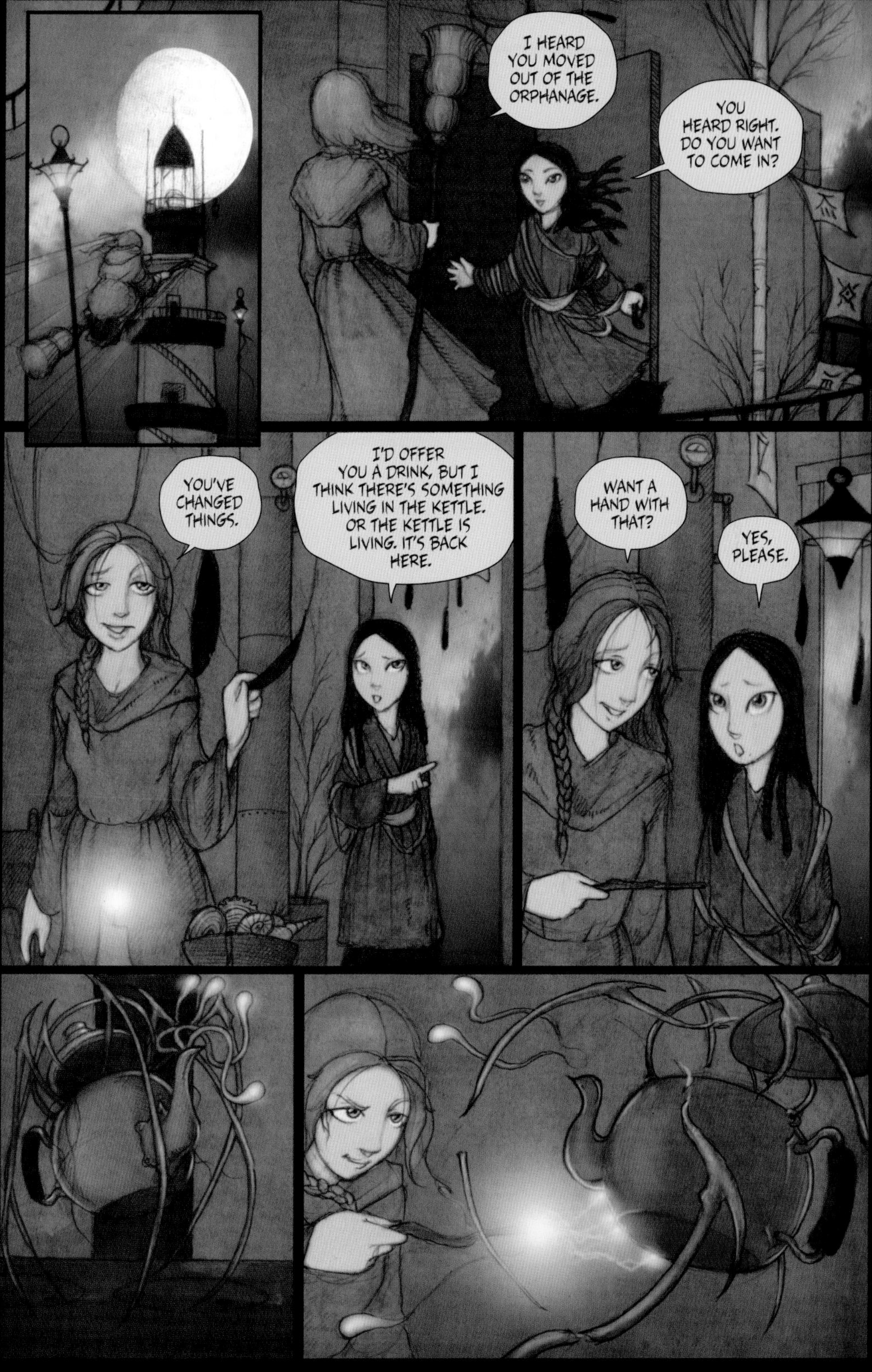
I HEARD YOU MOVED OUT OF THE ORPHANAGE.
YOU HEARD RIGHT. DO YOU WANT TO COME IN?
YOU'VE CHANGED THINGS.
I'D OFFER YOU A DRINK, BUT I THINK THERE'S SOMETHING LIVING IN THE KETTLE. OR THE KETTLE IS LIVING. IT'S BACK HERE.
WANT A HAND WITH THAT?
YES, PLEASE.

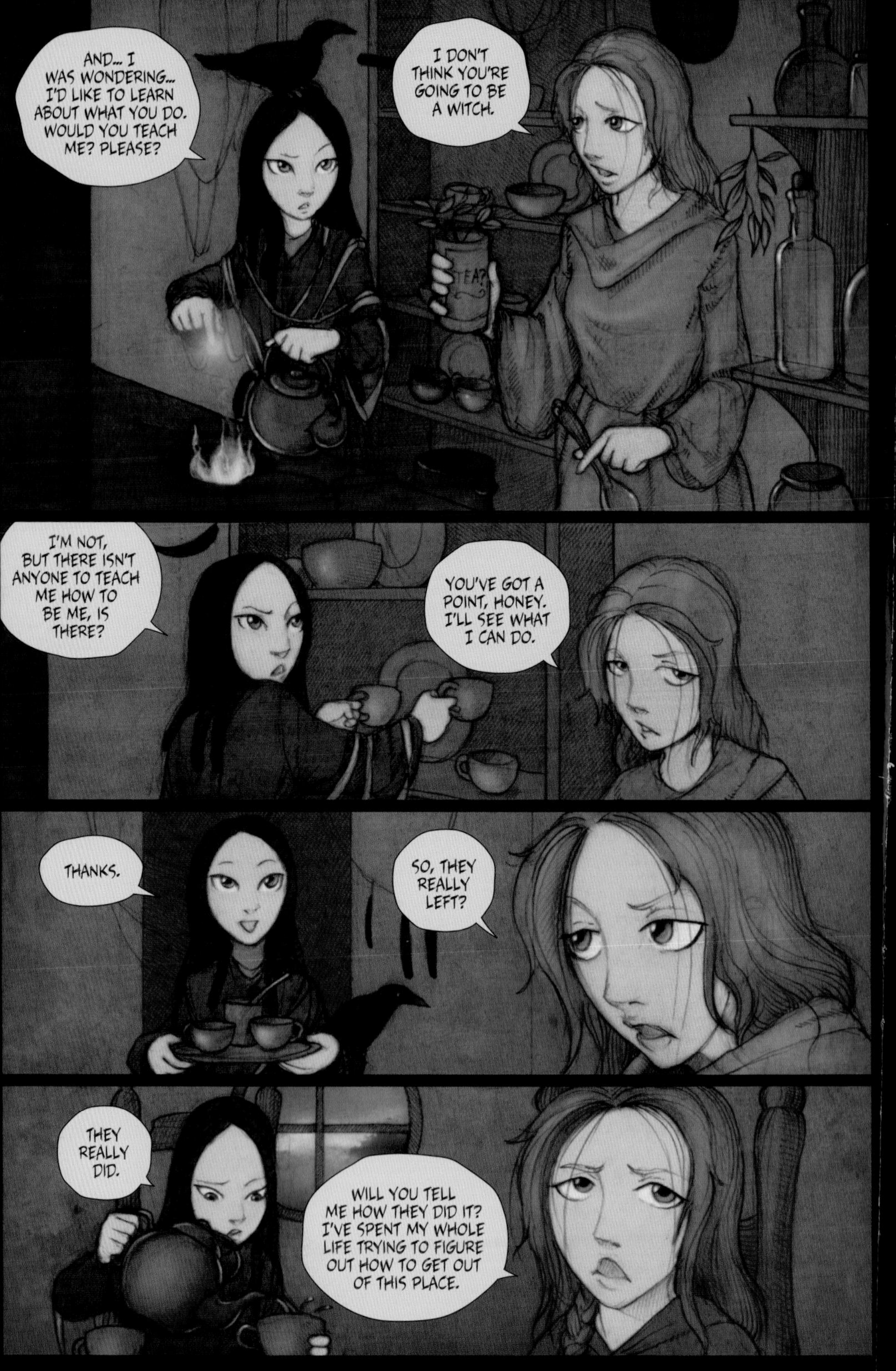
AND... I WAS WONDERING... I'D LIKE TO LEARN ABOUT WHAT YOU DO. WOULD YOU TEACH ME? PLEASE?
I DON'T THINK YOU'RE GOING TO BE A WITCH.
TEA?
I'M NOT, BUT THERE ISN'T ANYONE TO TEACH ME HOW TO BE ME, IS THERE?
YOU'VE GOT A POINT, HONEY. I'LL SEE WHAT I CAN DO.
THANKS.
SO, THEY REALLY LEFT?
THEY REALLY DID.
WILL YOU TELL ME HOW THEY DID IT? I'VE SPENT MY WHOLE LIFE TRYING TO FIGURE OUT HOW TO GET OUT OF THIS PLACE.

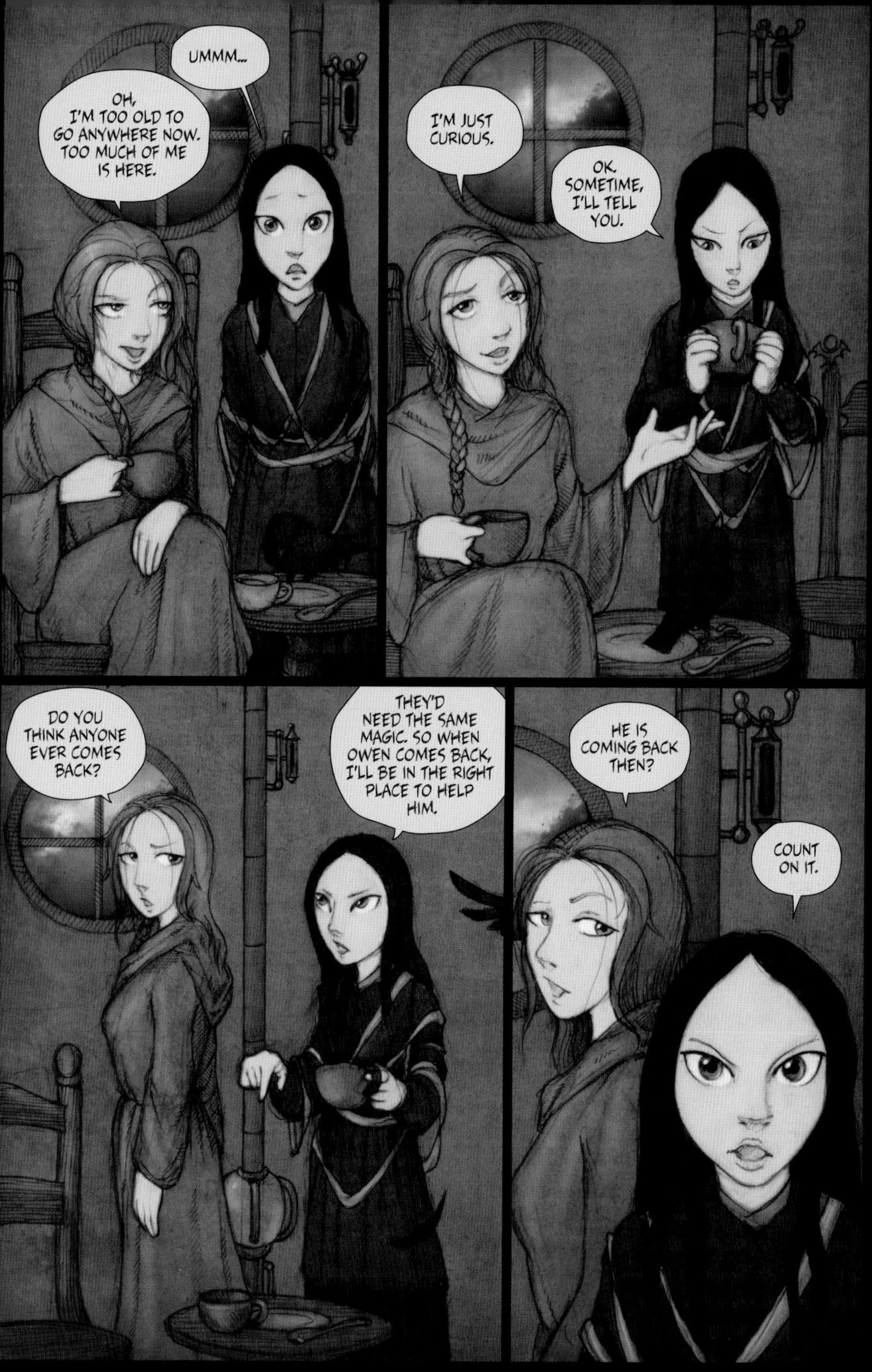
OH, I'M TOO OLD TO GO ANYWHERE NOW. TOO MUCH OF ME IS HERE.
UMMM...
I'M JUST CURIOUS.
OK. SOMETIME, I'LL TELL YOU.
DO YOU THINK ANYONE EVER COMES BACK?
THEY'D NEED THE SAME MAGIC. SO WHEN OWEN COMES BACK, I'LL BE IN THE RIGHT PLACE TO HELP HIM.
HE IS COMING BACK THEN?
COUNT ON IT.

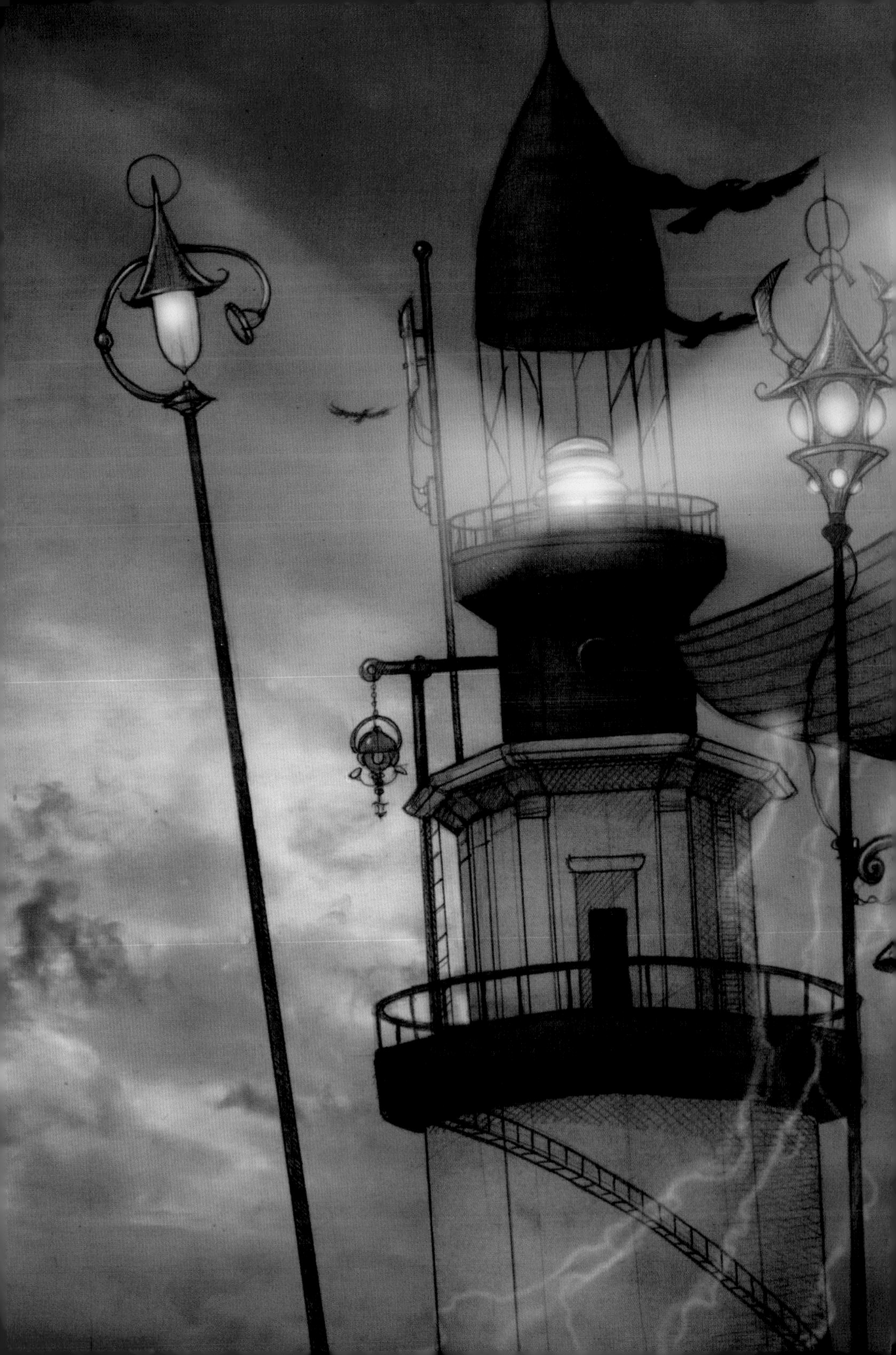

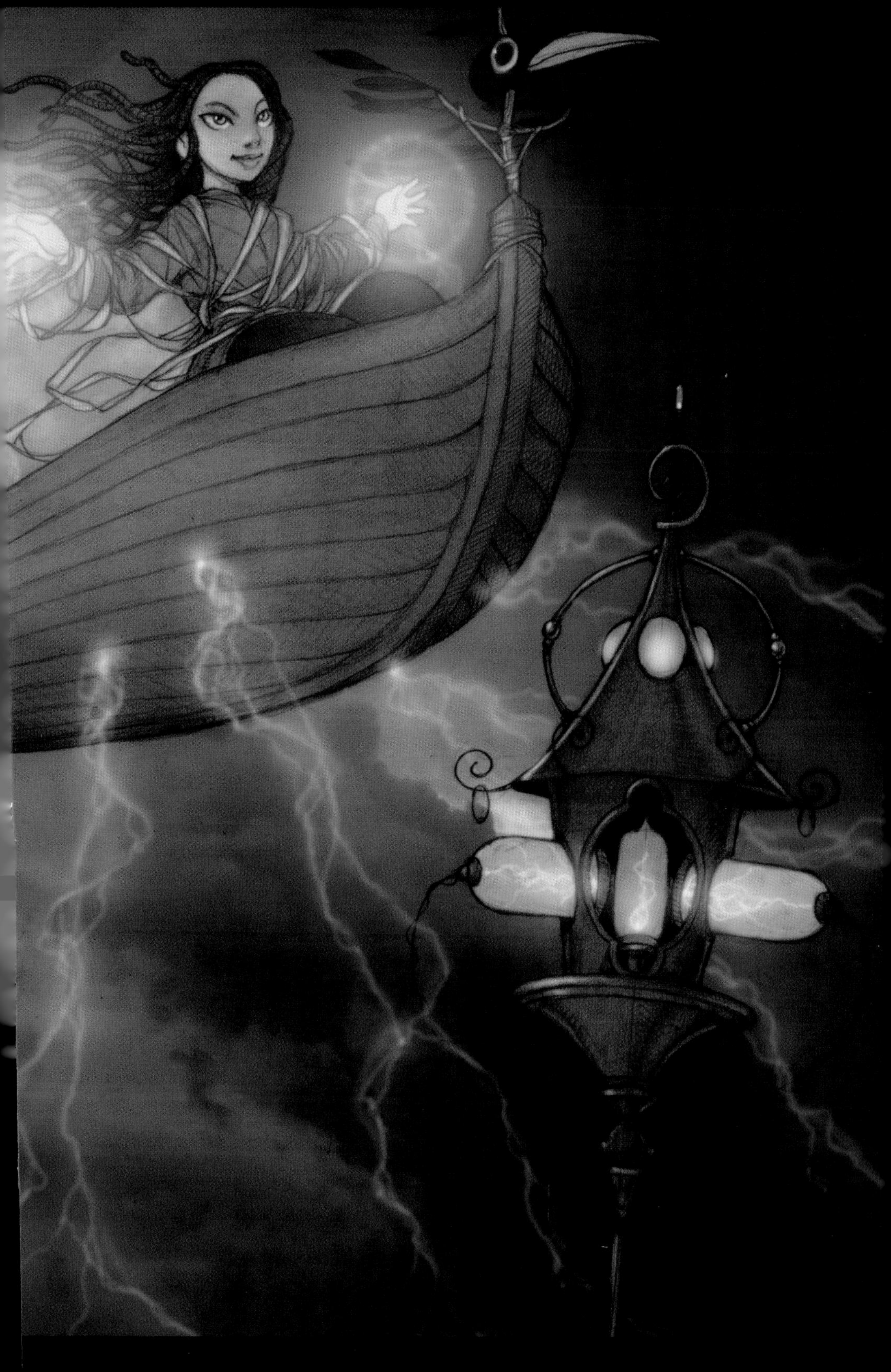

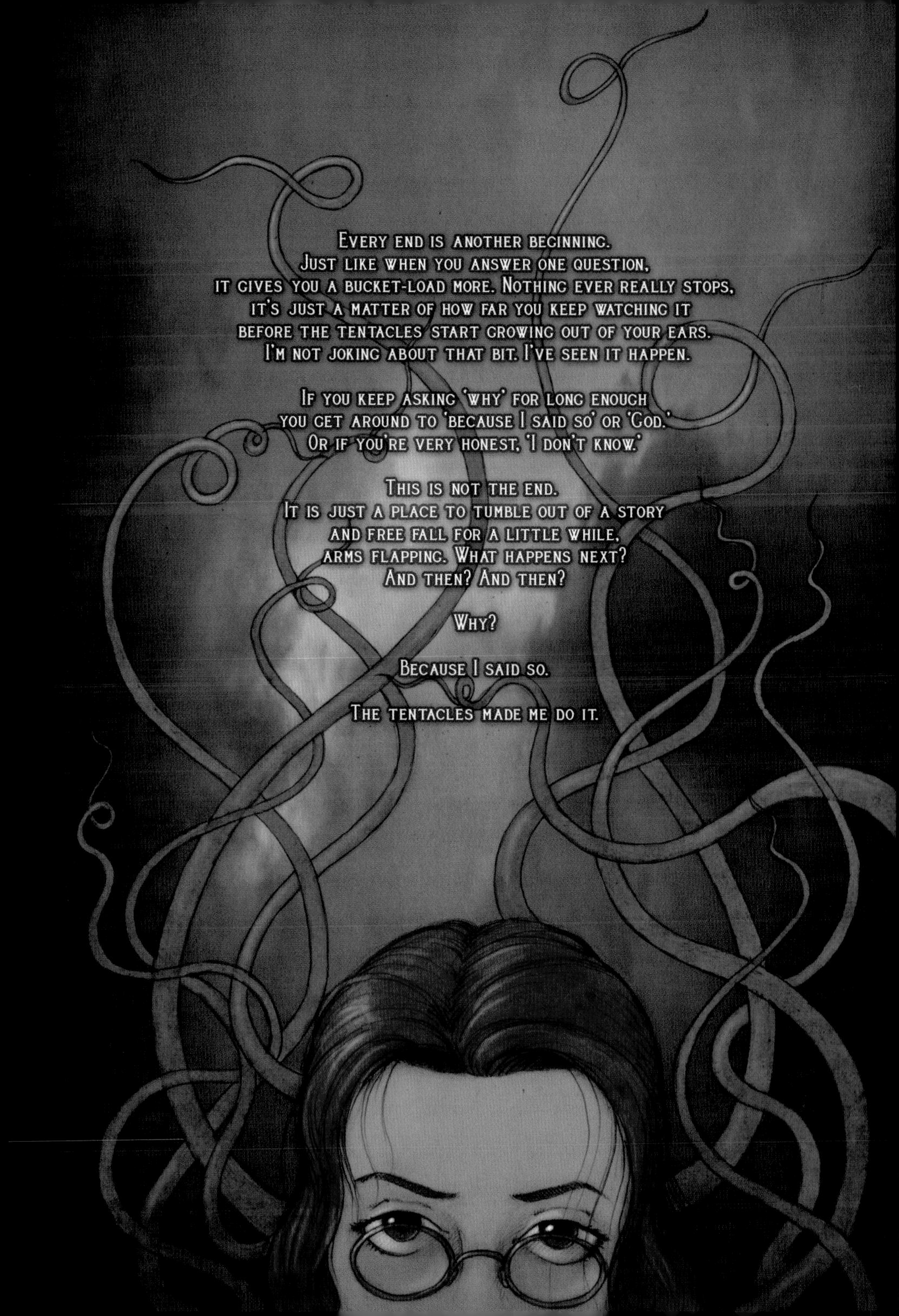
Every end is another beginning.
Just like when you answer one question,
it gives you a bucket-load more. Nothing ever really stops,
it's just a matter of how far you keep watching it
before the tentacles start growing out of your ears.
I'm not joking about that bit. I've seen it happen.
If you keep asking 'why' for long enough
you get around to 'because I said so' or 'God.'
Or if you're very honest, 'I don't know.'
This is not the end.
It is just a place to tumble out of a story
and free fall for a little while,
arms flapping. What happens next?
And then? And then?
Why?
Because I said so.
The tentacles made me do it.

Founding Families

The founding families of Hopeless, Maine are responsible for having commenced building the town in the late 1700s. They were not the first inhabitants of the island, nor the only ones to be present at the establishment of Hopeless as a town. Their status as founders owes to a combination of self-importance (The O'Stoats), sheer numbers (The Jones and Chevin clans), and being the ones to record the history (The Frogs). The island was never a welcoming place, and colonising it cost heavily in terms of human lives. And others. The abandoned churches and cemeteries of the island, as well as the empty cottages and ruined buildings around the town, testify to a time when Hopeless was a thriving and successful place for those who were willing to risk a short life expectancy.

Hopeless was founded as a town at the time when the gnii industry was at its height, and workers came to build and run the gnii processing plant on the island, which in turn generated other employment. In a matter of years, the gnii disappeared. Changes to winds and tides made it ever more difficult to leave the island or visit it by choice, such that the most usual method of arrival is shipwreck and near-drowning, if not some partial chewing by sea creatures.

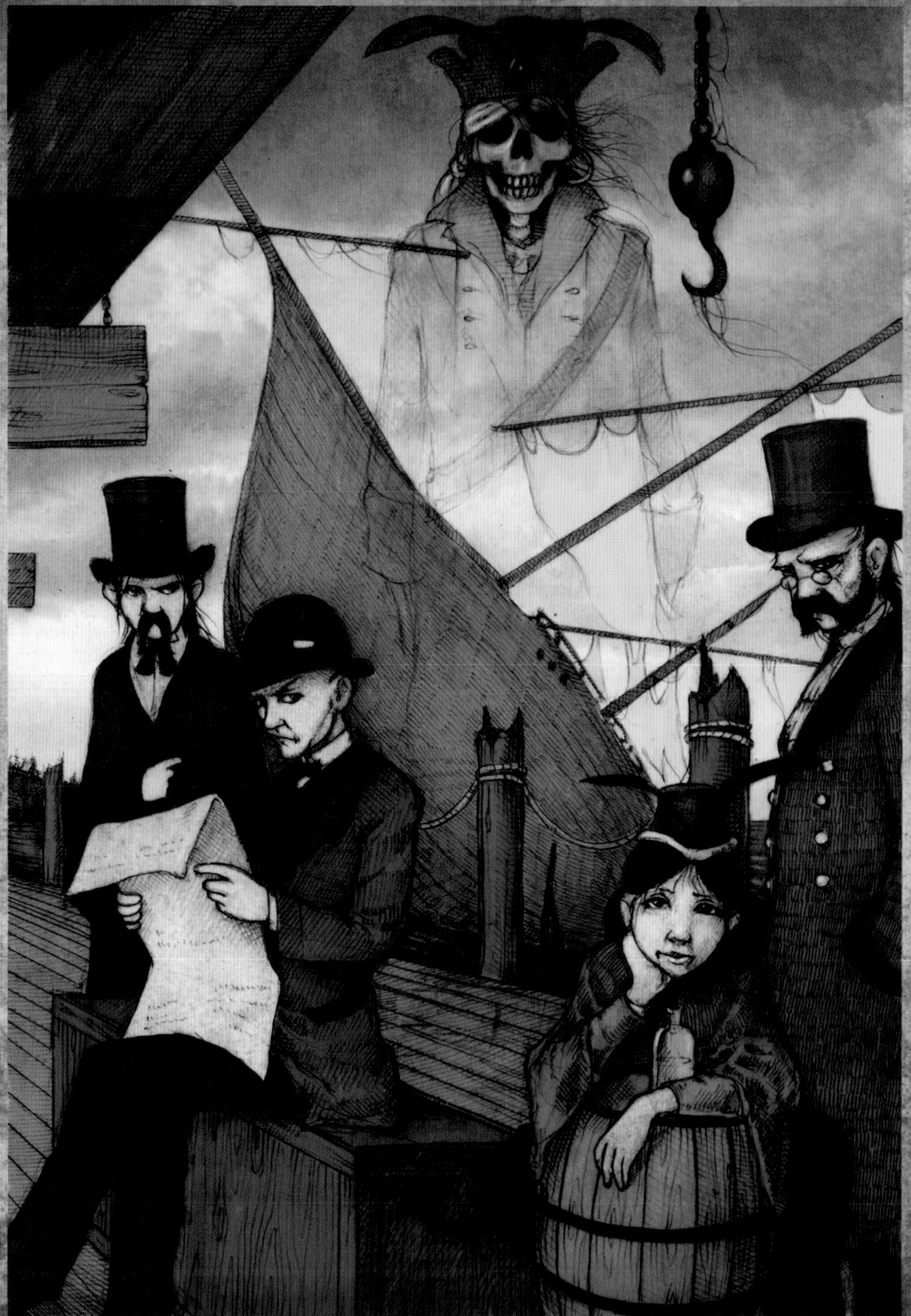

JONES

The Jones clan frequently claims to have descended entirely from the famous Welsh pirate Howel Llewellyn Aberystwyth Jones.

The aforementioned pirate captured three vessels before attempting to careen on Hopeless, and never getting afloat again. Joneses can be divided into those who feel that the pirate crew were all male (and all related and married locals) and those who believe in a crew of both genders, not excessively related, from whom today's clan descends. Either way, there is no doubt that the Joneses have been marrying their cousins far too often over far too many generations. Their capacity to be fruitful and multiply has resulted in a sufficiently large variety of Jones to suggest some genetic diversity, but even so, many of them are quite mad, possessed of unusual features, or a curious amalgam of the two.

The most prominent Jones on Hopeless is at present Frampton Jones, who runs the island's weekly news sheet: The Hopeless Vendetta. He inherited this post from his father, who first brought the printing press to Hopeless and dropped it in the sea whilst bringing it ashore. After years of salvage and repair, the press was rebuilt and the island's announcement chalkboard was taken to new heights with the addition of a deliverable news sheet. It was not until after Frampton took over the press from his father that he established they actually already had a typewriter, and set about building a more usable printing machine. Frampton is a pioneer of paper recycling and scientific exploration. He also owns the only camera in Hopeless Maine.

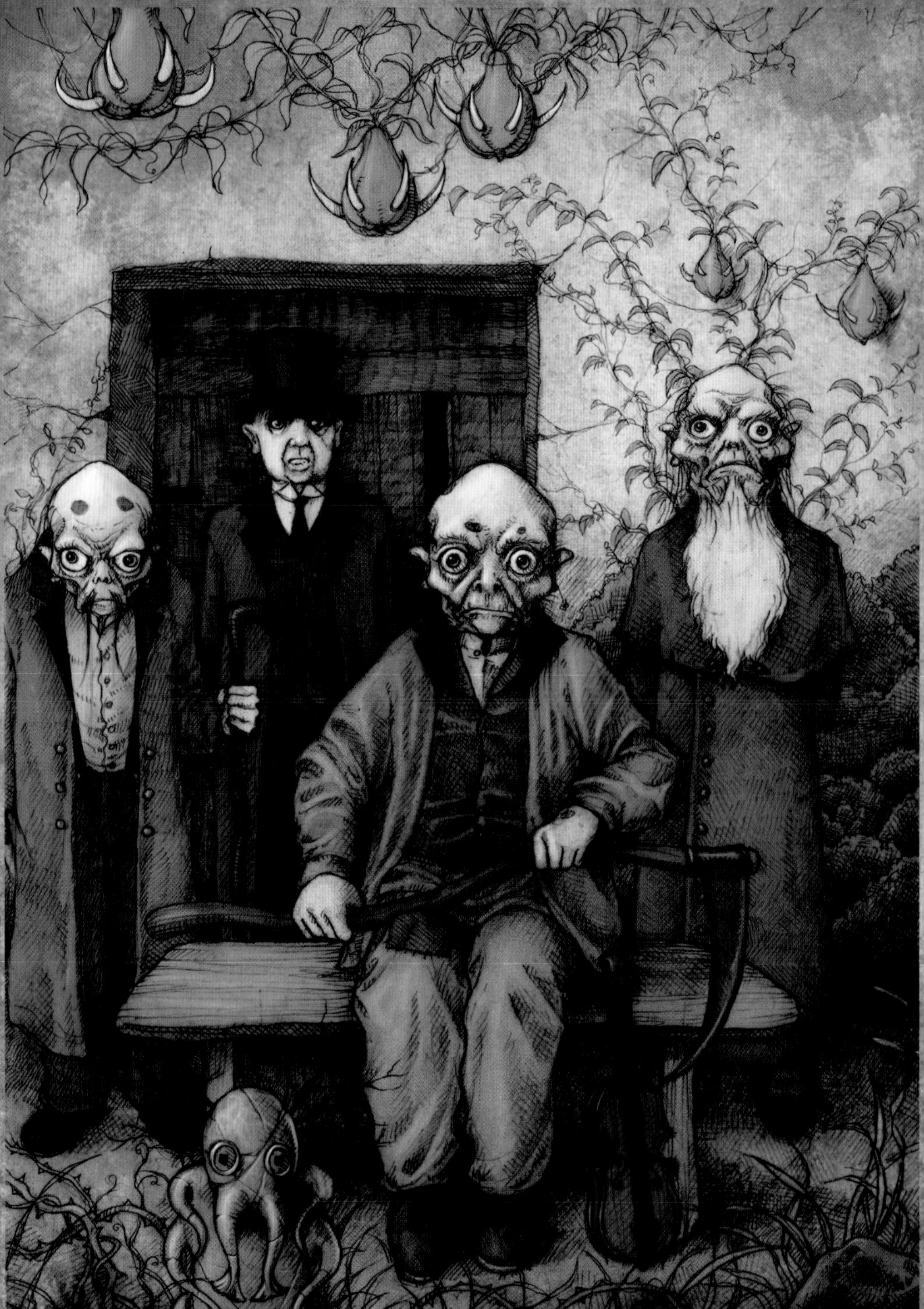

FROGS

It is evident that the Frog family will be the first founding line to become extinct. Never numerous, the Frogs have failed to reproduce in recent generations, and with Elgar Frog the youngest of them at sixty-one, time has clearly run out. There are no stories about where the original Frog settlers came from. Their names appear regularly in parish records and on gravestones but no particular achievement or activities have ever been ascribed to them. They are a quiet people, modest in their ways and manners, unassuming, but a continued presence from the earliest days of Hopeless, Maine. They have been a frequent voice for organised leadership within the community, but despite their efforts to get a proper council running, the island remains largely anarchic.

Descendants from female members of the line do exist and include pillar of the community Doc Willoughby. He has always been keen to assert his connection with the Frogs. Other relatives from lines of female descent are harder to identify but must certainly exist. Elgar Frog is the most prominent family member, as well as the youngest. He teaches music and provides tunes for town dances. Generally, the Frogs support more conservative approaches to dancing, namely the outright condemning of it. However, in matters of public entertainment and social contact between those who are young and unwed, Elgar Frog has proved to be the black sheep of his family. It is more usual for Frogs to be associated with librarianship, book selling and record keeping. In fact, a deceased member of the family still presides over the library, guarding the seventeen books that make up the total wisdom of Hopeless with a determination that defies the grave.

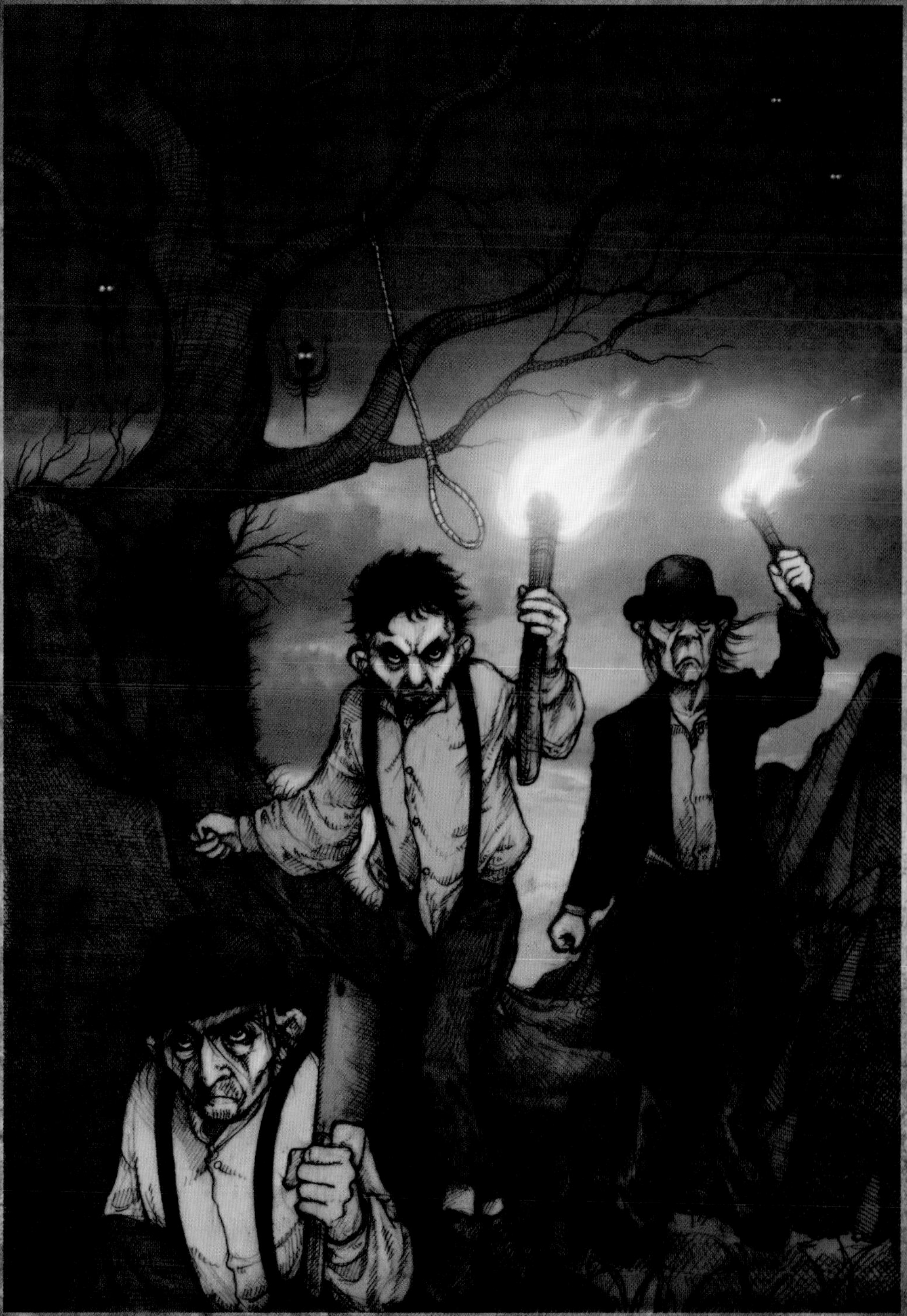

CHEVINS

When you need an angry mob with pitchforks, the Chevins can generally be relied on to make up numbers. As a family they have always been farmers, fishermen, wreckers, builders and otherwise busy, and take a pride in avoiding using their brains as far as is humanly possible. They have long standing family traditions around getting small mammals to fight each other, throwing live fish into unlikely places, and bringing torches along just on the off chance that some righteous burning will be called for. Frequently more active in their support of the church than the church leaders of Hopeless feel comfortable with, and equally active in their unofficial support of assorted vices, the Chevins have never been as respected as they wanted to be. They regularly marry into the Jones clan in a bid to improve their social standing, and this is probably the only reason that inbreeding on the island has been kept to a manageable level.

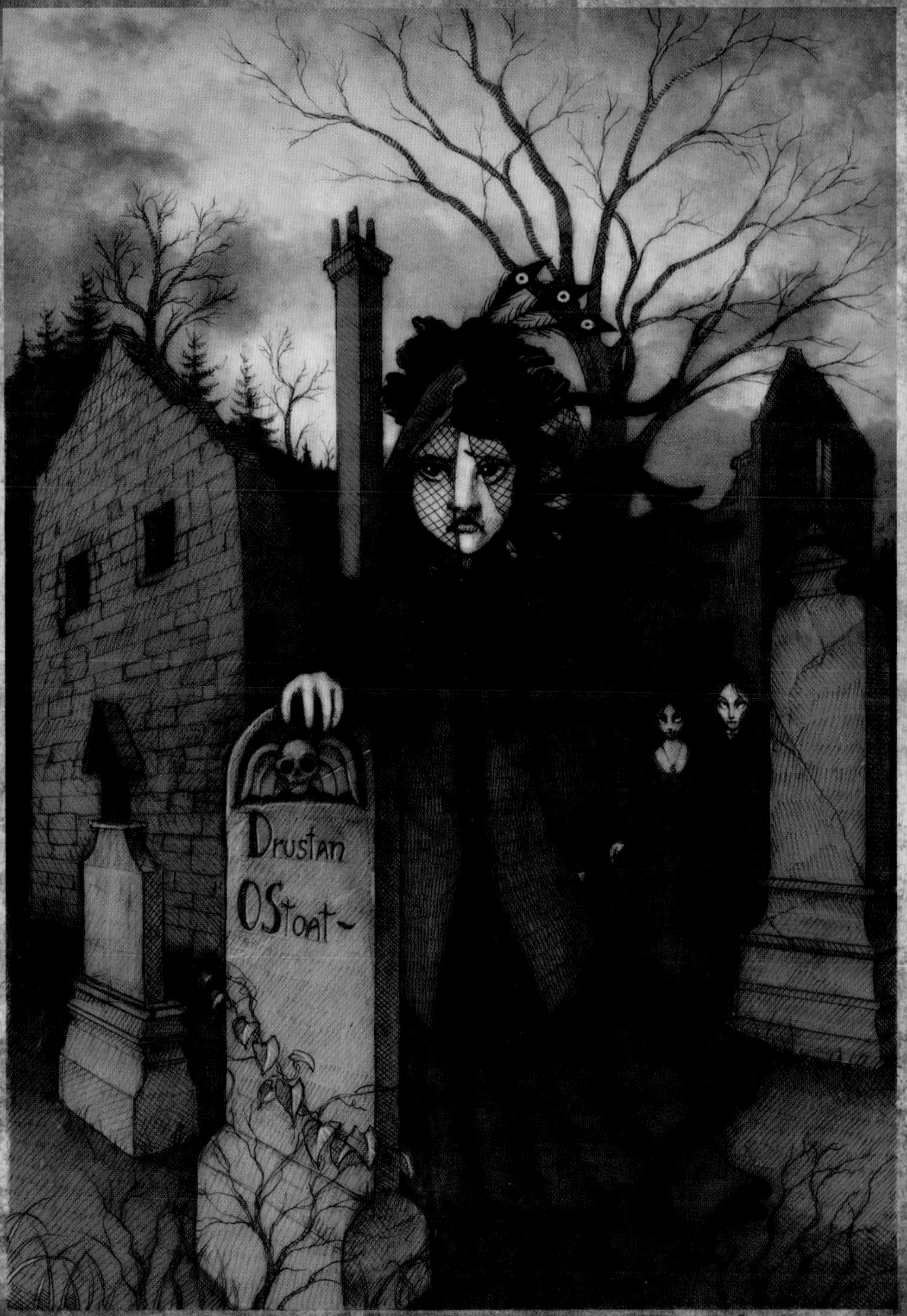
Drustan
OStoat~

THANK YOU!

Creating a graphic novel whilst living on a narrowboat has been far harder than we could have imagined. If we had imagined it, we probably wouldn't have tried. Narrowboat life means generating all your own electricity and having patchy internet access. On top of that, we don't have a car, so getting to places where things like broken bikes, and broken computers can be fixed is logistically very difficult. The short of it is that this book only happened because a number of absolutely brilliant people got involved to keep us afloat. People who have ferried us about, fixed bikes, sourced bikes, rescued broken computers, let us use internet, electricity, fed us and otherwise kept us sane.

So, this book is dedicated, with heartfelt thanks, to the people who made it possible - Trish and Keith Andrews, Martin Pearson, Sally Powell, Autumn Barlow, Rob and Sarah Gothard, and our brilliant, long suffering editor, Paul Morrissey.

We'd also like to thank all the kind and generous people who have supported the webcomic, helped promote us, and said encouraging things that kept us going. Lee Ann Farruga, Captain and Whisper, Neil, Jimmy Miz, Jamie Smart, and Stephen Raisin deserve special mention. And to everyone we haven't specifically thanked, please consider yourselves much loved and hugely appreciated. We want you to know that if you've been there for us along the way, if you've taken a moment to leave a comment, ask a question, or make a suggestion, you have made a huge difference to us.

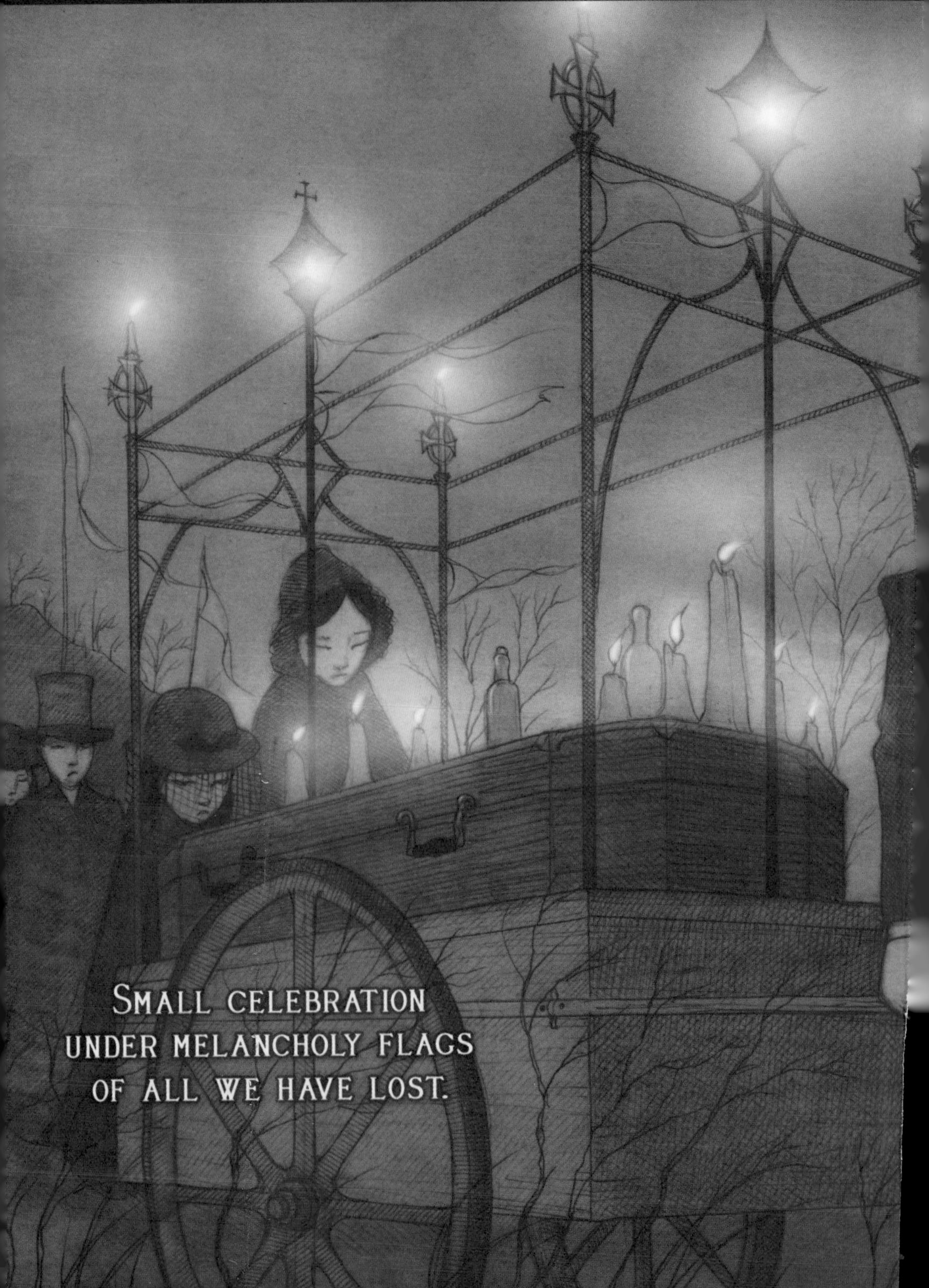
SMALL CELEBRATION
UNDER MELANCHOLY FLAGS
OF ALL WE HAVE LOST.

ABOUT THE AUTHORS

Along the way, Tom and Nimue Brown have lived in both America and the UK, including in a shed, a forge and on a narrowboat. They've made monsters for children and undertaken peculiar things in public, with spoons. Being a bit retro in their tastes, both Browns like to start the creative process with a blank sheet of paper (lined for Nimue) and either a pen or a pencil. Despite occasional luddite tendencies, they do have a website – **www.hopelessmaine.com** and a fascination with green technology. The Browns live with an eccentric child, are owned by a cat, are totally addicted to coffee and are easily bribed with cake.

In other bits of their working lives, Nimue writes novels and non-fiction Druid titles. Tom has created book covers and album art for all kinds of people. Fond of collaborative works, the Browns turn up in all sorts of unlikely places and are open to requests, from workshops at The Wildfowl and Wetland Trust to Professor Elemental's comic and beyond. Offers of cake always are seriously considered.

While the Browns have a longstanding love affair with all that is dark, gothic and serious, they also have a weakness for things playful and frivolous. As a consequence they feel very at home with Steampunks.

O'Stoats

The O'Stoats have always considered themselves to be the first family of Hopeless, Maine. Their aristocratic style has set them apart down the generations. They are by far the wealthiest family and have the most influence, but one also dogged by violence, murder and misfortune. There have also been longstanding accusations of nasty occult dabblings, resulting in deep mistrust from the largely God-fearing citizens of Hopeless. Very few members of the O'Stoat clan have ever died quietly of old age, in their own beds. Some of the bodies have never been found. Frequently, the murderers have never been found either, but it is generally felt that the O'Stoats keep their deaths very much in the family.

The status of the O'Stoats as a family remains uncertain at present. The child heir to the family name, Drustan O'Stoat, was viciously murdered some years ago. His parents, Melisandra and Durosimi, subsequently disappeared, although a number of people claim to have seen them since that time. Rumours of a second child remained little more than idle gossip for years, as no child had previously been identified as theirs. Salamandra is now the only known surviving O'Stoat, and her role in the disappearance of her parents is unknown. She is now the most prominent member of what has always been the most troubled and powerful family on the island.